Hellhounds and Hero Horses

Beasts of Myth and Legend

Retold and Translated by

Richard Marsh

Legendary Books

Legendary Books
Hellhounds and Hero Horses: Beasts of Myth and Legend
ISBN: 978-0-915330-18-8

Published by
Richard Marsh
15 Fontenoy Street
Dublin 7, Ireland
Phone 353-1-8827941
www.RichardMarsh.ie
Richard@RichardMarsh.ie

Also by Richard Marsh:
A World of Tricksters, Legendary Books, 2020
Meath Folk Tales, The History Press Ireland, 2013
Irish King and Hero Tales, Legendary Books, 2011
Irische Königs- und Heldensagen, the German edition of
Irish King and Hero Tales, Edition Narrenflug, 2014
Spanish and Basque Legends, Legendary Books, 2010
Tales of the Wicklow Hills, Legendary Books, 2007
The Legends and Lands of Ireland, Sterling, 2004

Front cover: Urco Ale label detail; coat of arms of the Republic of Adygea (see Nart Horses section).

Back cover: clockwise from top left; Black Shuck, Tam O'Shanter, Sleipnir and Odin (8th-century Tjängvide stone, Sweden), Piper and Wolves (Andorra stamp), Gelert's Grave, Peche Merle cave painting (Rakush), Saint Francis and Wolf. Centre: the Simurgh on the Iranian 500 rial coin. Bottom left: author and Val.

Frontispiece: Tuireann with Bran and Sceolán. Arthur Rackham from *Irish Fairy Tales* by James Stephens, 1920.

The mythology of a people is far more than a collection of pretty or terrifying fables to be retold in carefully bowdlerized form to our schoolchildren. It is the comment of the men of one particular age or civilization on the mysteries of human existence and the human mind, their model for social behaviour, and their attempt to define in stories of gods and demons their perception of the inner realities. … It helps us to see the myths of the past as man's attempt to embody his intuitive ideas about the human mind and its environment, to express truths dimly perceived which have roots in his innermost being. … In reaching out to explore the distant hills where the gods dwell and the deeps where the monsters are lurking, we are perhaps discovering the way home.

H. R. Ellis Davidson, *Gods and Myths of Northern Europe*, 1964.

Early Review

Richard Marsh's *Hellhounds and Hero Horses* introduces the reader to a vast menagerie of fantastic mythical beasts from around the world. Legends and anecdotes featuring the canine and equine title creatures receive the most attention, but Marsh does not stop there. The book includes tales of cats, birds, wolves, many reptiles and insects plus a variety of shape-shifters and shape-changers. He obviously has done his homework; the scholarly Introduction and extensive list of Sources make this a valuable reference book for anyone interested in pursuing this topic. After reading this book, you will never look at certain animals in the same way.

Wynn Montgomery
Storyteller
Erie, Colorado

CONTENTS

PÚCAS
Ireland

OTHER DOGS

HERO HORSES

CATS

BIRDS

WOLVES

SAINTS AND ANIMALS

SHAPE-SHIFTERS AND SHAPE-CHANGERS

Shape-shifters

Shape-changers

OTHER BEASTS

APPENDIX

Acknowledgements

I am grateful for the assistance of the following people and institutions in assembling this book.

The National Folklore Collection (Ireland), especially Director Críostóir Mac Cárthaigh and Claire Doohan, to quote from the Collection (NFC) and the Schools Collection (NFCS); Dr Mac Cárthaigh for the translation from "Scéal Spride" from the NFC in the Protective Púcas section; the Folklore of Ireland Society, for permission to quote Mrs O'Toole in "A Robin Warns of Danger" from their journal, *Béaloideas*; the National Library of Ireland staff generally, with particular thanks to Nora Thornton for her assistance in translating "The Porridge Púca"; public libraries in Santiago de Compostela in Galicia and Oviedo in Asturias; Minerva Barcala in Vilagarcía de Arousa, Galicia, for information on the local use of "urco" and the no-longer locally brewed Urco ale; Cristobo Carrín of Asturias for sharing his insight into the links between the human psyche and mythology; Alberto Álvarez Peña for explaining the Asturian Güestia and Güercu; Manuel Mandianes, Felipe Senén and Aurora for providing some surviving remnants of the urco tradition; David Clark of the Universidade da Coruña for introducing me to Manuel and Felipe; Miguel Ángel González González for information on the Huéspeda de Ánimas or Hueste of León; Carlos Saenz Saralegui for the contemporary account of the protective Black Dog in Argentina.

Preface

The 245 stories, anecdotes and incidents take precedence in this international collection of ultranatural activities of supposedly irrational animals as reported by presumably rational humans. Background information and context are integrated in the text where necessary to fully appreciate the narratives, and notes and related material are in the Appendix.

It is a convention in English to use human personal pronouns and adjectives – he/she, his/her, etc. – for animals that are named.

The source citation "NFC" refers to the Main Manuscript Collection in the National Folklore Collection (Ireland) housed at University College Dublin. "NFCS" is a manuscript in the Schools Collection, which consists of 740,000 pages of folklore and stories collected by more than 50,000 school children between 1937 and 1939.

A citation such as "Fuentelapeña §770" refers to a paragraph in that author's book, *The Entity Explained*, available online in Spanish: *El ente dilucidado*.

The Panchatantra, under that name or versions such as *The Fables of Pilpay/Bidpai*, is the source of some of these stories. It is a 300 BC collection of 87 fables and moral tales, many of which are older than the collection. The Jataka tales from the same period relate events in previous incarnations of the Buddha and can overlap with some stories from *The Panchatantra*. Adopted by international folklore, they can turn up in any culture.

Tags labelled AT refer to the Aarne - Thompson classification system of international folk tales.

Foreword

Csenge Zalka

Are you a dog person or a cat person? Some people have a firm stand on either side, and some just reply "yes." How about horses? Did you collect horse magazines when you were little, are you still a dedicated equestrian as an adult? Or maybe you find birds more fascinating? Are you a member of the birding community?

The animals that surround us, the ones we have the closest relationship with (domesticated or otherwise) have also inhabited our imagined landscape for millennia. They have been our companions, our role models, the embodiment of our wildest dreams of running or flying free. They have also lurked in the shadows, a warning or a threat we can't quite chase away even in our waking hours. Black dogs, fiery horses, devilish cats appear in our oldest tales to put the hero to the test.

Some of these creatures become real celebrities. How many of us learned in History class that Alexander the Great named several cities after his steed Bucephalus, or that Caligula wanted to make his favorite horse a consul? How could our most legendary heroes survive without their loyal steeds and even more loyal hounds? Some of the most intriguing beasts, like the kelpie or the púca, still hold considerable power in the social media and popular culture of today. Twitter's weekly #FolkloreThursday discussions are often dominated by Black Dogs, and folklorists have been latching onto the water-horse in Disney's *Frozen II* since the first trailer of the movie hit the Internet. These imaginary creatures are still with us, and we are still fascinated by them. Maybe even believe in them. Or at least feel a chill creep down our spine when we see glowing eyes in the shadows on our way home at night.

Richard Marsh dove deep into the treasure trove of legend and lore to assemble this collection. He is the most meticulous researcher I know, undaunted by nearly inaccessible sources or language barriers. He chases down leads like a hunting dog, gathers information like a worker bee, and treasures rare stories like a clever magpie. His enthusiasm and collecting fervor shows through his work. Each story comes with information of its origins and significance woven through its fabric – the mark of the storyteller who doesn't only research and respect stories, but also takes great enjoyment in sharing them. We are the fortunate audience of someone who can open up a treasure chest at any moment, and spill the gems of ages and continents at our feet.

Many of these stories come from primary sources – the closest we can get to the living oral tradition of a culture. Many of them are translated into English for the first time. It is worth noting that traditions less commonly known to English-speaking audiences, such as Basque folklore, are also present in this collection, showing diversity within Europe and beyond.

Tradition takes on many forms. Stories of shapeshifters speak to one of the oldest desires of humanity: to change our skin, transform into another creature's body, to see the world as a wolf, an eagle, a serpent sees it. Becoming something other than human terrifies and intrigues us and fills our stories with deep emotions. The legends of saints and animals, which also have a place in this collection, connect Christianity to much older beliefs and traditions. It shows how our admiration for nature finds a new place in a new faith.

We are at an important, crucial moment in our relationship with nature. Our story is interwoven with those of the animals that surround us; the creatures who have been with us since the very beginning. We have responsibility to them, and we also rely on them with our lives, just as heroes rely on their magic steeds or their animal helpers. Our oldest stories shed light on how much we owe them, and how desolate the world would be if they disappeared.

These are stories of wonder, exploration, and companionship. Let's walk forward with them together.

Dr Zalka Csenge Virág
International storyteller and researcher, author of *Dancing on Blades: Rare and exquisite folktales from the Carpathian Mountains* (Parkhurst Brothers, 2018)
Budapest, March 2nd, 2020.

Izena ba du, da – if it has a name, it exists.
Basque proverb

Introduction

For over 2000 years, philosophers, theologians and natural historians have been writing about the similarities and differences between rational and non-rational beings, that is, humans and animals, and the nature of their relationship. Pliny the Elder, Pope Saint Gregory the Great, John Moschus, Al-Qazwīnī, Ovid, Plutarch, the endlessly inquisitive Capuchin friar Antonio de Fuentelapeña, and other classical authors from around the world speak from beyond the grave in these pages. Alternately credulous and sceptical, they were the scientists and parapsychologists of their times, and their observations and interpretations serve to at least partially explain attitudes that have remained constant in myths, legends, folk tales and purportedly factual incidents in the modern age.

One reason those men put so much effort into explaining – to themselves as much as to their readers – how Nature operates is probably that they understood the inner workings of the human mind. Country people by necessity have an intimate knowledge of the lives and habits of animals, and it's vital for their well-being to be able to predict the actions of the domestic and wild beasts with which they share their lives and territory. To be on the safe side, perceptions of danger can be exaggerated and result in fantastic and entertaining cautionary tales – popular science developing into science fiction.

On the masthead of *The Folk-Lore Journal*, which is the source of some of these stories, is the motto *Alter et idem* – "Different and yet the same". The title of Dermot MacManus's book *The Middle Kingdom: The Faerie World of Ireland* reflects that "otherness" concept. Fantasy author Terry Pratchett called that book "probably one of the most influential books I've ever read".

Elementals

Elementals are chthonic creatures – of the earth: not human, animal, demon or angel – and are often classed among the fairies, but while fairies are described as human-like in form, elementals normally appear in the shapes of animals. Like the fairies, they originate in deep time, before the arrival of modern life forms, and are often hostile toward animals and humans, with the notable exceptions of the Simurgh, most of the Black Dogs and the Irish púca. They exist in an ultranatural realm. They are not aligned with the Devil, though religions tend to demonise them, and it is easy to see why some people reason with a false syllogism: the unknown is dangerous, danger is bad, the Devil is bad, therefore ...

Material but Invisible Beings

The physician, alchemist and astrologer Paracelsus wrote *The Book of Nymphs, Sylphs, Pygmies, Salamanders, and Other Spirits* (1566) "to describe the creatures that are outside the cognizance of the light of nature, how they are to be understood, what marvellous works God has created." In his 1676 book *The Entity Explained: A Unique New Discourse that Demonstrates that in Nature There Are Irrational Invisible Animals and Which Ones They Are*, Fray Antonio de Fuentelapeña seriously explores, in the context of orthodox 17th-century Catholic philosophy, the possibility of the existence of material but invisible beings in a parallel universe that we nowadays call the paranormal. "[Fray Antonio] is preoccupied by the trace of God in Nature but also considers the exception and the anomaly of His own laws." (Flor)

Cristobo Carrín, in his article "Monsters of the Underworld and Hell of the Asturians", points out that Lecouteux, following Le Goff, maintains that a serpent that was prevented by Saint Marcel from devouring the corpse of a woman who had led a bad life –

is a *genius loci*, that is, a spirit that guards a certain territory from the beginning of time, and which has to be appeased before digging, building, cultivating or in any way altering that territory. In the mythologies of Europe and the Near East these spirits take the form of terrestrial creatures of uncontainable force which dominated the world in an epoch before the birth of the gods. When the gods entered the scene, they conquered the monsters and enclosed them in a distant prison, thus permitting humans to prosper in a world relatively secure and ruled by stable laws.

That is the reason for fairy planning permission in Ireland. Normally, when people wish to build a structure on their own land, they are required to apply to the local government authority for permission and post a prominent notice informing neighbours who might be affected. To be safe, country people have been known to draw a plan of the proposed project and post it at the location in question. If the drawing remains undisturbed, it means that the fairies have tacitly granted permission. If it is torn to pieces, permission denied.

Some of the beasts in this book fit the descripton of a *genius loci*, especially the púcas of Ireland, the Black Dogs of England, the Galician urcos, and the spirits that inhabit the ancient stone boundary markers called *finxos* in Asturias.

Inter-species Cooperation

About 25,000 years ago, a segment of the wolf population decided en masse to throw their lot in with humans and become the first wild animals to be domesticated. These dogs-to-be reckoned that the advantages of relative security and free meals outweighed the risk of being abused or ending up in the stew pot themselves. It was only around 3500 BC that horses agreed a tacit referendum for the same reasons. These willing partners allowed people to hunt, work, travel and wage war more effectively.

Hellhounds

Fear of dogs is related to the visceral dread of being eaten alive by a carnivore, whence the primitive terror of the hellhound. I've never heard of a horse killing a person without provocation, but there are frequently reports in the media about dogs fatally savaging children and adults for no apparent reason – man's best friend becomes man's worst enemy.

Fortunately, there are far more news stories about dogs as helpers and life savers. However, you still need to be alert when walking down a street in what you take to be neutral territory, but which a dog regards as his.

Local stories, told as factual, of large ultranatural black dogs are widespread. In Spanish tradition, especially in Galicia, the fiery-eyed urco presages death or misfortune. The name comes from the Latin *Orcus*, meaning Hell or Pluto, the god of the infernal region, so it's literally a hellhound.

In rural Ireland, where everyone knows their neighbours' dogs, an unnaturally large, black, red-eyed dog that belongs to no one and is frequently encountered in a certain place is the friendly local púca (anglicised "pooka"). It may be startling to a stranger when it unexpectedly appears out of thin air, but it is not threatening, and I've never heard of anyone being harmed by one. In Britain the Black Dog more or less fills that role.

Hero Horses

Some people are afraid of horses, but that's mainly because of their size and the tenderfoot's complaint that they are uncomfortable in the middle and dangerous at both ends. Also, there is the real possibility of injury or death if you fall off. And never walk closely behind a horse if it has a red ribbon tied to its tail. That means it's a known kicker.

Two small but memorable incidents sowed the seeds for this book.

Cindy was 17 years old, employed at the entry level as a hotwalker (a person who walks horses after exercise or a race to cool them) on a Thoroughbred race track in Florida with ID that adjusted her age to the legal requirement. During a lull in activities one hot afternoon, she was looking for a cool and secure place to take a nap and decided to bunk in with a five-year-old mare who was one of the horses I looked after as a groom.

Years later, she reminisced: "I remember falling asleep curled up in Kankakee Miss's stall and you coming to wake me. She acted like she had given birth to a foal and had to protect it. What a sweet girl she was."

I was standing next to a moderate but challenging jump at a horse show. A girl aged about ten rode up to it on a full-sized horse. They jumped, but as they reached the top of the arc she started to slip off to one side. The horse swerved in mid-air to get under her, and they landed safely. I turned to a stranger standing beside me and said, "Did you see that?" He nodded, eyes wide with wonder.

Ordinary and Extraordinary Real Animals

The otherness of the familiar – *Alter et idem* – applies especially to ordinary flesh-and-blood animals doing extraordinary things that make them seem both human-like and more than human.

Human sense of humour: a YouTube clip shows a large dog sitting next to a half-filled bathtub and a cat sitting on the edge next to him, both looking into the water. The dog looks at the cat, back at the water, and then lifts a paw and casually nudges the cat into the tub.

Human helpfulness: on YouTube a bear scoops a floundering crow out of the water and gets a peck on the nose for his trouble. Also on YouTube, a medium-sized dog launches an unprovoked attack on a small boy, dragging him off his tricycle. A cat bursts seemingly out of nowhere and chases the dog away. A dog stole bread from its master to give to Saint Roch. And there are many reports through the ages of dolphins rescuing drowning humans.

More than human prescience: in the story "A Prescient Dog" (Other Dogs), a collie who "was always at hand when the boats were putting to sea" somehow knows that a storm is brewing and makes such a fuss among the fishermen that they decide not to go out that day. A storm comes, and many boats are lost. Another time the men ignore the dog's warning, and two of them are drowned in a sudden storm.

These and other incidents demonstrate that animals are not, as is often assumed, less than human: they're just other, a property that is magnified and exaggerated in the accounts of legendary and mythical beasts.

Are the Stories True?

Sánchez Vicente, in *La Cultura Popular Asturiana*, asserts strongly that many folklore and legendary beings were invented by literary romantics in the 19th century and that they never had currency among the population of Asturias, which probably applies to many of these stories from elsewhere. Folklorists and storytellers call this "fakelore". Others seem to have had their origin with the people, but as those oral sources have become extinct in modern times, so have their stories, except for their continued inclusion in books about fantastic creatures. I have found it difficult to collect stories about the Galician urco that are contemporary or even from the 20th century, unlike the eyewitness reports of púcas in Ireland and Black Dogs in Britain, which are plentiful.

On the other hand, accounts have been collected in recent years that indicate popular knowledge of the folklore characters, though perhaps some of the references are jocular. One example is the Asturian *sumiciu*, whose name Cabal derives from the Latin *sumere*, "to take":

> A thing that's lost, it has to be here because I just saw it and it's not here. Damn, the sumiciu has hidden it. You can even have a tool or something in your hand and it disappears. The sumiciu exists, it's true. A thing has disappeared and there is no way you can find it, and you

turn around and it appears again, but at the moment no matter how hard you look you can't find it. That's what's called the sumiciu.

(As told to Sordo Sotres, *Mitos Asturianos*, 1999)

So are the stories true? Books have been written on that topic, but none have expressed the answer as clearly as a 5-year-old girl, who, when another child asked a storyteller if a story he had just told was true, explained: "It might not be true on the outside, but it's true on the inside."

The reverse could be said of eye-witness reports of apparently unexplainable events. I once investigated repeated sightings of a flying saucer for a local newspaper. I asked a woman who said she had seen the object to phone me the next time it appeared and tell me exactly where it was in the sky. A few days later she did. I looked, and, as I had suspected, it was the planet Venus setting. The story was factual on the outside – she had really seen something – but mistaken in the woman's identification, so not true on the inside.

Many of the following stories probably report actual occurrences that were interpreted and pre-judged according to the witnesses' cultural background and beliefs.

HELLHOUNDS

URCOS

Northwest Spain

"Orcus represented Death. His name was also applied to the Underworld. He carried off the living by force and conducted them to the infernal regions."

New Larousse Encyclopedia of Mythology

Forms of the Urco

The urco in Galicia is the descendant of Orcus. It nearly always takes the form of a large black male dog with fiery red eyes, but it does not physically take people to the Underworld; rather it is regarded as a presage of death or misfortune, reflecting its original role as a psychopomp or guide to the Underworld. A similar creature is the Chilean Tue-Tue, said to be a shape-shifting wizard.

One reason for the prevalence of the urco in Galicia is probably that as the westernmost extremity of the Iberian Peninsula the region was associated with death and the underworld, prompted by the westward course of the sun, as Ireland was for the superstitious Roman soldiers in Britain. The Camino de Santiago, which follows the Milky Way and terminates at Santiago de Compostela in Galicia, is the route taken by souls on their way to the Otherworld. Also, several sites in Galicia are identified as portals to the Otherworld, such as Pico Sacro (Sacred Peak), 15 km from Santiago de Compostela.

Worship of Orcus was largely confined to rural areas, with variations on his cult surviving into modern times in the form of wild man festivals. So it is not surprising that remnants of folk belief in the urco still exist in rural Galicia. Unfortunately, remnants are all I have been able to find, unlike the many 20th-century reports in Ireland of a large black dog with fiery red eyes called the púca, which is not a portent of death, and the plentiful stories of the mostly benevolent Black Dog in Britain.

The Can do Urco (literally "Hound of Hell") is related to Cerberus, whose duty is to keep the inmates of Hell inside – he eats those who try to leave, according to the Greek poet Hesiod – not, as sometimes supposed, to keep the living out. In a radical reversal of the role of Cerberus, the goalkeeper in Vilagarcía de Arousa in Galicia is called "urco". That misunderstanding may have arisen from the fact that local micro brewer Cervexa Suevia until recently sold a strong ale called Urco, with the head of a snarling, ferocious, red-eyed black dog on the label and on the cover of this book.

The most common forms of the urco are dogs: white dog, black dog, Can do Urco, Can do Mar (which comes from and returns to the sea); also, half wolf and half serpent with scales and great strength in the tail. The Cadela Peregrina ("female pilgrim dog") is a white dog, a sign of death: don't stare at it.

King Pedro the Cruel, the Prophetic Boy and the Urco

Spain

Jerez is in the southwest of Spain, geographically, culturally and linguistically far from the urco's normal habitat in the northwest. "Urco" is a specifically Galician term and may have been unknown to the anonymous author of this ballad. The word does not appear in the Spanish original, but the monstrous black dog looks and acts like a death-presaging urco, and so I think the story belongs in this section.

Pedro, King of Castile and León 1350-1369, fully warranted the epithet "the Cruel", and not only for his many assassinations. His mother protested against his outrageous treatment of his French wife, Blanche of Bourbon, because she feared political repercussions, and so he exiled his mother. He imprisoned Blanche and is suspected of ordering her murder. He had his illegitimate half-brother Fadrique, the Master of the Order of Santiago, killed so he could give the post to his mistress's brother. After a battle in which his illegitimate half-brother Enrique, Fadrique's twin, defeated him, Pedro was lured into a meeting with Enrique, who stabbed him to death and became king.

The ballad (my translation), from Juan Timoneda's 1573 collection *Rosa Española,* is believed to have been composed within twenty years of Pedro's death. The action is set after Fadrique's murder in 1358 and before Blanche's in 1361.

A saker falcon is twice the size of a peregrine falcon, and well able to take down a heron, which was a popular prey for falconers. Pedro was aware of 12th-century laws, republished during his reign, which severely penalized the killing of falcons, including amputation of the right hand, imprisonment, and a fine one-fifth of the price for the murder of a human.

In Jerez King Pedro took his saker to a lake.
He spied a heron, loosed the saker, but by wretched fate
His bird attacked a peregrine, which plummeted instead.
At Pedro's feet the falcon fell, ominously dead.

A shiver went through Pedro as he watched the heron fly.
Higher soared the bird until it vanished in the sky.
From where the heron disappeared, he saw a murky shape
That floated earthwards, black and baleful. Pedro stared
agape.

The closer moved the frightful form, the more he shook with
fear.
And then it stood five steps away – menacingly near.
From the mass emerged a boy – a scowling shepherd lad –
Crying, groaning. Frowzy hair cascaded round his head.

Thorns projected from his feet, his body furred and sleek.
A bloody dagger in one hand; the other waved a snake.
From a shoulder draped a shroud, a skull hung from his
throat.
At his side a red-eyed urco howled, jet-black its coat.

In roaring tones the boy declared, "King Pedro, you are
doomed.
Your mother exiled, brother slain, your wife in prison
gloom.
God is angry, but if you repent and reinstate
Your queen, He'll grant to you an heir; if not, behold your
fate.

"Disaster will descend on you; the fault will be your own.
Your daughters will turn bad, and Don Enrique take your
throne.
Your death will come from dagger wounds; to Hell you will
be thrown."
The blackness, boy and urco vanished. Pedro stood like
stone.

A Poet's Fictitious Urco

A street in the centre of Pontrevedra in Galicia bears the name Rúa Andrés Muruais in honour of the 19th-century poet who, with the collaboration of other artists, reinvented the urco as a prank. Urco is now the King of the annual Carnaval, a freewheeling party like Mardi Gras that upends acceptable public behaviour before the austerity of Lent. (Carnaval is often called Entroido or Introido in Galicia.)

An article in the newspaper *La Vox de Galicia* 24 February 2001 describes the urco as "a fictitious personage, a demon of legend, that the poet Andrés Muruais revived in 1876 to create a carnival mockery." In the months preceding that year's Carnaval, Muruais and his friends circulated rumours that a horrific beast was seen in various parts of the city wreaking all sorts of havoc. It was identified as "The Urco". Panic seized the populace, and night guards were doubled for security. The monster was none other than Muruais himself, "dressed in skins wearing an animal mask, dragging chains and howling in lament".

Muruais enhanced the yarn by describing the beast in a pamphlet as "a fierce animal capable of swallowing twenty sacks of copper coins in one gulp as easily as a burro could swallow two grains of barley … in [the Urco] was lodged a soul of some important person in torment, which it carried about while committing a thousand acts of mayhem." One version of the story says that the founder of Pontevedra, Teucro, returned to defend the city. (Teucro was the brother of Ajax, and after the Trojan War he came to Galicia and established the city.) Teucro pretended to befriend the Urco and on the third day of Carnaval poisoned it.

But Muruais's parody account states: "The Urco had not entered Pontevedra, and far from being what was attributed to him, he was a powerful king, who from remote lands and accompanied by his court and army, came to visit the land of the Hellenes." He was welcomed by Teucro amid many ceremonies and processions. Then some of the warriors engaged in jousts, and the Urco challenged Teucro to break spears. On their first and only encounter, the Urco received a mortal wound and died.

The Death of Urco is recreated annually as a feature of Pontevedra's Carnaval, and the ritual is probably one reason why some concept of the urco survives in folk memory, as does Teucro, whose name has been adopted by the local handball team.

A Sensational Newspaper Report

Carril is a suburb of Vilagarcía de Arousa. Cortegada is a small island in the estuary of the River Ulla within easy swimming distance of the city. The tenants of Cortegada were evicted when the owner of the property gave it to King Alfonso XIII at the beginning of the 20th century. He visited it only once and took no further interest in it, possibly because he had heard that an urco was living there.

La Voz de Galicia carried the screaming headline on 15 June 2014: "Urco, the terrifying dog of Cortegada. An enormous black dog swam from the island to frighten the children of Carril."

The article says that one morning in the early 20th century, the residents of Carril were awakened during a storm by the howls of the urco. The children were especially frightened, huddled beneath their threadbare sheets and trembling from the cold and fear, visualising the terrifying figure of the black dog with sharp fangs, having often been threatened by their parents with the urco for refusing the few crumbs of food they were given or for not finishing their supper of leftovers. Fishermen working at night have reported feeling a blow on the boat when the dog is swimming from the island to Carril.

The Urco Today

The folk memory of the urco is mainly preserved in books and popular media, but it also remains not far beneath the surface in the consciousness of present-day Galicians.

Xosé Ramón Mariño Ferro reports that the people of his parish near Pontevedra believe in the Cadela Peregrina. His father-in-law assured him that the Peregrina exists. It's an animal like a dog that comes from the cemetery to announce a death, he explained. Mariño said he didn't believe it existed and challenged him to prove it. They went to the cemetery. "If it's there, let it come out," said Mariño. It didn't appear.

His grandmother was a saint and prayed frequently.

"Why don't you sleep?" he asked her one day.

"Because I want to feel when the urco passes."

"What is the urco?"

"It's like a calf that gives three yowls and all the dogs follow it howling."

"If you feel it, call me. I want to see it."

At midnight she called him. He only heard the third yowl. It was like the moo of a cow but louder. He wanted to go to the window to look, but his grandmother didn't let him. Then he heard many dogs howling continuously.

It is said that people on the point of death see through the window the figure of an enormous dog accompanied by a pack of dogs.

Archaeologist Felipe Senén, former director of the Archaeological Museum in A Coruña, told me this:

> In Galician tradition, the Can do Demo (Dog of the Demon) is a warning from beyond the grave, always negative, in the form of a dog of great size and with shining eyes. This image has stayed with me since childhood. It is an ownerless black dog of unknown origin that howls at the door of a house, announcing a death that happens without fail within days. I've never forgotten my childhood fears when at night I'd hear the howls.
>
> I believe I saw the urco once, on a visit to the "House of the Demon" in Anllóns in Ponteceso, a house with a poltergeist well documented and publicised, where doors and tables were moved and blows were heard and stones fell. When I left without seeing anything strange inside, I was accosted by a black dog with hostile eyes. I'll never forget it. On another occasion, in the same place, another large dog, also black, crossed in front of my car without letting me move. Coincidence?

> In many traditions in Galicia, the urco appears in festivals of a cyclical agrarian character, such as Carnaval or the Night of Saint John [Midsummer's Eve]. In Carnaval in some places, the idol made of straw and rags that presides over the field of the festival is the pagan "Urco" (King Urco in Pontevedra), and then on Ash Wednesday it is burned to ashes.
>
> [That happens elsewhere in Galicia in the Entroido.]

Anthropologist Manuel Mandianes, co-author with Antón of *O Ciclo da Vida* (The Cycle of Life), told me about this belief in the south of Galicia:

> In La Limia, a zone of Ourense, they speak of "La Negra", a black female dog that goes at the head of the procession of the dead in which there is a living person who will die soon. La Negra walks in front to indicate the way the procession should go. They say to a person who walks with little energy or stumbles and falls frequently, "You saw La Negra."

Aurora in Santiago de Compostela related an adventure of her aunt, Josefa, when she was about nine years old:

> In 1950, Josefa was gathering firewood in the woods near her home when she heard a strange and frightening noise. Having been told many stories about the urco – *can do urco* or *can do inferno* in Galician, literally, the "dog from hell" – she was afraid that the monster was about to attack her, and she scrambled up a tree. The bestial sounds continued intermittently through the afternoon, and when they finally ceased, she climbed down from the tree and ran home as fast as she could. Although she never saw the animal that was making the mysterious noises, she is convinced to this day that she nearly became the victim of a "*can enfermo*", as she understood the name. ["*Can enfermo*" means "sick dog".]

In Tolosa, Gipuzkoa, 480 km (300 miles) from Galicia, 70-year-old Francisco Jauregui Aguirrezabala told this story to Juan Garmendia Larrañaga in 1992 (*Mitos y Leyendas de los Vascos*). Neither author nor source called the creature an urco, but it fits the description.

Francisco was helping his uncle with the ploughing one day, and when they finished they adjourned to a cider bar for supper. They left about midnight. After half an hour along the road, Francisco noticed a dog the size of a donkey walking past them. He said to his uncle, "Did you see *that*?" The uncle said No and asked what it was that his nephew saw. He described the dog, but his uncle said he hadn't seen it.

They came to a crossroad and went separate ways to their homes. Francisco was nervous, and as a precaution he picked up three stones from the road. When he reached his house, he saw the same monstrous dog again, this time standing in front of him and barring his way. He threw the stones at the dog and it disappeared, but there was no sound of the stones falling to the ground. Francisco ran into the house and locked the door securely.

Fermín Apezteguia Telletxea, 62, from Ezkurra in Navarre told Larrañaga this story. A man from Vitoria-Gasteiz came to Ezkurra to meet with some charcoal-burners and stayed the night in a tavern. In the morning, as he was about to take to the road, his friends asked him if he was afraid of Otherworld beings – demons and suchlike. He said he had no fear of them. He set off, and at the head of the stream near the hermitage of Santa Cruz four large white dogs came out and planted themselves in front of him. Frightened, he returned to the tavern, where blood began to flow from his mouth. He died a short time later, convinced that he had met four demons in the shape of white dogs.

The dogs may have been a warning of danger ahead. The bleeding could have been caused by stress coupled with an underlying health issue such as an ulcer or alcoholic liver disease.

The Asturian Güercu and Güestia

"Andái de día, que la nueche ye mía."
"Walk by day, for the night is mine."

If you are out after midnight, especially on the Eve of All Saints Day (Halloween) or the Eve of Saint John's Day at Midsummer, you might encounter the Güestia and receive that warning from them.

Alberto Álvarez Peña searches the valleys and villages of Asturias to collect stories from the remaining tradition bearers. In *La Güestia y Otros Agüeros de Muerte* (The Güestia and Other Auguries of Death), he says that the Güestia is a procession of spirits, among which can be seen a person who has just died or is about to die, and so it is a type of presage or announcement of death similar to the Galician Santa Compaña (Holy Company) and urco and the Irish banshee and slua sí (fairy host). In Asturias it's also called Santa Compaña or Santa Compañía, and La Buena Gente (The Good People), which is a respectful term used for the fairies in Ireland.

> The Güestia consists of the souls of people who manipulated land boundaries in their lifetime in order to gain more property at the expense of their neighbours. Whoever sees the Güestia will die the following year. To avoid this sad ending, one must trace a circle with a cross inside or a pentagram on the ground and stand in it, and not speak to any of the Güestia or accept anything from them, because that will indicate that the person is dead and will be condemned to wander eternally.
> Álvarez Peña, *Un Paseo por la Mitología Asturiana* (2019)

Alberto clarified privately that those people who interfered with land boundaries to gain more land did so by moving the ancient stone boundary markers called *finxos* in Asturian or *mojones* in Castilian. The practice continues today, though not as much as before. The punishment to wander eternally is not for the stealing of land per se. The finxos that traditionally mark the territory are believed to be the residence of the *genius loci*, the spirit of the place, and it is the offence against that entity that brings retribution.

In his *Leyendas Asturianas de Difuntos* (2015), Alberto has more about the Güestia:

> We find some very interesting variants of the Güestia in Santianes (Pravia). They call it the Bueste and say that it was a pack of dogs that made its ghostly appearance at night, accompanied by "human beings who were like ghosts".* There are also descriptions where it is called La Guostia and La Pirriría,** and they say that it is a very tall, dark and terrible woman who appears surrounded by dogs, which at first look like small black shapes but on coming closer grow, increasing their size until the unfortunate person who sees them recognises the phantom dogs that accompany her.
>
> *Informant: Rogelio Meijide, 94. Collected 6 November 1998.
>
> **Informant: Marifé Alonso García. Collected 5 December 1998. She heard the story from her grandmother, Claudia Álvarez Morán, who died at the age of 75 in 1951.

The Asturian version of the urco takes a different form. In private correspondence, Alberto explained:

> In Asturias we call it *Güercu*, and it is also a presage of death, but it does not adopt the form of a black dog. In this type of story, someone encounters – nearly always at dusk – a neighbour or family member; it can be on the road or while working in the field, etc. The person greets the figure but they do not respond. They pass by without stopping, and when the person looks again they have vanished. On arriving home he mentions the incident, and he is told that what he saw is impossible, because

that individual has just died, whether in the same town or some distance away.

We also have black dogs, the sight of which implies the death of the person who sees them. They are generally interpreted as the incarnation of a soul or a dog from Hell that brings auguries of death. There are few stories of this type and they are not called "Güercu". In Tapia de Casariego they speak of the Can de Oliveros, a presage of death. In Santalla de Oscos, in a place where a person was killed, a large black dog would appear dragging chains.

The Huéspeda de Ánimas or Hueste of León

In León, the Huéspeda de Ánimas ("procession of spirits") or Hueste ("host") is similar to the Asturian Güestia and the Galician Santa Compaña, but its purpose is to announce the imminent death of the person who encounters it on the road, or of the terminally ill to whom it pays a visit. It wanders the roads to recruit those who are near death, or, in some cases, to petition the living to pray for the remission of their sins. Some authors derive *hueste* from the Latin *hostis* ("enemy"), but others say that the original form is *estantigua* – *hueste antigua* – "ancient host", with "host" being a neutral term for any travelling group.

Miguel Ángel González González tells me that animals can also be auguries of death. One is a crow or other bird giving three knocks on a window to announce the death of a relative. This is similar to a current Irish belief. You hear three knocks on the door, open it, and no one is there. Go to a window from where you can see the door. You hear three knocks again, and it is clear that no physical being has done it. Later, you learn that a relative died at the same time you heard the knocks.

BLACK DOGS

About Black Dogs

> The phantasmagoria of rural England are to a great extent due to the race-memory of the pagan gods. This is true of such figures as the Headless Horseman, the Black Dog, the White Lady, the now defunct fairies, and the ghost-coach. They are ... mythological, the detritus of a former religion.

> The spectres of Britain were purely hellish ... strangely featured and ugly ... looking stern and grim ... (quoting Gildas, 6th-century English historian)

> Of these spectres of Britain which still remain, the most interesting is the Black Dog phantom ...
> (Witcutt)

> That which is nearly always known as the Black Dog, is always black, and is always a dog and nothing else.
> (Brown)

There are two types of Black Dogs: harmful and harmless. Most are harmless or positively benevolent. They are sometimes included among the fairies, but they are more accurately classed as elementals or chthonic beasts: of the earth, not angel or demon or animal. Typical descriptions of their habits show them to be liminal creatures, from the Latin meaning "threshold/border"; that is, they are tied to a limited territory or a certain place like an ageless sentinel. Some say they are the ghosts of people who died violently.

"Black Dog" is their usual generic title, unless they have earned fame or infamy, like the Moddey Dhoo and Black Shuck. The Galician urcos, literally hellhounds – Cans do Urco – normally take the form of black dogs that foretell death but are not in themselves menacing.

The Irish púcas are non-threatening beasts that appear as black dogs, horses and other animals, and are often benevolent and even life-saving, though in the shape of horses they will take those foolish enough to mount them on a night-long tour over rough country.

This section is about black dogs, harmful and harmless, that are not identified as urcos or púcas, which are covered in other sections.

The Shape-shifters and Shape-changers section deals with those phenomena.

Black Dog Syndrome

Animal shelters report that black animals, especially big black dogs, are more difficult to find homes for because of superstitions and unconscious prejudice absorbed through horror films and fiction and popular tradition. They call it the Black Dog Syndrome. The hadith, a collection of the sayings of the Prophet Muhammad, is an example of a religious tradition.

"The black dog is a devil." Sahih Muslim Book 004, Hadith Number 1032.

"The Prophet of Allah (pbuh [peace be upon him]) ordered to kill dogs, and we were even killing a dog which a woman brought with her from the desert. Afterwards he forbade to kill them, saying: Confine yourselves to the type which is black." Abu Dawud Book 010, Hadith Number 2840.

Frightening or Dangerous Black Dogs

The Moddey Dhoo
Isle of Man

For he was speechless, ghastly, wan
Like him of whom the Story ran
Who spoke the spectre hound in Man.
Sir Walter Scott, "The Lay of the Last Minstrel", 1805

The Moddey Dhoo (Manx: "Black Dog") is typically described as a large black dog the size of a calf with eyes "blazing like saucers" which induces fear into those who encounter it but is not reported to be harmful. The earliest written account seems to be a passage in George Waldron's 1726 *A Description of the Isle of Man*, which Walter Scott followed closely in his novel *Peveril of the Peak*, 1823:

> Through one of the old churches in Peel Castle, there was formerly a passage to the apartment belonging to the Captain of the Guard, but it is now closed up. An apparition, called in the Manx language, "The Mauthe Doo," in the shape of a large black spaniel with curled shaggy hair, was used to haunt Peel Castle; and has been frequently seen in every room, but particularly in the Guard Chamber, where, as soon as candles were lighted, it came and lay down before the fire in the presence of all the soldiers, who at length, by being so much accustomed to the sight of it, lost great part of the terror they were seized with at its first appearance. They still, however, retained a certain awe, as believing it was an evil spirit, which only waited permission to do them hurt, and for that reason forbore swearing and all profane discourse while in its company. But though they endured the shock of such a guest when altogether in a body, none cared to be left alone with it.
>
> It being the custom, therefore, for one of the soldiers to lock the gates of the Castle at a certain hour, and carry

the keys to the Captain, to whose apartment, as I said before, the way led through a church, they agreed among themselves, that whoever was to succeed the ensuing night, his fellow in this errand should accompany him that went first, and, by this means, no man would be exposed singly to the danger; for I forgot to mention that the *Mauthe Doo* was always seen to come from that passage at the close of day, and return to it again as soon as the morning dawned, which made them look on this place as its peculiar residence.

One night, a fellow being drunk, and by the strength of his liquor rendered more daring than ordinary, laughed at the simplicity of his companions, and, although it was not his turn to go with the keys, would needs take this office upon himself to testify his courage. All the soldiers endeavoured to dissuade him, but the more they said, the more resolute he seemed, and swore that he desired nothing more than that *Mauthe Doo* would follow him, as it had done the others, for he would try if it were Dog or Devil.

After having talked in a very reprobate manner for some time, he snatched up the keys and went out of the Guard-room. In some time after his departure, a great noise was heard, and no one had the boldness to see what had occasioned it, till the adventurer returning, they demanded the knowledge of him; but as loud and noisy as he had been at leaving them, he was now become sober and silent enough, for he was never heard to speak more; and though all the time he lived, which was three days, he was entreated by all who came near him, either to speak, or if he could not do that, to make some signs, by which they might understand what had happened to him, yet nothing intelligible could be got from him, only that, by the distortion of his limbs and features, it might be guessed that he died in agonies more than is common in a natural death.

The *Mauthe Doo* was, however, never seen after in the Castle, nor would anyone attempt to go through that passage, for which reason it was closed up, and another way made. This happened about 1666.

[About the Moddey Dhoo]: a man told me last year that it was not a dog at all, but the spirit of a man imprisoned in the Castle "for his sins".

The Moddey Dhoo species is not yet entirely extinct. One which has long haunted a locality near Ramsey is more deserving of fame than the Black Dog of Peel Castle, if only because he has been seen oftener and more recently. In 1927 a friend of mine met him one night at Milntown corner as she turned into Glen Aldyn. "He was black, with long shaggy hair, with eyes like coals of fire. I was frightened and would not pass, so we looked at each other, and the dog gave me a chance to pass him. It happened just before my father died."

(Gill)

That is the behaviour of the Galician urco.

Tibicena/Guacancha
Canary Islands

"The devil appears frequently by day and by night in several forms, including that of a hairy dog and other shapes called Tibicenas." (Arias Marín de Cubas, 1687)

The Tibicenas – Guacanchas in Tenerife – were demons in the bodies of big black dogs with red eyes that lived in caves and preyed on animals and people especially at night. (Galindo, 1632)

Shakra and the Black Dog
India

Shakra, king of the gods, saw that people had fallen away from religion and righteousness, so he disguised himself as a woodsman and changed his charioteer into a fearsome black dog with four large tusks and came into a large city. The dog chased everyone into their houses and howled in front of the king's palace.

"Why is your dog howling?" the king asked Shakra.

"He's hungry. Feed him."

The king ordered food to be taken out to the dog, but he quickly ate everything they sent and then devoured the king's horses and elephants before going on to consume all the food in the city.

"Why?" the king wanted to know.

"My dog will eat all my enemies, and my enemies are those who are evil. If there is no evil in the world you will be safe."

And then Shakra and the dog disappeared.

Black Shuck
England

> Is this the skeleton of legendary devil dog Black Shuck who terrorised 16th century East Anglia? Folklore tells of SEVEN FOOT hell hound with flaming eyes. (Headline, *The Daily Mail*, 16 May 2014)

Archaeologists found the skeleton of a dog alternately described in the *Mail* article as 7ft tall and 7ft long and weighing 200 pounds. "It was discovered a few miles from two churches where Black Shuck is said to have killed worshippers during an almighty thunderstorm in August 1577. What's more, it appears to have been buried in a shallow grave at precisely the same time as Shuck is said to have been on the loose, primarily around Suffolk and the East Anglia region."

The following is paraphrased and distilled from *A straunge and terrible wunder wrought very late in the parish church of Bongay* ..., a pamphlet published by Abraham Fleming in 1577.

On Sunday 4 August 1577, "to the amazing and singular astonishment of the present beholders and absent hearers, at a certain town called Bongay [Bungay], not past ten miles distant from the city of Norwich, there fell from heaven an exceeding great and terrible tempest, sudden and violent," with thunder and lightning at nine in the morning. The congregation in the parish church were "in a manner robbed of their right wits" because of the roaring and violence of the storm.

Suddenly, in the midst of the tumult, a black dog appeared in the church. It ran down the aisle and, passing between two people kneeling in prayer, "wrung the necks of them both at one instant clean backward." It gave a man "such a grip on the back, that therewithall he was presently drawn together and shrunk up, as if it were a piece of leather scorched in a hot fire." The man apparently survived miraculously. The marks of the beast's claws remain on the stones and the door as testament to the veracity of the report.

On the same day in the town of Blibery (Blythburgh), twelve miles from Bungay, the same creature entered a church and "slew two men and a lad and burned the hand of another person."

The story is referenced in the song "Black Shuck" on The Darkness's 2003 album *Permission to Land* and in a local rhyme.

> All down the church in the midst of fire,
> the hellish monster flew,
> and, passing onward to the quire,
> he many people slew.

The image of a black dog features in Bungay's coat of arms, and their football team is called the Black Dogs.

Reports of Black Shuck's death centuries ago seem to be premature. An American airman stationed at an East Anglia RAF base reported recently that when he was on guard duty alone one night, he encountered a large dark dog with red eyes in a locked hanger. The Yare Valley in Norfolk is reputed to be one of Black Shuck's haunts. It is described as a "huge, uncanny dog" the size of a horse and smelling of sulphur.

Dóelchú and the Death of Celtchar
Ireland

Ulsterman Celtchar mac Uthechair was all one could wish for in a warrior. With prominent ears and nose he was big and ugly with a temper to match. One of the reasons for his permanent foul mood was an unhappy encounter with the Connacht warrior Cet mac Matach. Not only that, but Cet had mocked him over the matter at a feast given by the hospitaller Mac Dathó. During a debate over who should have the Champion's Portion of food, Celtchar had boasted about killing Conganchnes mac Dedad, which incident is recounted below. That might have qualified him for the Champion's Portion, but then Cet sat down next to the pig and dared anyone to challenge him. Celtchar stood up.

"Ah, Celtchar," said Cet. "Do you remember the time I came to your house and you threw a spear at me and I threw one at you that took away your baby-makers? Since then, you have suffered from what the doctors call retention of urine, and you haven't produced any more sons or daughters."

Celtchar sat down.

So it's understandable that when he discovered that his wife had been unfaithful to him with Blái Briuga – though it wasn't entirely the man's fault, since *she* had seduced *him* – he went looking for revenge.

Blái knew he was in trouble, so he took refuge in the palace of King Conor. Conor was playing fidchell (a board game similar to chess) with his champion, Cúchulainn, and Blái was leaning over the board between them watching, when Celtchar tracked him down. He hurled his spear, and it went through Blái's chest and stuck in the wall behind him. A drop of blood trickled down the shaft and landed in the middle of the fidchell board.

"Well, Cúchulainn," said Conor.

"Well, indeed," said Cúchulainn.

They measured the distance from the drop to the edges of the board where the two were sitting to see which was the nearer, because that was the one who would be responsible for punishing Celtchar for the murder in the king's palace in front of the king. It was determined that the drop was closer to Conor.

The blood-eric or fine that Conor imposed required Celtchar to free Ulster from the most dreaded pests that would come in his lifetime.

The first pest was Conganchnes mac Dedad, who was ravaging Ulster and killing people in revenge for the death of his nephew, Cú Roí mac Dara mac Dedad, at the hands of Cúchulainn. The horn skin of Conganchnes made him impervious to weapons. To get around this problem, Celtchar offered to let Conganchnes marry his daughter, Niamh. Then he asked Niamh to find out how to kill him. The result was that Celtchar put a sleeping spell on Conganchnes and pounded red-hot iron spits through the soles of his feet and into the marrow of his shins. When he was dead, Celtchar cut off his head and raised a cairn – a heap of stones – over it.

The second pest was the Mousy-dun, a grey-tan dog that a widow raised from a pup she found in a hollow oak. When it grew up, it killed her sheep, cattle, son, and herself, and then went on to devastate the kingdom. Celtchar cut an alder log nearly the length of his arm, hollowed it out and boiled it in honey, herbs and grease, then placed it at the entrance of the beast's den. When the Mousy-dun bit into one end, its teeth got stuck in the soft, gluey wood, and its mouth was left wide open. Celtchar reached in the other end of the log, put his hand down the dog's throat, and pulled out its heart.

A year later, some cowherds heard whimpering from the cairn that Celtchar had erected over the head of Conganchnes. Inside they found three pups: a tan, a spotted and a black.

They gave the spotted one, Ailbe, to Mac Dathó, King of Leinster. She defended the whole kingdom and was famous all over Ireland, and she was the occasion for a major disturbance at the feast mentioned above. Queen Maeve of Connacht and King Conor of Ulster both politely requested the dog be given to them, with an implied “or else”. Mac Dathó was in a quandary: if he gave the dog to one of them, the other would invade his land and take the cattle and slaughter the people. His wife suggested he invite the Ulstermen and the Connachtmen, who had been at war for over three hundred years, to a feast to collect the dog and let them fight it out among themselves, and that’s what he did.

During the ensuing brawl, Mac Dathó let Ailbe loose to decide for herself which group she preferred, and she chose to fight on the side of Ulster, because Connacht was losing. She was eventually killed by Maeve’s charioteer in County Meath, where a standing stone, Lia Ailbhe, was erected in her memory near Clonalvy, the Meadow of Ailbe.

The tan one went to Culann the Smith, where it served as a guard dog. It attacked the boy Setanta as he approached the house one night, and he killed it in self-defence.

“It’s a great loss,” said Culann. “That dog wasn’t the weakest of the dogs that came out of the head of Conganchnes.”

To compensate Culann, Setanta offered to be his guard dog for a year while he raised and trained a replacement, thereby earning his name: Cúchulainn, the Hound of Culann, who became one of the two greatest heroes in Irish legend.

The black pup was given to Celtchar, who named him Dóelchú – “Chafer-hound” – for his resemblance to the black chafer beetle. This became the third pest. He would obey only Celtchar, and one day when Celtchar was away the dog escaped and started killing the cattle and sheep of Ulster.

“Rid us of this pest,” said Conor.

Celtchar went to where the dog had last been seen and called to him. Dóelchú came running to his master and lay down licking his feet.

“I won’t be blamed for what you do,” said Celtchar, and he ran his spear into the dog and brought out the heart on the tip of the spear. He held it aloft for everyone to see. A drop of blood trickled down the shaft and went through Celtchar into the ground, and so he died.

Miguel and the Black Dog
Cantabria and the Basque Country

Miguel, a cheerful and hard-working charcoal-maker from Gipuzkoa in the Basque Country, travelled west through Bizkaia in search of a place where he could ply his trade. Just across the border in Cantabria, he found a stand of arbutus (*madroño*), whose wood burns hotter and longer than oak – ideal for the making of charcoal – in a river valley east of the village of Otañes, which is six kilometres from the port town of Castro Urdiales on the Bay of Biscay. On the day he arrived, he built a simple cabin overlooking the bridge at the bend in the road where it crosses the river, and on the next day he began felling trees to make charcoal to sell to one of the blacksmiths in Otañes.

He relieved his solitude by singing and by calling out compliments to the women carrying baked goods to sell in Castro Urdiales every Tuesday and Sunday, and he struck up friendly and pleasant conversations with all who passed by. Among those bakers' vendors was the beautiful young Agustina, who crossed the 410m Monte Otañes on her westerly journey from the village of Sopuerta to Castro at sunrise and back again at sunset, 15 km in each direction. She rode a fine mule and was always accompanied by a small black dog. She broke her morning and evening journeys to stop and chat with Miguel, and the dog, nimble as a squirrel, climbed up the bank to the cabin to eat a piece of cornbread that Miguel left out for it.

One Sunday afternoon he was still asleep after working all night making charcoal. Two French tinkers on horseback stopped to rest by the side of the road in an alder thicket near the bridge. They took the saddle-bags off the horses and left them to graze in a nearby field. From where they sat as they ate their lunch, they could see Miguel's cabin, as well as the stretch of the road leading east from Otañes.

"The other day when we passed by here," said one, "there was a charcoal-maker up there in that cabin. I don't see anyone now. I wonder where he is."

"As it's Sunday, he's probably in Otañes changing his clothes and washing the charcoal dust out of his throat with a pint."

"So let's wash the dust of the road out of ours with a slice of ham and a couple of sips of wine."

And so they did, and soon they were merry enough.

"I wonder if anyone's sleeping in that cabin?" one said.

"We'll see," said the other, and he shouted "Yoo-hoo!" There was no response.

"No one's there, so maybe we can charge a toll for anyone who wants to cross the bridge."

"The problem is that there are no people on the road."

"Quiet! I hear someone coming."

Now they could hear the jingle of the cascabeles of a mule and a woman's voice singing, and soon Agustina appeared on her way home riding her fine mule followed by the small black dog.

"It's one of the bread vendors coming from Castro Urdiales. She should be carrying three or four pesos."

"Which we wouldn't earn in three or four days making pots."

"She looks like a lively one."

"Better and better."

"And that's a superb mule."

"Suitable for a man of my weight."

"Money, maid and mule – a three-way win."

Agustina called out when she was opposite the cabin: "Miguel?"

The little black dog climbed the bank to the cabin for its usual treat. Miguel remained asleep. Hearing no reply, Agustina continued along the road. When the dog heard the bells jingling as the mule moved on, it ran back down the bank to join its mistress. After passing the bridge, Agustina noticed the tinkers on the road, lounging against a boulder. The sight made her nervous, but she continued on her way, trying to appear calm.

"Good evening, gentlemen," she said.

"Hello, lovely lady," one of the tinkers said. "Where are you coming from?"

"From Castro."

"You know that you have to pay a toll for the bridge, don't you?"

"What bridge?"

"The one you just crossed."

"How much do I have to pay?"

"All the money you have," said one, grabbing her as the other took hold of the mule's halter.

"Jesus, save me!" cried Agustina, as the tinker swept her off the mule and carried her to the alder thicket.

The little dog launched itself at the legs of his mistress's attacker, but the tinker kicked it out of the way, crippling it.

"Save me, Holy Virgin!" Agustina shouted. "Miguel, Miguel, help!"

The dog dragged itself up to the cabin and barked desperately. Miguel woke up and heard Agustina's calls for help. He looked out the window and saw one tinker holding the mule, while there was violent movement in the bushes. He was overcome with terror, thinking that there might be more than one evil-doer assaulting Agustina, and he didn't dare leave the cabin. The dog stood at the door howling miserably, while the weakening voice of Agustina cried, "Miguel, help. They're killing me."

When the dog saw that Miguel did not pick up his axe and go to help his mistress, it ran out the door. Soon Agustina's cries stopped, and Miguel saw the tinkers mount and ride east toward Bizkaia, while the dog howled incessantly. Once they had gone, Miguel took the road in the opposite direction to Otañes to report the attack. In the growing dark of the evening, and with the mournful cries of the dog still audible behind him, he rebuked himself for his cowardice in not trying to protect Agustina. As he reached a chestnut grove at the edge of the village, he suddenly saw in front of him the little black dog, growling fiercely with eyes that glowed like live coals. Then it disappeared as suddenly.

The village magistrate and the doctor accompanied Miguel to the scene of the crime to treat the victim if there was still time, or recover the body if not. On the way, Miguel saw the dog repeatedly crossing in front of him, staring at him with those burning red eyes. The others did not see it, but as they approached the alder grove they could hear the sad cries of the dog next to its mistress. The doctor was able to revive her briefly, but she expired after describing her killers. They carried the body into Otañes, followed by the dog, but Miguel stayed in his cabin.

In an effort to dispel his fear, Miguel built a bonfire in front of the door and managed to fall asleep, but whenever he woke during the night, he could see the dog sitting next to the fire, showing its teeth with the eyes glowing. So in the morning, he threw a lump of cod across the embers, along with the piece of cornbread he had saved the previous day, to mollify the dog. Then he went down to the river to have a drink before returning to work at the charcoal making. But when he bent down to wash his face in a pool in the river, he saw in it the dog baring its teeth. He looked up at the rocks on the bank, thinking the dog had climbed up there, and he was seeing a reflection in the water. But, no, the dog was nowhere in sight. A sense of dread crept across him that he couldn't explain.

All day long he saw the dog at his side, and he thought he could still hear the desperate cry of "Miguel, Miguel" from the alder grove. That evening, he made a wooden cross and planted it where the blood of Agustina still stained the ground, and then he took the road across the border for Galdames in Bizkaia.

He ran into friends there from Gipuzkoa who were also charcoal-makers. He told them what had happened, and they said he should stay there and work, while two of them would go and finish his task at Otañes. He was happy to accept the proposition, but in the evening he saw before him the black dog staring at him with flashing eyes and menacing teeth. The same thing happened the following days and nights, unsettling his imagination and giving him no peace or sleep. Then one day he didn't see the beast, and he relaxed, until it suddenly appeared three paces in front of him, as usual baring its teeth and with eyes of fire. He angrily picked up his axe and brought it down on the animal, splitting it in half. He slept that night, content that he had rid himself of his persecutor. But the next day the dog appeared again, more irritated than ever, with no mark of injury on its body.

He told his friends that he was going to Bilbao and take a ship to San Sebastián to see if he could free himself of the dog.

"That dog must be the devil," they said. "If it appears again, make the Sign of the Cross, and you'll see how it disappears."

He went down the mountain to Güeñes and followed the Cadagua River until just before he reached Alonsotegui on the west side of Bilbao. At the side of the road there was an iron cross mounted on a stone column with the inscription: "Here died Don Diego de los Hoyos on the 9th of December 1675. Pray for him." The monument had stood for nearly two centuries, impervious to damage by the elements, as a symbol of the Redemption. Hat in hand, Miguel approached the cross saying an Our Father, when he saw the black dog at the foot of the cross with glittering eyes and menacing teeth.

It wasn't the devil that pursued and threatened him, it was God – and his own conscience.

He boarded a ship in Bilbao, thinking that at least during the voyage to San Sebastián he would not be pursued by the horrible vision, but he was wrong. Late in the afternoon, as the ship approached San Sebastián, Miguel saw the black dog on the deck in its usual threatening attitude.

He stayed for a few days at the family home, but he had now lost his reason. The black dog continued to haunt him, and one afternoon he went to the beach with the intention to end his misfortune by ending his life. The black dog appeared along the road, and this stiffened his resolution. When he arrived, he made his way to the top of a rock at whose foot the waves crashed furiously enough to guarantee a swift departure. But as he gazed around at the picturesque city and colourful gardens and surrounding landscape, and listened to the bells and songs of a festival, he thought that life is beautiful in spite of misfortunes, and he renounced his intention to abandon it voluntarily.

As he climbed down from the rock, he heard a scream from the far end of the beach, and he saw a head that appeared and disappeared between the waves.

"Miguel, Miguel!" came the desperate cry.

It was the same sound that had never left his memory, and he launched himself into the sea with the abandon and anxiety of a father racing to rescue his child. Moments later, he was holding in his arms a young girl, who the waves kept trying to tear from his grasp. Long and hard was the battle, but finally Miguel, battered and bruised and half dead from emotion and fatigue, managed to stumble on to the beach and deposit the girl into the arms of her grateful family. Her father, a wealthy banker from Madrid, wept and shook the calloused hand of the labourer who had saved his daughter.

Miguel took the road home exactly at sunset, the hour when the black dog was most likely to make its presence known, but this time it didn't appear. Several days passed with no sight of the dog. One day the wealthy banker came to the door and handed Miguel a purse containing a hundred ounces of gold, in gratitude for the rescue of his daughter.

That is my translation and paraphrasing of "El Perro Negro" by folklorist, poet and novelist Antonio de Trueba (1819-89) from *Cuentos Populares*, 1864. Some of the stories in the book are localised international folk tales. Others are romanticised but fact-based historical legends. De Trueba was born in poverty and lived to the age of 15 in Galdames, about five km from Agustina's village of Sopuerta. In his youth he worked in the mines locally and a blacksmith shop in Madrid. This is his account of how he heard the basis of the Black Dog story.

He and his brother and some cousins were crossing Monte Otañes on the night of 28 September 1859 when they met a young man from nearby Las Muñecas known to his brother. The man explained that he was searching for a stray sheep, had heard that the group was on the road, and decided to join them for safety – "because I don't pass this way at night alone."

"Why? Are there robbers here?"

"No. In this land you are well advised to carry a bag of coins in your hand so no one bothers you."

"What are you afraid of?"

"The black dog."

The young man told them about the murder and the apparitions of the black dog as he led them to the wooden cross that Miguel had erected in memory of Agustina. De Trueba said he was so frightened that he thought he could see the dog among the alders. He said the murder took place "12 or 14 years ago", presumably dating from the publication of the book. It sounds as if he heard a real local tale – and the belief in a phantom Black Dog or urco is widespread in the Basque Country and the north of Spain – but he probably added fictitious details.

A hundred ounces of gold is worth about €100,000 today. A charcoal-maker was among the lowest on the social scale, just above the knacker, who rendered dead animals to make ingredients for useful products like soap and stank as a result of his trade.

The Hanging Judge and the Black Dog
Ireland

John Toler (1745-1831) was Solicitor-General then Attorney General in charge of prosecuting rebels – or suspected rebels – after the 1798 Rebellion. When he was appointed Lord Chief Justice in 1800 as Lord Norbury, the Lord Chancellor was prompted to say, "For God's sake make him a bishop or even an archbishop, but not a Chief Justice." His contemporary, Daniel O'Connell, the leading advocate of his time, said, "He did not understand, nor was he capable of understanding, a single principle of law." A modern historian has described him as "one of the most black-hearted and sadistic scoundrels who ever wore scarlet and ermine" (Hale). Even *The Dictionary of National Biography* saw fit to comment: "His indifference to human suffering … disgusted even those who thought the occasion called for firmness on the part of government." A modern account echoes contemporary opinion: "His knowledge of law was negligible and his style of administration was ludicrous." (Lysaght)

So it is not surprising that Lord Norbury, labelled The Hanging Judge, turns up in local legends. A Brendan Behan short story alerted me to one of them. A man is hired to collect and deliver a coffin. Between the collection and the delivery, he comes to a pub and decides to stop for refreshment. Several drinks later, he emerges to find his cart empty. The coffin: "And where was it, only gone, like Lord Norbury with the devil." This is the tale behind that expression.

Lord Norbury owned a town house at Number 3 Great Denmark Street near Dublin's city centre. His country home was a few miles away in Cabra. One night, he called on his coach driver to take him from town to Cabra. When the coach arrived in Cabra, the driver opened the door for his passenger, only to find the coach empty. He said later that about halfway through the journey the coach seemed unusually light, and he concluded that the devil had snatched Lord Norbury en route.

Norbury wrongfully convicted a man for sheep-stealing, and the victim's widow on her deathbed cursed the judge that he would never have a peaceful night's sleep. A widow's curse is matched only by that of a priest or a poet for effectiveness, and it is known that Norbury was an insomniac for the rest of his life.

It is still told in the Cabra area that Norbury in the form of a large black dog dragging a chain was seen near his house until it was demolished in 1939. A block of flats was built on the site in 2003 to commemorate Norbury's hanging of Robert Emmet, leader of a failed revolt, in 1803.

Some say that the ghost of the Hanging Judge still prowls the neighbourhood.

The Black Thing on the Handlebars
Ireland

John Skehan spent his working life with the Irish national radio and television broadcaster, RTÉ. He told me that he didn't believe in ghosts and suchlike, but he did have a strange experience that he couldn't explain. His voice was perfect for radio – low, soft, warm and reassuringly calm – and his off-air personality was the same.

In his early twenties, he was cycling one day through the hills in the south of the country, when a black shaggy Thing leapt from the bushes and settled on his handlebars and sat there staring at him. John indicated with his hands that it was the size of a large cocker spaniel, but it was no kind of animal that he had ever seen before.

"I didn't know what it might do if I stopped," he said matter-of-factly, "so I kept on cycling. After what was probably only a minute or so but seemed like an hour, it leapt off. So I continued cycling and wondered: what on earth was that?"

The Cailín Deas Curse
Ireland

Among suggestions in Seán Ó Súilleabháin's *A Handbook of Irish Folklore* for folklore collectors to ask about is "dogs sing *Cailín Deas Crúidhte na mBó* [the pretty girl milking the cow] to delay priest on sick-call." The implication is that the dogs – some say they were black – were demons whose intention was to prevent the priest reaching the dying man in time. This is how I heard and tell the story.

In the north of County Cork, a priest was called out to attend a dying man and administer the Last Sacraments. On his way, there came to his ears the most literally enchanting music he had ever heard. The tune was "Cailín Deas Crúidhte na mBó". He paused to listen, and when the tune finished he discovered he had been there for hours, and he knew that it was fairy music. He hastened to the dying man's house to find that the man had died without receiving Extreme Unction. He cursed the tune instead of admitting the delay was his fault, and it is said that in that part of County Cork people refuse to play it because of the curse.

Pat Connery has been playing her uillean pipes at the entrance to the Monastic City at Glendalough in County Wicklow for many years, and "Cailín Deas Crúidhte na mBó" is in her repertoire. When I take people to Glendalough, we stop in front of Pat, and I tell the story as an example of genuine non-touristic folklore and ask her to play the tune for us.

There is real magic in the tune. Whenever I play it on the harp, no matter what key I use, it always comes out with a different flavour.

Benevolent Black Dogs
England

Ethel Rudkin's article about Black Dogs in Lincolnshire in the journal *Folklore* (1938) is regarded as a benchmark in the study of the phenomenon. She said she had seen a Black Dog in 1926 at the ruined Dunwich Abbey before she was aware of the local tradition, and so believed those who said they had seen one, and she vouched for the sincerity of her informants. These are quotes and paraphrased snippets from the article.

A man shot at a Black Dog and his gun-barrel broke.

It is often seen near Roman roads and probable ancient trackways and "does not cross a parish boundary".

As she cycled, a schoolmistress regularly saw a Black Dog trotting along the grass verge beside her. She would become aware of its presence and then become aware that it wasn't there: she didn't actually see it appear and disappear. She said she liked to know that it was there.

A lay preacher walking home at night saw a large Black Dog suddenly appear at his side. A brave and strong man, he later said that he'd rather deal with a man than a dog, but he felt the dog was there to protect him.

A woman on her way home "noticed that a very large dog was walking behind her; this was a strange dog to her, one she had never seen before. Presently she passed some Irish labourers, and she heard them say what they would do to the lone woman if 'that (something) dog hadn't been with her.'"

"It leaps into the road and runs before the spectator, leaping back over another gate farther on. It always comes and goes on one's left." The dog "always left them at the same hand-gate." Several people report that it appears and disappears at the same place.

A woman walking alone to visit a sick friend at night was joined by a large black shaggy dog at a certain point. It walked with her to a certain point and vanished. On her way home two hours later, the dog joined her where it had left her and vanished again where it had first joined her. She thought it was "nice of the old Dog to wait for her".

A woman walking home alone at night noticed a large Black Dog following her. Annoyed, she gave it a good wallop with her umbrella. She almost fainted when the umbrella went through the animal.

Children were discussing stories of the Black Dog, and they asked their nurse what she would do if she met with one. "I shall put 'im i' my pocket," she said. On her way home, the Dog appeared and said, "Put me in yer pocket, put me in yer pocket."

Some call it a boggart in Lincolnshire, with the usual description of a Black Dog. One walked into a house, strolled around the kitchen and then walked out.

One informant told Mrs Rudkin: "No matter 'ow dark a night it is, you can allus see the Dog because 'e's so much blacker."

A Black Dog Survey
England

Theo Brown shared some of his findings in "The Black Dog", *Folklore* 1958, after giving due deference to Mrs Rudkin.

> It is always associated with a definite place or "beat" on a road. It is always an individual.
>
> Only in North Devon is there a patch of Black Dogs following a number of parish boundaries, according to Mrs Barbara Carbonnel, which suggests a topographical dog of great antiquity.
>
> At Uplyme in Devon, the Black Dog used to patrol the Dorset boundary along Dog Lane, behind the Black Dog Inn. [See also "The Resident Avoca Púca."]
>
> Some of the city dogs may be prehistoric.
>
> At least six churches have Black Dogs, and two rectories have them inside.
>
> Miss Ruth Tongue states that she knows of three cases in Somerset where a black dog was secretly buried in a churchyard to protect a new extension.
>
> ... it is apparent that the dog occurs on sites where violent death of any kind has taken place.
>
> It is to be remembered that the Black Dog in all Scandinavian countries is believed to be the devil.
>
> In two places it has been suggested by the local people that the Black Dog is someone dressed up by smugglers, etc.
>
> At Hatfield Peverell (Essex) a man struck at the dog, and man, horse, waggon and load were all burnt to ashes (surely an excessive penalty?).
>
> Horses and dogs are terrified when they see the Black Dog.

Saved from Robbers
England

A man travelled a mile through a wood one night. As he entered the wood, a large black dog joined him and accompanied him until he emerged from the wood. On his way back shortly afterwards, the dog met him at the entrance to the wood and trotted along beside him until he exited. Years later, he discovered that two condemned prisoners had confessed that they had planned to rob and kill him that night, but they changed their minds when they saw the dog with him.

(Briggs)

The Midwife and the Black Dog
England

This story from Tollesbury in Essex seems to be little known outside the area. The most comprehensive account I've found is that given by the unnamed son of the unnamed midwife to Stanley Coren in his *Gods, Ghosts, and Black Dogs*, 2016.

In the 1960s, the midwife would be called at all hours to attend women in labour, cycling along roads she had known from childhood. She was obviously a brave woman, but there was one area that made her nervous whenever she had to pass it, especially at night: Tolleshunt D'Arcy.

When she was a child, several children had mysteriously disappeared in that district. One night, a priest came across a large black dog scratching at the ground. He stopped, and the dog ran away. Curious, the priest inspected the spot where the dog had been digging and found the remains of a child. Other bodies were then discovered, and a man was arrested, but he escaped and committed suicide. Personal tragedy had evidently unhinged him. He said that he had lost two wives in childbirth, and he felt that children were evil and deserved to die. His body is believed to be buried where he had disposed of the children's bodies at Tolleshunt D'Arcy.

Returning home late one night from a delivery, as she passed Tolleshunt D'Arcy the midwife glanced up the hill and saw the figure of a man dressed in black. He was moving at a speed and in a direction that meant he would soon intercept her on the road. Then she saw a large black dog with fiery red eyes on the road in front of her. She stopped, assuming the dog belonged to the man and that he would call it to him. But the dog walked beside her, keeping itself between her and the man and growling at the man, who stopped. The dog stayed with her until the lights of Tollesbury came into view, and then it disappeared.

The following day, the midwife related the incident to the local vicar and his wife. The vicar's wife suggested that the midwife was carrying the scent of childbirth after the delivery, and this may have awakened the spectre of the murderer. Also, regardless of whether the dog that had exposed the grave was physical or a spirit, it may have been the same spirit or a revenant that accompanied the midwife when the spectre of the killer appeared.

The Cadejo
Central America

The cadejo resembles the Black Dog though with goat's feet. The name may derive from *cadena*, the Spanish for "chain", because it is often seen dragging a chain. It is believed that it originated with the indigenous people as a psychopomp, conducting humans to the Afterlife, more or less the function of the urco. With the European influence of Christian dualism, now the white cadejo is blue-eyed and benevolent, guarding late-night travellers, including drunks, against attack, especially from the malevolent fiery-eyed black cadejo. However, if the black cadejo is the type that is the Devil in disguise, even the white cadejo might not be able to stop it.

In El Salvador, two brothers visited a wizard. He asked them to help by gathering firewood. They neglected to do this, and they ate all his food. When the man discovered this, he cursed a part of the road that led to their village. As the brothers were walking home, they heard voices, but they turned their backs on them – it's well known that you shouldn't do that – and they were transformed into a white and a black cadejo. When they arrived home in their new forms, they were exiled to roam the roads forever.

A similar tradition is current in the north of Argentina, according to my Argentinian friend, Carlos Saenz Saralegui. He told me that if a black dog bars your way, it is because there is danger ahead, and you should not proceed. A white dog means the road is safe. Carlos did not recognise the term "cadejo".

See also "A Protector Coyote" in the Shape-shifters section.

PÚCAS

Ireland

Puck: Old English *púca*; Old Norse *púki*. "The ulterior history of the name and the question whether it was originally Teutonic or Celtic, is unsettled."

Oxford English Dictionary

Forms of the Púca

The púca (pooka) is a non-threatening beast that in Ireland normally appears as a pony-sized black dog with fiery red eyes. At worst, it can startle a person when it materialises out of thin air, but it is generally congenial and benevolent, or at least neutral, and has been credited with saving lives. Confusingly, water horses like the Scottish kelpie, which typically take a human foolish enough to mount them on a wild ride before dumping him in a river, are also called púcas in Ireland.

> I find the Pooka a difficult spirit to define or even to name in a satisfying way, for so many experts use many different forms of the name and describe many different appearances and behaviours of this spirit. Its exact type seems peculiar to Ireland, but the form in which it appears can vary so from place to place, from century to century, and even from person to person that it can easily become quite bewildering.
>
> (MacManus)

> At this time of the year [1 November] that vicious and terrifying apparition the Pooka, which the peasantry describe as resembling a cross between a mule, a bullock, and a big black pig, was very liable to be met with by the unwary if out late at night. By all accounts, to be in a runaway motor would be preferable to a ride on the Pooka's back, which it is his object to bring about.

(FitzGerald, "Customs Peculiar ...", 1908)

It is well known that you should not pick blackberries after the First of November, because on November Eve (Halloween) the púca pisses on the bushes. Most sources use the euphemism "spits" or: "On November Eve the fairies pass over all such things and make them unfit to eat," as a priest told Evans-Wentz.

> In Co. Carlow & gen. in Leinster (as well as I know) the púca is an enchanted horse, which lies on the grass as quiet as a lamb in some conspicuous spot until some unwary individual decided to go for a ride on him. God help him who goes for a nocturnal ride on a púca. Seven tours of the earth is nothing to him, hell for leather the whole time & at the end of the joy ride he invariably flings off his victim into the middle of a brake of briars, nettles, etc.
>
> If a man caught his horse or a neighbour's horse after dark, no power on earth would persuade him to get up on it. And many a man wouldn't mount his own at night even if he saw him coming out of his own stable. Sure it might be the púca.
>
> Verbatim from the National Folklore Collection, NFC 462:356
>
> Collector: Peadar MacDomhnaill, January 1938
>
> Source: John English, Co. Limerick

Puck and the Púca

Shakespeare's "shrewd and knavish sprite call'd Robin Goodfellow", alias Puck, in *A Midsummer Night's Dream* is a loose borrowing of the horse form of the púca.

> I'll follow you, I'll lead you about a round,
> Through bog, through bush, through brake, through brier:

Sometime a horse I'll be, sometime a hound,
A hog, a headless bear, sometime a fire;
And neigh, and bark, and grunt, and roar, and burn,
Like horse, hound, hog, bear, fire, at every turn.

Robin Goodfellow is also lumped in with things that go bump in the night or cause panic in the woods, as with the man in one of Pilpay's fables who "ran home as if a thousand robin-goodfellows or raw-head and bloody-bones had been at his heels."

Another aspect of the Irish púca is his helpfulness, as related in "The Kildare Pooka" and "The Piper and the Púca" below. A fairy points out this quality in *A Midsummer Night's Dream*:

Those that Hobgoblin call you and sweet Puck,
You do their work, and they shall have good luck.

The following two stories are from *The Middle Kingdom: The Faerie World of Ireland* (1959), in which Dermot MacManus relates anecdotes about the Fair Folk told to him by people he knew personally and who had no reason to lie. The opening to the first story goes like this: "In 1952 a friend of mine, Margo Ryan, a charming and intelligent girl, encountered the Pooka in a way that is typical."

A Redcross Púca

It was a midsummer evening with light still lingering in the sky. As Margo walked along a quiet back road near the village of Redcross in the County Wicklow hills, she heard the soft patter of steps and turned to see an enormous black dog keeping pace with her. She felt no fear and put her hand out to pet it, but her hand went through the dog. It moved slightly away to the side but kept pace with her, then came closer. Again she tried to pet it, but her hand met nothing but air, even though the animal looked solid. It moved on ahead and continued walking in front of her until it vanished from the middle of the road.

"Let there be no doubt about it whatever," MacManus emphasises: "it did not run off but actually vanished from where it stood in the centre of the road."

That and other stories in *The Middle Kingdom* and from other sources suggest that the dog-form púca is territorial. Like any dog – or, indeed, a robin or a shopkeeper – it takes a keen proprietorial interest in those passing through its realm. One of MacManus's tales has an intriguing difference: a fearsome-looking beast with a playful sense of humour.

A Northern Ireland Púca

In 1928 a young man home on break from university was fishing in a drought-diminished stream in County Derry, when he noticed a large black dog walking towards him in the shallow water. As it drew near, the man realised that it was no ordinary big dog; it was the size of a pony, and he felt a strong sense of horror. He dropped his fishing tackle and climbed a young ash tree that bent alarmingly with his weight. As the dog passed by it looked up at him with a malevolent leer and a mocking grin, as if it enjoyed terrorising a human just for fun.

The Resident Avoca Púca

Tommy was about 18 years old, working at the Handweavers in Avoca, County Wicklow, when I was living there in the 1980s. One day in conversation he mentioned the friendly local púca, which I had not heard about before. He said that where he lived with his mother at a bend in the Vale Road about a mile and a half (2 km) south of Avoca Village at Garnagowlan, they frequently saw a large non-frightening black dog with fiery red eyes in the early evenings.

It was years later that I came across a curious entry in the authoritative *The Place-names of Co. Wicklow* by Liam Price under Garnagowlan. Unusually, Price was at a loss to discover the meaning or the story behind the name on the Vale Road: "The Black Dog: Perhaps it was originally the name of an inn." If so, how did the inn get its name? That spot is not suitable for an inn, and it's barely half a mile from the Woodenbridge Hotel, established in 1608 and claiming to be the oldest hotel in Ireland. Price was working from the Ordnance Survey map of 1839, so the name The Black Dog obviously originated long before then. That is strong evidence that the Avoca púca is an ageless elemental: a chthonic or earth spirit.

One of the driving principles behind Price's decades-long research was what he called "historical continuity": "when the stories themselves were forgotten, place-names contained in them still survived, and have lasted down to our own day."

Compare the "Uplyme in Devon" entry about the Black Dog Inn in Black Dogs.

Poulaphuca
("Pool of the Púca")

Many years ago, I asked a waitress at the Poulaphuca Inn near Blessington on the border of Counties Wicklow and Kildare if she knew how the pool under the waterfall behind the hotel, part of the course of the River Liffey, came to be named the Pool of the Púca. She made up a yarn on the spot about a púca being knocked down by a car, probably inspired by the fact that a lorry had recently crashed through the parapet of the bridge over the waterfall. I asked her if she knew the real story, and she admitted that she didn't. Here it is, paraphrased from Padraic O'Farrell's *Irish Ghost Stories*.

In 1813, before the bridge was built, the Kildare Hunt, known as the Killing Kildares, was chasing a fox, when an unfamiliar large black riderless horse joined them as they neared the waterfall. The fox leapt across the gorge but failed to get a grip on the opposite ledge and fell into the pool. The strange horse made the jump successfully, and the hounds attempted to follow it but fell into the pool. The fox managed to swim to safety, but most of the hounds were lost.

The mysterious black horse was described afterwards as a púca with fiery red eyes and a diabolically triumphant neigh, but it sounds more like a water horse.

The Kildare Pooka

A Literary Folk Tale by Patrick Kennedy

Mr. H-----R-----, when he was alive, used to live a good deal in Dublin, and he was once a great while out of the country on account of the "Ninety-eight" business [the 1798 Rebellion].

But the servants kept on in the big house at Rath-----, all the same as if the family was at home. Well, they used to be frightened out of their lives after going to their beds, with the banging of the kitchen door and the clattering of the fire-irons, and the pots, and plates, and dishes. One evening they sat up ever so long, keeping one another in heart with telling stories about ghosts and fetches and that when – what would you have of it? – the little scullery boy that used to be sleeping over the horses, and couldn't get room at the fire, crept into the hot hearth, and when he got tired listening to the stories, sorra fear him but he fell dead asleep.

Well and good, after they were all gone, and the fire raked up, he was woke with the noise of the kitchen door opening, and the trampling of an ass on the kitchen floor. He peeped out, and what should he see but a big grey ass, sure enough, sitting on his currabingo, and yawning before the fire. After a little, he looked about him, and began scratching his ears as if he was quite tired, and says he, "I may as well begin first as last."

The poor boy's teeth began to chatter in his head, for says he, "Now he's goin' to ate me;" but the fellow with the long ears and tail on him, had something else to do. He stirred up the fire, and then he brought in a pail of water from the pump, and filled a big pot, that he put on the fire before he went out. He then put in his hand – foot, I mean – into the hot hearth, and pulled out the little boy. He let a roar out of him with the fright, but the pooka only looked at him, and thrust out his lower lip to show how little he valued him, and then he pitched him into his pew again.

Well, he then lay down before the fire till he heard the boil coming on the water, and maybe there wasn't a plate, or a dish, or a spoon on the dresser, that he didn't fetch and put into the pot, and wash and dry the whole hum' of 'em as well as e'er a kitchenmaid from that to Dublin town. He then put all of them up in their places on the shelves, and, if he didn't give a good sweepin' to the kitchen after all, leave it till again. Then he comes and sits fornent the boy, let down one of his ears and cocked up the other, and gave a grin. The poor fellow strove to roar out, but not a dheeg 'ud come out of his throat. The last thing the pooka done was to rake up the fire, and walk out, giving such a slap o' the door that the boy thought the house couldn't help tumbling down.

Well, to be sure, if there wasn't a hullabulloo next morning, when the poor fellow told his story! They could talk of nothing else the whole day. One said one thing, another said another, but a fat, lazy scullery girl said the wittiest thing of all. "Musha!" says she, "if the pooka does be cleaning up everything that way when we're asleep, what should we be slaving ourselves for, doing his work?" "*Sha gu dheine*," [*Sea, go deimhin*: yes, indeed] says another: "them's the wisest words you ever said, Kauth: it's meself won't contradict you."

So said so done. Not a bit of a plate or dish saw a drop of water that evening, and not a besom was laid on the floor, and everyone went to bed soon after sundown. Next morning everything was as fine as fire in the kitchen, and the lord mayor might eat his dinner off the flags. It was great ease to the lazy servants, you may depend, and everything went on well till a foolhardy gag of a boy said he would stay up one night and have a chat with the pooka.

He was a little daunted when the door was thrown open, and the ass marched up to the fire. He didn't open his mouth till the pot was filled, and the pooka lying snug and sausty before the fire.

"Ah then, sir!" says he, at last, picking up courage, "if it isn't taking a liberty, might I ax who you are, and why are you so kind as to do half of the day's work for the girls every night?"

"No liberty at all," says the pooka, says he. "I'll tell you, and welcome. I was a servant here in the time of Squire R.'s father, and was the laziest rogue that ever was clothed and fed, and done nothing for it. When my time came for the other world, this is the punishment was laid on me – to come here, and do all this labour every night, and then go out in the cold. It isn't so bad in the fine weather, but if you only knew what it is to stand with your head between your legs, facing the storm, from midnight to sunrise on a bleak winter night!"

"And could we do anything for your comfort, my poor fellow?" says the boy.

"Musha, I don't know," says the pooka; "but I think a good quilted frieze coat would help to keep the life in me, them long nights."

"Why then, in throth, we'd be the ungratefulest of people if we didn't feel for you."

To make a long story short, the next night but two the boy was there again; and if he didn't delight the poor Pooka, holding up a fine warm coat before him, it's no matter! Betune the pooka and the man, his legs were got into the four arms of it, and it was buttoned down his breast and his belly, and he was so pleased, he walked up to the glass to see how he looked.

"Well," says he, "it's a long lane that has no turning. I am much obliged to yourself and your fellow-servants. Yous have made me happy at last: good-night to you."

So he was walking out, but the other cried, "Och! sure you're going too soon: what about the washing and sweeping?"

"Ah, you may tell the girls that they must now get their turn. My punishment was to last till I was thought worthy of a reward for the way I done my duty. You'll see me no more."

And no more they did, and right sorry they were for being in such a hurry to reward the ungrateful pooka.

(Verbatim from Kennedy. Also in Yeats.)

The Piper and the Púca

A Literary Folk Tale by Douglas Hyde

Translated literally from the Irish of the *Leabhar Sgeulaigheachta* (Story Book).

In the old times, there was a half-fool living in Dunmore, in the county Galway, and although he was excessively fond of music, he was unable to learn more than one tune, and that was the "Black Rogue". He used to get a good deal of money from the gentlemen, for they used to get sport out of him. One Oiche Shamhna (November Eve – Halloween) the piper was coming home from a house where there had been a dance, and he half drunk. When he came to a little bridge that was up by his mother's house, he squeezed the pipes on, and began playing the "Black Rogue" (an rógaire dubh). The Púca came behind him and flung him up on his own back. There were long horns on the Púca, and the piper got a good grip of them, and then he said:

"Destruction on you, you nasty beast, let me home. I have a ten-penny piece in my pocket for my mother, and she wants snuff."

"Never mind your mother," said the Púca, "but keep your hold. If you fall, you will break your neck and your pipes." Then the Púca said to him, "Play up for me the 'Shan Van Vocht' (an t-seann-bhean bhocht – The Poor Old Woman)."

"I don't know it," said the piper.

"Never mind whether you do or you don't," said the Púca. "Play up, and I'll make you know."

The piper put wind in his bag, and he played such music as made himself wonder.

"Upon my word, you're a fine music-master," says the piper then, "but tell me where you're for bringing me."

"There's a great feast in the house of the Banshee, on the top of Croagh Patric tonight," says the Púca, "and I'm for bringing you there to play music, and, take my word, you'll get the price of your trouble."

"By my word, you'll save me a journey, then," says the piper, "for Father William put a journey to Croagh Patric on me, because I stole the white gander from him last Martinmas."

The Púca rushed him across hills and bogs and rough places, till he brought him to the top of Croagh Patric. Then the Púca struck three blows with his foot, and a great door opened, and they passed in together, into a fine room.

The piper saw a golden table in the middle of the room, and hundreds of old women (cailleacha) sitting round about it. The old woman rose up, and said, "A hundred thousand welcomes to you, you Púca of November (na Samhna). Who is this you have brought with you?"

"The best piper in Ireland," says the Púca.

One of the old women struck a blow on the ground, and a door opened in the side of the wall, and what should the piper see coming out but the white gander which he had stolen from Father William.

"By my conscience, then," says the piper, "myself and my mother ate every taste of that gander, only one wing, and I gave that to Moy-rua (Red Mary), and it's she told the priest I stole his gander."

The gander cleaned the table, and carried it away, and the Púca said, "Play up music for these ladies."

The piper played up, and the old women began dancing, and they were dancing till they were tired. Then the Púca said to pay the piper, and every old woman drew out a gold piece, and gave it to him.

"By the tooth of Patric," said he, "I'm as rich as the son of a lord."

"Come with me," says the Púca, "and I'll bring you home."

They went out then, and just as he was going to ride on the Púca, the gander came up to him, and gave him a new set of pipes. The Púca was not long until he brought him to Dunmore, and he threw the piper off at the little bridge, and then he told him to go home, and says to him, "You have two things now that you never had before – you have sense and music (ciall agus ceól)."

The piper went home, and he knocked at his mother's door, saying, "Let me in, I'm as rich as a lord, and I'm the best piper in Ireland."

"You're drunk," said the mother.

"No, indeed," says the piper, "I haven't drunk a drop."

The mother let him in, and he gave her the gold pieces, and, "Wait now," says he, "till you hear the music, I'll play."

He buckled on the pipes, but instead of music, there came a sound as if all the geese and ganders in Ireland were screeching together. He awakened the neighbours and they all were mocking him, until he put on the old pipes, and then he played melodious music for them, and after that he told them all he had gone through that night.

The next morning, when his mother went to look at the gold pieces, there was nothing there but the leaves of a plant.

The piper went to the priest, and told him his story, but the priest would not believe a word from him, until he put the pipes on him, and then the screeching of the ganders and geese began.

"Leave my sight, you thief," said the priest.

But nothing would do the piper till he would put the old pipes on him to show the priest that his story was true.

He buckled on the old pipes, and he played melodious music, and from that day till the day of his death, there was never a piper in the county Galway was as good as he was.

Douglas Hyde (1860-1949) was a collector of folk tales and songs before he became the first president of Ireland after independence. His English translation is from Yeats.

The Hill of the Speaking Steed

It is the general opinion of many old persons versed in native traditional lore, that, before the introduction of Christianity, all animals possessed the faculties of human reason and speech; and old story-tellers will gravely inform you that every beast could speak before the arrival of St. Patrick, but that the Saint having expelled the demons from the land by the sound of his bell, all the animals, that before that time had possessed the power of foretelling future events, such as the Black Steed of Binn-each-labhra, the Royal Cat at Clogh-magh-righ-cat (Clough), and others, became mute; and many of them fled to Egypt, and other foreign countries.

(O'Kearney, also Graves)

Dun-Binn-each-labhra, which is now called *Binneach Luna*, in the province of Ulster; the reason the hill was called *Binn-each-labhra* (hill of the speaking steed) was this: namely, in the days of Samhain (All-hallows) [Halloween], a plump, sleek, terrible steed was wont to emerge as far as his middle from the hill, and speak in

> human voice to each person; he was accustomed to give intelligent and proper response to such as consulted him, concerning all that would befall them until Samhain of the ensuing year. The people used to offer valuable gifts and presents to him at the hill, and they adored him until the time of Patrick and the holy clergy.
>
> (O'Kearney, also O'Keeffe)

The parish of Dunbin, near Dundalk, County Louth, is said to take its name from Dun Binn Eich, the Fort of Horse Hill, which may be the site of Binn-each-labhra, the Hill of the Speaking Steed.

Douglas Hyde wrote to W. B. Yeats about the tale: "This tradition appears to be a cognate one with that of the Púca."

See "The King of the Cats of Cruachan" in the Cats section for the story of the Royal Cat at Clogh-magh-righ-cat.

Protective Púcas

There was a spirit long ago who was master of the district stretching from the top of Coomakesta to the cross at the edge of town, on the far side of Goleen. She killed a Casey man on the bridge at Cahirsiveen. She killed a soldier at Garranbane, and she killed a carpenter at Coomakesta. Well, there was a man walking the road one night and the horse approached him, and he figured it wasn't a horse but a wild pooka, and they came to a place where there was a gravel quarry at the side of the road at Cuan Trae, and the pooka entered the quarry and told the man to follow him.

"If I do," he said, "it will be like going from the cold into the heat."

"She is north of Murreagh," said the pooka, "knocking sparks off the road."

Well, the man stood inside the pooka, and the pooka was shaking. Soon he heard the noise approaching, as she drew great sparks from the road. She passed them and they came out, and the pooka said to the man:

"Well, I had planned to get you up on my back for a ride, but I suppose you've had your fill of the spirit, and I'll leave you alone."

(Translation by Críostóir Mac Cárthaigh from "Scéal Spride" NFC 146:281-2)

Collector: Tadhg Ó Murchú

Source: Muiris Ó Ríordáin, age 67, who heard it from Pádraig Ó Muircheartaigh, age 80, many years before.

County Kerry 1935

One night a young cowherd was on his way home from socialising, when something leapt at him and knocked him off the footpath into a bush and flung itself on top of him. Suddenly a flash of crimson light sped harmlessly along the path. The thing lifted itself off the man and let him get up. He could now see that it was a young horse.

"I just saved your soul there," said the colt. "You would have been killed if you had been on the footpath. That was a sprite."

"Who are you?" said the lad.

"I'm the Púca."

They went their separate ways, and the cowherd never saw either the púca or the sprite again.

(Ó Cróinín: my version from the Irish of Amhlaoibh Í Luínse)

A Púca Warns of Impending Death

The ghost of a friend who had died when they were boys accompanied Sheridan into adulthood and even went with him when he socialised. One night when he was playing cards with a group of friends, the ghost ordered him urgently to go home. Sheridan ignored the command, but when he noticed a large black dog under the table "with fiery red eyes and green saliva dripping from its mouth", he left. A short time later there was a fight and one man was killed.

(County Longford folklorist Pádraig Mac Gréine via O'Farrell)

A Púca Prevents an Ambush

This story was told to me by a man as factual. He had heard it from a man who believed it really happened.

During the Irish War of Independence (1919-1921), a young member of the IRA (Irish Republican Army) was rushing on his bicycle to deliver an urgent and important message to a group of rebels near Enniscorthy, County Wexford, when he saw a huge black dog standing defiantly in the middle of the road. He slowed down and then walked his bike in hopes that the dog would move if he didn't alarm it. But the dog stayed where it was. The man got the strong impression that the dog was not going to let him pass, even if he got off the road and walked around it through the fields. So he turned around and took an alternative route of an extra ten miles and delivered the message.

Many years later, the son of that man told about the incident in a pub. One of his listeners asked him the precise date when it happened and where, and after receiving the answer he told this story.

"My father was in the Auxiliaries* during the War of Independence. On that date he was with a group of Auxiliaries and Black and Tans** who were waiting along that road to ambush that messenger, and they knew his name. They had received information that he would be coming along the road with a message that it was vital they prevent going through. They had orders to kill the man. My father had been a schoolmate and friend of the messenger, and he told me, 'I was just hoping and praying that my friend would not use that road.'"

*Auxiliaries: the Auxiliary Division of the Royal Irish Constabulary (the Irish national police force) consisting of former British Army officers. They specialised in assassinations.

**Black and Tans: an infamously brutal force of former British Army non-commissioned officers and lower ranks. They took care of the rough work.

The Porridge Púca

The creature in this story collected from Cork storyteller Amhlaoidh Í Luínse in the 1940s is called a púca but obviously does not fit the usual description. It's probably a ghoul. This is an example of the generic use of "púca" for anything that might frighten children into being home before dark.

A man wanted to get married but hadn't found a suitable prospect. Three girls offered to be his wife. He said he'd marry the one who retrieved his blackthorn stick that he had left in the graveyard. One of them accepted the challenge.

She had just got the stick when a voice from one of the tombs spoke: "Open the tomb."

She opened it, and a man ordered her to put him on her back and carry him to the house of one of her neighbours.

"Get oatmeal and milk and make porridge."

She found oatmeal but no milk.

"Get water if you can't find milk," said the púca.

There was no water.

"Light a candle and bring two dishes."

She did that. Then he got a knife and went to where two boys were sleeping. He pricked them with it and drew blood and stirred it into the oatmeal to make porridge and poured it into the two dishes. He began eating and ordered her to eat as well.

She pretended to eat the bloody porridge, but when he wasn't looking she dumped it into her apron.

"It's a pity what you've done to those two boys," she said.

"If there had been milk or water in the house that wouldn't have happened," said the púca.

"Is there anything that will bring their souls back to their bodies?"

"Only if you put a bit of the bloody porridge in their mouths, but we ate it all." Then he told her that there was a pot of gold buried near the bushes in the park next to the house.

When she got outside she put her apron with the porridge in a hole in a ditch without the púca noticing. Then she left him back in the tomb and went home to bed. She woke up when her mother told her about the two boys found dead in their beds.

She went to the wake and said to the father of the boys, "If I bring your boys back to life, will you give me that park next to your house?"

The father said, "Don't joke. It's not possible to bring them back to life."

"It's no joke. I'll do it if you give me the park."

He agreed. She got the porridge and put a bit of it into the mouths of the boys, and as soon as she did so, the boys came back to life.

After the wedding, she and her husband – the walking-stick man – dug up the gold and found an inscription on the pot that directed them to three others. They became wealthy, and all because of the Porridge Púca.

(Condensed and paraphrased from the Irish in Ó Cróinín, with the vital assistance of Nora Thornton of the National Library of Ireland.)

OTHER DOGS

The Dog is beyond all others the most faithful to Man, and the Horse next. … A female puppy in a bitch's first litter can see fairies.

(Pliny – *Natural History*, Book VIII, Chapter XL)

Dogs in Heaven

India and widespread

On their last journey, the heroes of the epic Mahabharata of India, the Pandava brothers and their communal wife, all die except the just and merciful king, Yudhishthira, who continues the trek with only his dog for company. Indra, king of the gods, arrives with a chariot and offers to take him to heaven. Yudhishthira mounts the chariot with his dog, but Indra says, "There is no place in Heaven for persons with dogs." Yudhishthira refuses to go, saying that it would be unjust to leave his faithful companion.

The dog reveals that he is the god Yama, the embodiment of Dharma or righteousness, and this was just a test. He encourages Yudhishthira to go with Indra. Yudhishthira finds that heaven is full of his enemies, and his brothers are missing, so he insists on being taken to them. Indra's servant leads him to a place of punishment where his brothers are being tormented. Yudhishthira decides to stay there. Indra says it was the final test, and all are taken to heaven.

That incident has been freely adapted by many storytellers. This is my version.

A man and his dog were out walking in the countryside on a warm sunny day. The man took pleasure in watching the dog running and sniffing through the fields, when he suddenly had a thought.

"Wait a minute. My dog died ten years ago. Why is he here now?"

Then he remembered being seriously ill in hospital.

"Oh, maybe I'm dead, too."

As he continued walking, that suspicion was confirmed when he saw a large colourful sign above an ornate gate that read "Heaven". He approached the sentinel at the gate and identified himself and said, "I think I'm dead. Can I come in?"

"Certainly," said the guard, and he opened the gate. The man called his dog to join him.

"Ah, no," said the guard. "You can come in, but we don't allow dogs in Heaven."

"Well," said the man. "If my dog isn't allowed in, then I don't want to go to Heaven."

He and his dog continued walking along the road. He was getting thirsty, and he noticed that his dog's tongue was lolling out. They arrived at a dirt lane with a wooden pole across it as a gate. A man leaning casually on the pole greeted the man and smiled at the dog.

"It's getting a bit hot," said the dog's companion. "Any chance of a drink of water for the dog and myself?"

"Come on in and welcome. There's a pump with a cup for you and a bowl for the dog. Help yourself."

"What is this place?" said the man after refreshing himself.

"This is Heaven."

"But we just passed a place down the road that has a sign saying it was Heaven."

"No, that's Hell. They probably told you the dog couldn't come in with you."

"That's right. Why don't you have a sign saying this is Heaven so people won't be confused?"

"Well, the way it is, anyone who would go to Heaven and leave their dog behind doesn't deserve Heaven. That sign over the gateway to Hell saves us a lot of trouble sorting out who gets in here."

Sheehan's Bastard-hound
Ireland

I used hear my father saying – the bed o' heaven to his soul – that he used be in the habit o' goin' to *cuairt* [visit] to Sheehan's in Faha. The Sheehans kept a bastard-hound and he used have great welcome for my father every time he used to go to *cuairt* in it. Sometimes my father used come home from *cuairt* early, and sometimes it used to be late on him.

Any night that he'd chance to be comin' home late the bastard-hound was sure to keep company with him until he brought him home as far as his own door, and then he'd make off home again. If my father came home early the hound would not follow him at all. 'Tis the way that some dogs have great understanding, and they know when a person is in danger. (Verbatim)

Ref: NFC 405: 21
Collector: Seán Ó Flannagáin
Informant: Séamus Ó Cealla
Recorded in 1937, Co. Galway

Rescuer Dogs

A farmer who lives near the Garry Bog at Ballymoney [Ireland] told me that one dark night when he was crossing the bog, he missed his way in the dark, and might have stepped into a bog-hole had not a large brown collie appeared and walked before him. The dog led him out of the bog, then disappeared. He believed it to be the ghost of a dog he had been very fond of years before.

(Verbatim from Foster)

A farmer was caught on top of a hill in Somerset by a sudden mist, and he was aware of the dangers of trying to descend under the conditions. He worried that he might not survive the cold, when he felt damp fur. Assuming it was his sheep dog that had come to look for him, he followed the dog to his front door, "where he heard his own dog barking inside. He turned to look at the dog who had guided him, which grew gradually larger and then faded away."

(Briggs)

The Wolfhound of Antrim Castle

Northern Ireland

Mary Langford married Sir Hugh Clotworthy, who built Antrim Castle on the shore of Lough Neagh in Northern Ireland in 1613. One day, Lady Mary was walking along the lakeshore, when she heard a growl. She looked around and saw a wolf about to pounce. She fainted, and when she revived, she saw the dead wolf and a wounded wolfhound, which was licking her hand.

She tended her saviour's wounds, but when he recovered, he disappeared. Some years later, the castle guards heard the baying of a wolfhound during the night. They raised the alarm and lit torches, by the light of which they could see a group of rebels approaching the castle. Because of the wolfhound's warning, the surprise attack was thwarted.

One version of the story says that a trail of blood led to a dead wolfhound that had been hit by a stray bullet. Alternatively, after the battle a stone wolfhound miraculously appeared near the gateway. More realistically, Sir Hugh ordered a stone replica to be sculpted and raised to one of the castle's turrets as a token of gratitude. The sculpture has been moved several times and at last report was in the garden.

(All story sources consulted give Mary's name as Marian or Marion, but biographical data confirm that "Mary" is correct.)

A Prescient Dog
Scotland

A fisherman in Crovie had a collie dog. He was always at hand when the boats were putting to sea. One morning when the men were on the beach making ready to go to the fishing, the dog got into a great state of excitement, rushed about, and laid hold of the men when putting the lines into the boats. His conduct was such that the men did not go to sea. Scarcely had they got their lines back to their houses, than a great storm suddenly burst over the Firth. Several boats were lost from the other villages.

On another occasion, the owner of the dog was going with his boat to the south to sell his dried cod and ling. The dog was to be taken along with him. The boat was to sail from Gardenstone, another village about a mile distant. It was with the utmost difficulty the dog could be induced to follow his master. But no sooner did he reach the boat, than he bolted, and ran back, rushed into the house, and hid under one of the beds. He was taken by force from his hiding-place and carried to the boat.

The voyage was performed, and the boat was returning, and had come as far north as Stonehaven, when a heavy storm came down, the boat was driven ashore in the early morning, and two of the crew perished. The third one escaped through the intervention of the dog. He had become entangled about the wreck and could not free himself. The dog ran to the town, went up to the first man he met, began barking and pulling at him in such a way as to arouse his attention. Off the dog went. The man followed, and soon saw what had happened. The fisherman was rescued. This took place many years ago, but the dog still lives in the memory of the fisher folks.

(Verbatim, Gregor, 1886)

Gelert's Grave
Beddgelert, Wales

This is the inscription on the plaque at the grave, which is pictured on the back cover.

> In the 13th century Llewelyn, prince of North Wales, had a palace at Beddgelert. One day he went hunting without Gelert, "The Faithful Hound", who was unaccountably absent.
>
> On Llewelyn's return the truant, stained and smeared with blood, joyfully sprang to meet his master. The prince alarmed hastened to find his son, and saw the infant's cot empty, the bedclothes and floor covered with blood.
>
> The frantic father plunged his sword into the hound's side, thinking it had killed his heir. The dog's dying yell was answered by a child's cry.
>
> Llewelyn searched and discovered his boy unharmed, but nearby lay the body of a mighty wolf which Gelert had slain. The prince filled with remorse is said never to have smiled again. He buried Gelert here.

The story has been popularised by several poets, of whom the prolific Anon is the most succinct and least maudlin.

A pious monument I'll rear
In memory of the brave,
And passers-by will drop a tear
On faithful Gelert's grave.
Anonymous

David Pritchard (d. 1821) was the landlord of the Beddgelert (now Royal Goat) Hotel. He localised an ancient legend and borrowed the names of a local saint, Celert, and a famous 13th-century prince, Llewelyn, to concoct this story to boost tourism. A document from 1269 records the name of the village as Bedkelerd, the Grave of (Saint) Celert.

In various forms, the legend can be found in:

The Panchatantra (300 BC) – mongoose kills snake;

The Book of Sindibad (pre-13th century) – dog kills snake;

Gesta Romanorum (14th century) – greyhound kills snake.

See "King Sindbad and his Falcon" in the Birds section and "The Saviour Gnat" in Other Beasts for similar tales.

Clever Nart Dog

North Caucasus

The Narts wanted to test Bataraz's cleverness in battle, so they arranged an ambush with a hundred attackers. Bataraz sped away from them until they were well strung out, and then he turned and brought them down one by one as they arrived. Asked later where he had learned that trick, he said, "From my dog."

He explained, "One day my dog was following me through a village when he was attacked by a pack of the village dogs. He ran off immediately. Some of the dogs were faster than the others, and when he saw that he turned and took them on one by one as they caught up."

(Colarusso, *Tales*)

A Psychic Dog

Italy

There was a dog in Rome in the time of the Emperor Justinian of such a notable instinct that at a demonstration of his tricks, many of the onlookers would throw their rings into a heap, and at the command of his master the dog could give each ring to its owner without any errors. Also, when his master asked which of the people were married, single or widowed, he would pick them out by grasping their clothes, again with no errors.

(Fuentelapeña §767)

HERO HORSES

The Importance of the War Horse

We will consider more in particular the nature and noble properties of the warlike horse, the most noble of all the animals and having advantages in many ways for human life, whom none among the beasts can surpass, because although the ox helps man with his work, and the dog is faithful, and the elephant is strong and docile, and the sheep is productive, all of this is found in the horse, and so it is given preference. ... It is the strongest and fiercest of the domesticated animals that serve human use, strong in body and spirit.

(Huerta/Pliny – Lib VIII, Cap XLII, Note by Huerta)

There are horses that are so bellicose and love the battle so much that even when they are in their pastures or stables, if they hear the sound of war they become enraged and ferocious. We see this in the coasts and maritime places; when the trumpets sound "To arms" at any hour, as if the horses could smell war, they whinny and snort until they see the rider mounted, and then without need of rein or spur they go flying away.

It's even said that there have been horses that would pick up weapons from the ground and give them to their riders. So says Pliny, but it seems difficult.

It seems they understand the commands and urgings of the captains, because when the captains are giving a speech to the soldiers, the horses stay quiet and calm, and when the speech is finished they get excited like the soldiers themselves and show courage.

(Fuentelapeña §§780, 775, 781, after Huerta/Pliny)

In longer narratives, only those portions of the stories are told where the horse is featured.

The Adventures of Bayardo and Rinaldo

France

Belgian postage stamp 1946
"Sons of Aymon Astride Bayard"

"Stand, Bayard, stand!" The steed obeyed
With arching neck, and bended head,
And glaring eye, and quivering ear,
As if he loved his lord to hear.
(Sir Walter Scott, *The Lady of the Lake*)

Bayardo was the mount of Rinaldo, one of the four sons of Aymon, who were nephews of Charlemagne. Among the horse's attributes was the ability to lengthen himself to accommodate all four brothers. Statues of Bayardo, usually carrying the four brothers, are found in several European locations, most notably the Flemish town of Dendermonde, where a parade featuring the horse and riders occurs every ten years. The image also appears on Netherlands postage stamps.

This account consists of excerpts and retellings from the anonymous 12th-century French chanson de geste *Quatre Fils Aymon* (The Four Sons of Aymon); Torquato Tasso's 1562 epic poem *Rinaldo*; Matteo Maria Boiardo's 1495 *Orlando Innamorato*; and Ludovico Ariosto's 1532 *Orlando Furioso*. The quoted verse material is from John Hoole's

1792 translation of Tasso's *Rinaldo*, and the quoted prose is from *Bullfinch's Mythology*, 1863, 1881. Some of the prose scans and may have been lifted directly from a verse format. The basic stories date from the 12th century.

Young Rinaldo had been hearing reports of his cousin Orlando's heroic success in fighting the invading Moors with Charlemagne's army, and he felt ashamed that he was living a life of idleness with friends in Paris:

> Ah, what avails it now in thought to view
> Those honours that my great forefathers knew?
> Arrayed in steel behold Orlando goes
> And hews down squadrons of the Pagan foes ...
> While I my hours to empty pleasures give,
> In ease and indolence luxurious live ...

So he left the city and soon arrived in a forest glade, where he heard a horse neighing. It was a "stately courser", saddled and bridled, tied to a tree. Leaning against the tree was a full set of weaponry decorated with gold and gems – "A warrior's arms, that seemed in every part / The wondrous work of more than human art" – including a golden shield bearing Rinaldo's ancient family crest of a panther rampant. He donned the suit of armour, untied the horse and leapt into the saddle. He hefted the spear but left the short one-handed sword, because he had vowed when he was dubbed a knight by Charlemagne that he would never use a falchion in battle until he had won such a weapon in a fight with a famous chief.

Then he set off "to meet some peril worthy of his arm", and after several days of wandering he entered the Ardennes Forest. He rode all night, and just as dawn was breaking he encountered an old, white-haired man who appeared to be a pilgrim, walking along with the aid of a staff. He stopped and looked up at Rinaldo and said solemnly:

"You're as good as dead if you continue in that direction. Many a warrior wandering here, who trusted in his mortal strength, has soaked the ground with his life's blood. You should know that in this forest lives a mighty steed whose force exceeds that of every steed in every land. Boars and lions hide when they hear the crashing of trees as he makes his way through the forest. His skin is impervious to spear and sword. I advise you to find yourself a cave or den, because I think I hear him coming now."

"Let him flee who fears," said Rinaldo. "I stand firm."

"I see my words have fuelled your zeal," said the sage. "These eyes have never met a knight like you, so I'll tell you how to tame that courser's power. Use every art and artifice to throw him to the ground. Once you do that, he will gently bow to your command. Here's his story.

"Far-famed Amadis of Gaul was driven by a tempest to an island now called the Dangerous Isle. There he subdued this steed, whose name is Bayardo, and took him to Gaul. When Amadis left this world, the wizard Alquife brought the horse to this forest and placed a spell on him: no knight but one of the bloodline of Amadis would be able to tame him. Since that far-off age, no one has seen the horse, but there are signs that the time has come for the spell to be broken.

"I must leave you now. Remember – only when Bayardo has been laid on the ground will you gain control over him."

With that, the old man vanished. Unbeknownst to Rinaldo, it was his cousin in disguise – the wizard Malagigi, who had placed the arms he now bore and the steed he now rode at the tree for him to find. Malagigi was one of those who had detained him in Paris with fun and frolic for his own protection, until his strength had fully developed and the stars indicated it was safe to send him on his adventures.

Searching through the forest for Bayardo, Rinaldo encountered two knights having a meal. They invited him to share their food, and during the conversation Rinaldo told them that he was seeking the magic horse.

One of the knights, Isolero from Spain, said with a frown, "Stranger knight, forget this adventure you call your own. It's my task, and you would be mad to compete with me."

"I will not yield my claim on the horse," replied Rinaldo with a smile, "and I resent your insult."

Isolero drew his sword and said, "Give up your endeavour or die."

His companion, an English knight, who, backed by several others, had tried to capture the horse and reckoned himself fortunate to have survived, said, "If you two work together, you might be able to accomplish your objective."

Isolero ignored the advice and attacked Rinaldo without warning, splitting his shield and damaging his armour. Recovering from the shock, Rinaldo wrenched a large stone boundary marker from the earth and heaved it at the Spaniard, leaving him unconscious on the ground. When Isolero awoke, he started to renew the attack, but his friend managed to hold him back.

"If you both insist on this foolhardy venture, your only chance to succeed is to work together. Go to the horse's cave, then one of you engage the beast, while the other stands aside and watches how the combat goes and observes the horse's tactics. And then he can join the attack with an advantage."

The knights agreed to follow his advice. In the morning, guided by the Englishman, they set off for Bayardo's den. Along the way the other knights noticed that Rinaldo was not carrying sword or spear or shield.

"Does death have such charms for you that you go into battle without weapons?" they said.

> For arms (he cried) a dauntless heart I bear.
> With this the brave can every peril dare.

The Briton left when they arrived at the cave. Scarcely had Rinaldo and Isolero dismounted and tied their horses securely, when Bayardo came prancing from the cave, ears pricked and neighing defiantly. The earth shook when he stamped an imperious hoof. He was a thick-maned bay, whence his name, with a silver star on his aristocratic head. Broad and muscular of chest, large and firm shouldered, with white hind legs, he kicked out, smashing trees and rocks. Rinaldo fell instantly in love with the majestic beast.

Probably sensing Isolero's fear and the fact that the Spaniard's intention was not to tame the horse but to kill him, Bayardo attacked him first. Isolero set his spear to meet the charge, but Bayardo shattered it with no harm to himself. Isolero stepped aside and drew his sword. Bayardo wheeled and charged again. Isolero hit the horse directly on the star and was puzzled that it had no effect. Again the horse charged, and again Isolero struck the star. This time Bayardo felt the blow and bowed his head, but attacked again and knocked the Spaniard senseless to the ground.

Weaponless, Rinaldo ran to the horse and struck him in the jaw with his fist, drawing blood. Bayardo tried to grab his arm, but Rinaldo landed a blow on his forehead. He managed to dodge attacks by teeth and heels by staying close to the horse's side, until he slipped and was caught by a kick. A second blow would have finished him, but it missed the knight and struck and felled an oak. One of Bayardo's feet got stuck in an upturned root, and while he was off balance, Rinaldo grasped him and wrestled him to the ground.

> Then ere his feet Bayardo backward drew,
> On these his nervous hands Rinaldo threw
> And firmly held – while here and there the steed
> Impetuous snorts and struggles to be freed.
> He bends his neck, displays his threatening teeth,
> While smoky clouds his flamy nostrils breathe.
> With neighings shrill he makes the woods resound.
> At length great Aymon's son th' advantage found,
> And, by his arts o'erthrown, Bayardo pressed the
> ground.

As Malagigi had predicted, once the horse was brought to earth his ferocity was replaced by a calm but proud acceptance of his defeat, in the same way warriors often become friends following single combat. He nickered as Rinaldo stroked his neck and chest. The knight removed the saddle and bridle from the other horse and placed them on Bayardo.

On their way through the forest, Rinaldo and the recovered Isolero, having reconciled their differences, encountered a knight who mistook Rinaldo for an enemy and suddenly attacked him. Battle ensued.

> While thus the knights in sanguine strife engaged,
> An equal fight their fiery coursers waged,
> And each, by turns, with furious teeth, with strokes
> Of spurning heel, his rival's rage provokes.
> Bayardo, fiercer than the fiercest steed,
> Than every beast of wild or savage breed,
> Rushed on the foe with such resistless force
> As drove at once to earth the knight and horse.

The stranger knight was trapped under his horse and seriously injured. He would have died had Rinaldo not rescued him and Isolero not treated his wounds. Apologies tendered and accepted, they parted company.

Soon Rinaldo and Isolero came across two lifelike statues of Tristram and Lancelot fashioned by Merlin, mounted and carrying spears. A sign warned: "These spears are reserved for warriors whose martial strength and skill surpass these."

Isolero impetuously grabbed the lance in Tristram's hand but was knocked to the ground. Rinaldo carefully reached out, and the statue's head bowed and its hand opened, relinquishing the weapon.

Continuing their journey, they came across Charlemagne's queen and her ladies, among whom was Rinaldo's love, Clarice. He and Isolero killed or drove away the queen's guard, and Rinaldo carried Clarice off by force, although she didn't object too strongly once he assured her of his honourable intentions.

They were soon accosted by a mysterious knight, himself and his steed dressed all in black – "Horrid his mien, and on his shield he bore / A speckled dragon in a lake of gore" – who demanded that Rinaldo surrender Clarice to him. Isolero attacked the stranger and was quickly defeated. Rinaldo loosed Bayardo's rein, but the horse fell with a spellbound paralysis, trapping Rinaldo beneath him. The stranger struck the ground with his spear. The earth opened, and out galloped four fiery steeds drawing a chariot. The knight took Clarice into the car and drove off with her. When he was out of sight, Bayardo was released from the spell. Rinaldo later discovered that the knight was Malagigi, and he had safely delivered Clarice to her friends.

Rinaldo arrived at a tournament hosted by Charlemagne. Without revealing his identity, he took on all comers. A gigantic Saracen, Atlas, armed with the famous falchion Fusberta and mounted on a horse nearly the size of an elephant, challenged him.

> Alike impetuous charged each fiery steed.
> Of slenderer make, but sprung of fiercer breed,
> Bayardo drove to earth the rival beast
> And gave to cruel death a welcome feast.

Rinaldo confiscated Fusberta as spoils and thus finally earned his sword.

Gradasso, King of Sericane, had successfully passed through Spain on his way to France to obtain his greatest desire: Bayardo and the unbreakable sword of Orlando, Durandal, which had previously belonged to Hector of Troy and Orlando had won from the giant Jutmundus. He challenged Rinaldo to single combat. If he lost, he would release all of his prisoners and return to his country. If he won, he would get Bayardo. Rinaldo accepted the challenge, but he was led away through a magic spell by Malagigi, who was pursuing an agenda of his own involving a damsel in distress, and so Bayardo was forfeited to Gradasso.

Astolpho, "the handsomest man living" but famously inept as a warrior, accidentally came into possession of a magic spear, not knowing that it would unhorse any knight it touched. He met Gradasso in combat and unseated him, taking Bayardo as his prize, but then fled from Orlando, "owing his escape to the strength and fleetness of Bayardo".

Then Agrican took Bayardo from Astolpho and Orlando took him from Agrican.

Meanwhile, Rinaldo had escaped Malagigi's spell and was wandering on foot through the forest when he met a weeping damsel. She told him that a vile enchantress had captured her lover, along with Orlando and others. They rode on her horse until they came to a cave in which was a wonderful steed guarded by a giant and a griffin.

> This horse was a creature of enchantment, matchless in vigor, speed, and form, which disdained to share the diet of his fellow-steeds – corn or grass – and fed only on air. His name was Rabican. ... He was coal-black, except for a star of white on his forehead, and one white foot behind. For speed he was unrivalled, though in strength he yielded to Bayard.

Rinaldo made short work of the guardians and took the horse. Later, Orlando, mounted on Bayardo, and Rinaldo on Rabican found themselves on opposite sides in a battle and engaged in combat, but Bayardo refused to fight against Rinaldo, and so Orlando got the worst of the encounter. Orlando abandoned Bayardo in favour of Brigliadoro, and Bayardo was returned to Rinaldo. Orlando lost both Brigliadoro and his famous sword, Durandal, to a "base woman whom he had rescued", but he found and appropriated a magic sword "capable of cutting even through enchanted substances".

Sacripant, king of Circassia, was escorting the wicked enchantress Angelica, Princess of Cathay, through the forest. He challenged Rinaldo's sister, "the fair and illustrious Bradamante", who unseated him and killed his horse. Sacripant and Angelica both rode her palfrey, but soon afterwards they saw "a gallant and powerful horse, which, leaping the ravines and dashing aside the branches that opposed his passage, appeared before them, accoutred with a rich harness adorned with gold."

> "If I may believe my eyes, which penetrate with difficulty the underwood," said Angelica, "that horse that dashes so stoutly through the bushes is Bayard, and I marvel how he seems to know the need we have of him, mounted as we are both on one feeble animal." Sacripant, dismounting from the palfrey, approached the fiery courser, and attempted to seize his bridle, but the disdainful animal, turning from him, launched at him a volley of kicks enough to have shattered a wall of marble.
>
> Bayard then approached Angelica with an air as gentle and loving as a faithful dog could his master after a long separation. For he remembered how she had caressed him, and even fed him, in Albracca. She took his bridle in her left hand, while with her right she patted his neck. The beautiful animal, gifted with wonderful intelligence, seemed to submit entirely. Sacripant, seizing the moment to vault upon him, controlled his curvetings, and Angelica, quitting the croup of the palfrey, regained her seat.

Suddenly, Rinaldo appeared on foot. Seeing Sacripant mounted on Bayardo, he denounced him as a thief and demanded that he surrender Bayardo and Angelica. They fought. Normally, the mounted man would have the advantage, but: "The faithful animal loved his master too well to injure him, and refused his aid as well as his obedience to the hand of Sacripant, who could strike but ineffectual blows, the horse backing when he wished him to go forward, and dropping his head and arching his back, throwing out with his legs, so as almost to shake the knight out of the saddle." Angelica fled. Sacripant dismounted, and they continued the battle on foot until a messenger informed them that Orlando was now in possession of Angelica, so they called a truce, and Rinaldo galloped off on Bayardo, leaving Sacripant horseless.

Rinaldo and his brothers had slightly offended Charlot, the spoilt and unworthy son of Charlemagne, and the emperor condemned them to death. The brothers' mother, Aya, sister of Charlemagne, negotiated a pardon – on condition that Rinaldo surrender Bayardo to Charlot. As it was the only way to save their lives, Rinaldo reluctantly agreed. The brothers brought Bayardo to Charlemagne, who accepted them back into favour. Rinaldo formally presented the horse to Charlot and said, "Do with him as you think best."

Charlot ordered his servants to take Bayardo to a bridge over a river and throw him in. They did so. The horse sank to the bottom, surfaced, saw Rinaldo and climbed out of the river to stand beside him. Charlot then had a millstone tied to each hoof and two around his neck. They threw him in the river again. He shrugged off the stones and returned to Rinaldo. Charlot ordered Rinaldo to stand where Bayardo couldn't see him, and they repeated the operation. This time when Bayardo surfaced and didn't see Rinaldo, he sank to the bottom and, according to some sources, was never seen again. But more of the old chronicles record that a mysterious horse whose description closely matches that of Rinaldo's faithful steed was for long afterwards seen in the Ardennes, perhaps in search of his beloved companion.

Could it be that the Bayard in the *Lady of the Lake* quote above, the steed of "Fitz-James", King James V of Scotland (1512-1542) in disguise, was the immortal Bayardo?

Rinaldo was so distressed at the loss of Bayardo that he vowed never to ride a horse or carry a sword again, and he became a hermit. However, he was persuaded to join the Christian army to liberate Jerusalem. He fought on foot, wielding his pilgrim's staff to good effect. Later, he worked as a stonemason, but he was so efficient and diligent that the other workers were embarrassed, and they killed him out of envy.

Broiefort, Ogier the Dane's Horse

France and Avalon

When Ogier, son of the first Christian king of Denmark, was born, five women came from the Otherworld bearing gifts suitable for a warrior-to-be. A sixth, Morgan le Fay, sister of King Arthur, claimed him for her own. She promised him that he would not die until he had come to visit her at her home in Avalon.

Ogier grew into a seven-foot-tall adult with a physique to match, and he rode an equally mighty war horse won in combat with a giant Saracen. This was a black Arabian with a white star and forefeet named Broiefort, who despite the rider's weight could gallop for three days without stopping. As a result of a dispute with Charlemagne, Ogier was imprisoned, and Broiefort was given to an abbot. The abbot mounted the horse and rode him to his mountaintop abbey, but Broiefort, accustomed to the combined weight of Ogier and his armour, barely noticed the rider, and he galloped off at speed, bounding over rocks up the steep slope. When he arrived at the abbey, he came to such a sudden halt that the terrified abbot was tumbled from the saddle and sprawled on the ground in front of a group of nuns. Angry and embarrassed, he condemned Broiefort to the role of a common draught horse, dragging stones for the construction of a chapel. For seven years Ogier languished in his prison cell, while the horse was overworked, underfed and beaten. But salvation for both was at hand.

Charlemagne discovered that an army led by Ogier's brother, Guyon, now King of Denmark, and another one led by Ogier's friend and admirer, Carahue, King of Mauritania, were on their way to Paris to liberate him. At the same time, a Saracen force had captured Bordeaux and was fast approaching Paris. Charlemagne had no option but to release Ogier. He offered him his choice of horses in the royal stable, with the exception of his own charger, Blanchard, but they all collapsed under Ogier's weight.

Broiefort was sent for, and it was a scrawny, harness-chafed, dispirited beast that appeared before Charlemagne.

However, when Ogier called to him, he lifted his head and neighed with joy. Ogier mounted, and the horse proudly leapt and capered with all his old vigour.

Bruhier, the leader of the Saracens, had challenged Charlemagne to name a champion to meet him in single combat. That, of course, was Ogier. They met on the Plain of St Denis on the north side of Paris. When Bruhier saw Broiefort, he scoffed: "Is that horse meant to be the match of my own Marchevallée?"

To Bruhier's surprise, when the knights charged across the battle ground at full speed, it was Broiefort who carried his rider more than halfway. Unfortunately, while they were fighting with swords, a deflected blow struck Broiefort, and that was the end of the brave and faithful steed. But Ogier won the combat.

He mounted Marchevallée and charged into battle just as Carahue's army arrived, and the combined forces routed the Saracens. When Guyon came soon afterwards, Charlemagne and the two kings decided to take the war to the Saracens in the Holy Land, with Ogier on Marchevallée leading the French knights. Following their success, Guyon and Carahue returned to their kingdoms, and Ogier boarded a ship for France, apparently without Marchevallée.

Papillon, Morgan le Fay's Horse

France and Avalon

Partway through the voyage, the ship suddenly refused to answer to the helm, and it sped like an arrow towards a black headland and crashed into it. Ogier was the only survivor of the wreck. As he started to explore the strange land, he was suddenly confronted by a fire-breathing horse and two monstrous sea-goblins covered with shining scales. He drew his sword, but the goblins made no move to attack him, and the horse knelt down, inviting him to mount. His name was Papillon. Ogier leapt on his back, and the horse raced up the rocky side of the headland and galloped on until he reached a magnificent palace. He made his way into a garden, where he knelt in front of a fountain as a signal for Ogier to dismount.

A beautiful young woman awaited him. As he stared at her, his armour fell off by itself. She walked towards him and placed a crown of flowers on his head. At once, his memory left him: his companions and combats, Charlemagne, all vanished from his mind. He was conscious of nothing but the dazzling woman in front of him: Morgan le Fay.

Some accounts say a hundred, others two hundred, years passed, but none of them report on how they spent the time, ever-young, in Avalon. One day, Morgan playfully snatched the flower crown from Ogier's head, and suddenly he remembered who he had been. He told her he wanted to visit his friends in France, and she reluctantly agreed to let him go.

He mounted Papillon, and soon they came to the sea coast, where the sea-goblins that had greeted him were waiting. One of them took Papillon on his back and the other took Ogier, and they swam to France, where they landed on the southeast coast. Papillon made short work of the journey to Paris. The people Ogier met soon got over their confusion about who he was. The queen was especially interested in his stories of the events he had taken part in, and Bulfinch explains: "It is to the corrections which Ogier was at that time enabled to make to the popular narratives of his exploits that we are indebted for the perfect accuracy and trustworthiness of all the details of our own history."

The Saracens were once again causing trouble, and Ogier and the fire-breathing Papillon led the Franks to victory. He was praised by the king and became a favourite of the court, but soon the king died, and Ogier proposed to the queen. She was about to accept, but as Ogier was kneeling at her feet, a crown of flowers suddenly appeared on his head, and he disappeared in a cloud.

The jealous Morgan le Fay had come to reclaim him. He lives now in Avalon, along with King Arthur, and when the time comes for Arthur to return to this world, perhaps Ogier and Papillon will accompany him.

Sharatz and Marko

Serbia

According to history, Marko Mrnjavčević (1335-1395) was the son of King Voukashin and Queen Yevrossima; oral tradition says his mother was a *veela* (fairy) and his father a *zmay* (dragon). His main weapon was a club made of steel, silver and gold weighing a hundred pounds. He drank prodigiously but was never drunk.

At the end of their conjoined lives, Marko said of his faithful companion, "Better steed never trod our earth than Sharatz. ... Never will I be severed from my beloved steed!"

But a heroic horse's lot is not an easy one. Earlier, as he tightened the girth in preparation for a pursuit of the veela Raviyoyla, who had shot his blood-brother, Milosh, in the throat and heart, he whispered in Sharatz's ear:

> Lo, Sharo, thou on whom I depend for speed! Oh, thou must overtake, now, the veela Raviyoyla, and I shall shoe thy hoofs with pure silver and gild them with the finest gold. I shall cover thee with a silken cloak reaching to thy knees, and on it I shall fasten fine silk tassels to hang from thy knees to thy hoofs. Thy mane shall I intertwine with threads of gold and adorn it with rare pearls. But, woe to thee if thou reachest not the veela! Both thy eyes shall I tear out, thy four legs shall I break, and I shall abandon thee here and thou shalt for ever creep from one fir-tree to another, exactly as I should if I lost my dear brother Milosh!
> (Petrovitch)

They caught up with the fleeing veela, and after Marko battered her with his mighty club, he made her gather medicinal herbs to heal Milosh. Afterwards, Milosh found that his singing voice was much improved, and his heart was stronger. Raviyoyla warned her veela sisters, "Do not shoot any heroes in the mountains with your bows and arrows, so long as the Royal Prince Marko and his Sharatz are alive."

Whether or not Marko was of fairy origin, there was certainly some magic about Sharatz, whose name means "Piebald". When Marko was given his choice of foals as a reward for working for a man for three years, he tested them one by one by picking them up by the tail and swinging them around. He chose the one that he couldn't even lift.

One day, as they neared the top of a mountain, Sharatz stumbled and began to weep. Marko recognised the signs that one of them was going to die. A veela confirmed that time had run out for Marko. Complaining that his life had been too short at a mere three hundred years, Marko cut off Sharatz's head so that no Turk would ever ride him, then buried him. He threw his club into the sea, saying, "When my club returns from the depths of the ocean, then shall come a hero as great as Marko!"

(Petrovitch)

Toruchaar and Manas

Kyrgyzstan

Paraphrased and retold from the Kyrgyz verse epic *Manas*, c. AD 1000

Based on a translation by Elmira Köçümkulkïzï

"Horses are considered the wings of a man." (Köçümkulkïzï)

Manas is a living epic consisting of about half a million lines which first took shape a thousand years ago and continues to evolve. Its many versions are still performed by specialists who tell-chant the story over a period of three days. My retelling of a portion of the epic featuring the horse is partly prose paraphrase and partly an imitation of the verse form: 7-8 syllables to the line with alliteration and end rhyme.

Jakïp had long wished and prayed for a son. His wife, Chïyïrdï, was pregnant. She had an intense craving for tiger meat, which Jakïp obtained with much difficulty. She ate it and was satisfied. Jakïp demanded that the Kyrgyz keep this a secret from their enemies, to which they agreed. The learned men predicted that she would give birth to a lion. As she neared the end of her term, Jakïp, unable to stand the tension, went out to his horses. He promised to himself that if the baby was a girl he would kill the piebald mare for a feast, and if it was a boy, he would name him Manas and kill ninety animals. Whoever came to tell him he had a son would have as a reward his choice of Jakïp's stallions – and camels and anything else from his herds, and if that wasn't enough, even a flask of Jakïp's own blood.

He fell asleep and dreamed that a barefoot, bald old man with a white beard came and told him that the dun mare had foaled a stallion and at the same time the Creator had given him a son whose name would be Manas. Boy and colt, man and steed, would be as one. The divine messenger said of the horse:

> He will be a super steed,
> Gallop six months straight at speed.
> Strong as stone will be his bones,
> Never age and lose his teeth
> Till full sixty years have flown.
> Red as blood will be his tail,
> Flowing mane like a silk veil.

Jakïp woke from his dream to find that the dun mare had indeed dropped a foal.

> Toruchaar he named the colt.
> Muscles bulging, big and bold,
> He leapt three times across the mare
> And stamped the earth and grew threefold.

Fearless: flowing tail and mane
Marked the horse a hero's steed
Fit for Jakïp's son indeed.

A friend galloped up with the news that Jakïp's wife had given birth to a boy.

Manas jumped out strong and stood,
In his right hand dripping blood,
In his left hand yellow gold –
Signs that we should take as good,
Signs of what the future holds:
He will cut the foeman down
Like the harvest – to the ground.

A grey-black mane is on his neck.
A tiger from his right side leapt
And jumped three times across the lad.
A lion from his right side stepped.
At that the women all went mad.
The tiger vanished, but the child
And the lion still looked wild.

At the age of eight, Manas was so big and strong that he was constantly causing trouble and embarrassment to his father. "Your son turned out to be a rascal," Jakïp said to Chïyïrdï. So he gave the boy to a shepherd to look after for the next four years. During that time, Manas killed a giant who had killed four of Manas's boy-troop, and he bullied his young followers, slaughtered the shepherd's sheep and generally made a nuisance of himself to everyone else. When he was twelve years old he had reached his full growth, and the shepherd demanded that Jakïp take his son back.

When Manas led the Kyrgyz into battle against the Kalmyks, their oppressors and arch-enemies:

Toruchaar was Manas's steed.
Wind and bullet he'd out-speed,
Never stumbled, never slipped.

With lungs of iron and copper-kneed
He galloped tireless with ears pricked.
Clash of sword and battle roar
Would the mighty mount ignore.

Where he ran the ground would crack,
Leaving powder in his track.
Breathing fire and snorting smoke
He would spearhead the attack,
Graceful as a mountain goat,
Forceful as a raging flood,
Broad chest smeared with foam and blood.

Rakush – Faithful Steed of Rostam

Greater Iran

From The *Shahnameh* – Book of Kings

Quotes from Helen Zimmern's 1883 translation, some slightly modernised, are in italics.
See also two Simurgh tales in Other Beasts.

"The world is subject unto me, and Rakush is my throne, and my sword is my seal, and my helmet my crown."

This great Persian epic myth was set in its present form in the tenth century by the poet Ferdowsi in 50,000 rhyming couplets. It is largely based on historical events around the fifth century BC. Greater Iran encompasses modern Iran, Afghanistan, and much of the surrounding area east of Turkey.

The kingdoms of Iran and Turan had been at each other's throats for several generations. The throne of Iran was vacant, and Poshang, King of Turan, took advantage of that weakness to send his son, Afrasiyab, to invade. The men of

Iran called on their long-time champion, Zal son of Saum, and asked him why he wasn't leading the army to defend the kingdom.

"I have always done what was right for Iran," he said, "and all my life I have feared no enemy but old age. But that enemy is now upon me, so you'll have to look to my son, Rostam, to defend you, while I serve as his advisor."

Zal called his son and said, "Your lips still smell of milk, and your heart should desire pleasure, but Iran is in danger, and I must send you forth to deal with our enemies."

Rostam replied, "You know that my heart desires war rather than pleasure. So give me a steed of strength and the mace of Saum, your father, and let me go to meet the hosts of Ahriman."

Ahriman is the spirit of Evil incarnate.

Zal smiled at these manly words of a stripling, and he commanded that all the herds of horses from Kabul and their home territory of Seistan be gathered for his son to choose from.

And they were passed in order before Rostam, and he laid upon the backs of each his hand of might to test them if they could bear his weight of valour. And the horses shuddered as they bent beneath his grasp and sank upon their haunches in weakness. And thus did he do with them all in turn, until he came unto the flocks of Kabul. Then he perceived in their midst a mare mighty and strong, and there followed after her a colt like to its mother, with the chest and shoulders of a lion. And in strength it seemed like an elephant, and in colour it was as rose leaves that have been scattered upon a saffron ground. Now Rostam, when he had tested the colt with his eyes, made a running knot in his cord and threw it about the beast. And he caught the colt in the snare, though the mare defended it mightily.

Then the keeper of the flock came before Rostam and said, "O youth puissant and tall, take not, I counsel thee, the horse of another."

And Rostam answered him and asked, "To whom does this steed belong? I see no mark upon its flanks."

And the keeper said, "We know not its master, but it is rumoured to be the Rakush of Rostam. And I warn thee, the mother will never permit thee to ride on it. Three years has it been ready for the saddle, but none would she allow to mount thereon."

Then Rostam, when he heard these words, swung himself upon the colt with a great bound. And the mare, when she saw it, ran at him and would have pulled him down, but when she had heard his voice she allowed it. And the rose-coloured steed bore Rostam along the plains like unto the wind. Then when he was returned, the son of Zal said to the keeper, "What is the price of this dragon?"

But the keeper replied, "If thou be Rostam, mount him, and retrieve the sorrows of Iran. For his price is the land of Iran, and seated upon him thou wilt save the world."

And Rostam rejoiced in Rakush (whose name means "Lightning"), and Zal rejoiced with him, and they made ready to stand against Afrasiyab.

Rostam went to Mount Alberz to persuade royal-blooded Kai Kobad to occupy the throne. In the ensuing battle, Afrasiyab was defeated, and the warriors dubbed Rostam "Tehemten" (strong-limbed) for his deeds of prowess. Afrasiyab reported to his father and told him his imperialistic efforts were hopeless against the new champion of Iran. Poshang took his son's advice to heart and wrote to the newly installed Shah to say that he renounced his territorial ambitions: *"For why should we seek the land of another, since in the end each will receive in heritage a spot no larger than his body?"*

Kai Kobad's successor, Kai Kaous, foolishly invaded Mazinderan in north-western Iran against the advice of Zal, and he and his army were captured by the Deevs (demons) headed by the White Deev. He managed to smuggle out a grovelling letter to Zal, apologising for ignoring his advice and begging him to come to the rescue. Zal called Rostam.

"The hour is come to saddle Rakush and to avenge the world with thy sword. As for me, I number two hundred years, and have no longer the strength to fight with Deevs.

But thou art young and mighty. Cast about thee, therefore, thy leopard-skin and deliver Iran from bondage."

Rostam eagerly accepted the mission. Zal continued:

"There are two roads to Mazinderan. The one Kai Kaous took is safe but longer; the shorter one is dangerous. Speed is vital, so you need to take the shorter."

Rostam set off, *and Rakush caused the ground to vanish under his feet, and in twelve hours was a two days' journey accomplished.* In the evening, Rostam unsaddled Rakush and caught a wild ass and cooked it for his dinner. Then he lay down in the reeds to sleep, afraid of neither wild beasts nor Deevs.

But a lion had made its lair among the reeds, and when it came home and saw the man sleeping and the horse standing nearby, it thought they would make easy prey. It attacked Rakush, but the horse struck out and kicked the lion in the forehead, and then tore its skin with his teeth and continued to stamp on it till it died. The sound of the struggle awoke Rostam, and he said, "Who told you to fight a lion? If it had killed you, who would have carried me to Mazinderan?"

He went back to sleep, and Rakush felt downhearted at the unjust rebuke.

They spent the next day crossing a desert, nearly dying of thirst, and just as Rostam was about to give up he spied a sheep and followed it to a cool, clear spring. They drank their fill, and Rostam gave Rakush a much-needed bath. He caught and cooked another wild ass and lay down to sleep, unaware that he was trespassing on a dragon's territory. He warned Rakush not to fight any beasts but to wake him up if there was an attack.

The dragon approached in the middle of the night, angry to see the man and the horse near its den. Rakush stamped a hoof and swished his tail noisily, waking Rostam. But when Rostam looked around, the dragon had disappeared.

"That was unkind of you to wake me for no reason," Rostam said to Rakush, and he went back to sleep.

The dragon came again, and again Rakush woke Rostam, but the dragon had disappeared, and then it happened a third time.

"If you do that again, I'll kill you and make my way to Mazinderan on foot."

When the dragon approached the horse the fourth time, Rakush wasn't sure what to do. Rostam had forbidden him to fight a wild beast on his own, but what if he woke his master and the dragon disappeared again? He took a chance and stamped his hoof and neighed. Rostam sprang up in fury, but the dragon wasn't able to hide in time, and Rostam saw it. He threw on his armour and unsheathed his sword and went to meet the beast.

"Who are you and what are you doing here?" the dragon asked.

"I am Rostam son of Zal, and I am my own invincible army."

The dragon laughed and quickly leapt on Rostam and wound itself around him and began to crush him. Rostam was helpless. But Rakush jumped on the dragon from behind and tore at it with his teeth, as he had done with the lion, freeing Rostam to use his sword, and between them they destroyed the beast. Rostam praised his steed and washed him in the spring, and they continued their journey.

They survived an incident with a witch and rode into a land of darkness, where Rostam gave free rein to Rakush until they found themselves in a land of light. In a subsequent adventure, Rostam's army was vastly outnumbered, but Ferdowsi, the author of the epic, sums up the result, generously giving top billing to the horse: *wheresoever Rakush and Rostam showed themselves, there was great havoc made in the ranks*. They rescued Kai Kaous and his men, and the Shah bestowed a further title on Rostam: Jahani Pehliva – "Champion of the World".

One day Rostam was feeling restless, so he filled his quiver with arrows and saddled Rakush, and they set off hunting towards the east. They crossed the River Oxus (Amu Darya, the border between modern Tajikistan and Afghanistan) and arrived in the wilds of Turan near the city of Samengan. Rostam chased a herd of wild asses until he tired of the sport, then he killed an ass and roasted and ate it.

When he had finished the meal and had broken the bones and sucked out the marrow, he lay down to sleep while Rakush grazed.

As he slept, seven knights from Turan passing by noticed Rakush. They tried to catch him with their lariats, and he charged them and bit the head off one and trampled another. However, there were too many of them, and they captured him and took him into Samengan.

When Rostam awoke and found that his horse was missing, he followed the hoofprints into the city. News of his unusual arrival on foot reached the ears of the king, Samenganshah, who asked him what had happened to his horse. Rostam explained, and Samanganshah said, "Rakush is so well known that he can't remain hidden for long. Don't worry. We'll find him for you. Meanwhile, be my guest."

That night, Samanganshah's daughter, Tahmineh, visited Rostam in his room. She introduced herself and said that she had fallen in love with him from reports of his heroic deeds, wanted to marry him and bear him a son, and if he rejected her she would never marry. Rostam was persuaded when she said that if he accepted her offer she guaranteed she would find Rakush for him.

They were married, but as soon as Rakush was returned to him, Rostam departed. Nine months later, unbeknownst to Rostam, Tahmineh gave birth to a son, Sohrab. When Sohrab came of age he was ready to find his father and make him king of Iran and himself king of Turan. *"But a horse is needful unto me, a steed tall and strong of power to bear me, for it beseemeth me not to go on foot before mine enemies."*

Tahmineh ordered the herds to be paraded for Sohrab's inspection. *Sohrab surveyed the steeds and tested their strength like as his father had done before him of old, and he bowed them under his hand, and he could not be satisfied. And thus for many days did he seek a worthy steed. Then one came before him and told of a foal sprung from Rakush, the swift of foot. When Sohrab heard the tidings he smiled and bade that the foal be led before him. And he tested it and found it to be strong. So he saddled it and sprang upon its back and cried, "Now that I own a horse like thee, the world shall be made dark to many."*

Rostam's father, Zal, had a son late in life. This was Shugdad, who the Mubids predicted would bring ruin to the family. When the boy reached manhood, Zal thought it might prevent misfortune to send him to Kabul, whose king was forced to pay tribute to Rostam. The king saw an opportunity to use Shugdad to relieve himself of the imposition. He and Shugdad came up with a plan to kill Rostam. The king pretended to insult Shugdad, Shugdad went to Rostam to complain, and Rostam came to Kabul to settle the matter. Meanwhile, the king ordered a series of seven pits to be dug along a road, all lined with up-pointed swords and spears and concealed with branches and soil.

When Rostam arrived, the king apologised, and Rostam forgave him. The king invited Rostam to join him for a hunt, and Rostam accepted, suspecting no foul play. Shugdad rode his horse alongside Rostam and Rakush, keeping to the safe side of the road and forcing Rostam to the side with the hidden pits. When they reached the first trap, Rakush suddenly stopped, suspicious of the scent of the freshly turned soil. Rostam urged him to move forward, but Rakush refused.

Then Rostam took a whip and struck him, and before this day he had never raised his hand against his steed. So Rakush was grieved in his soul, and he did that which Rostam desired, and he sprang forward and fell into the pit. And the sharp spears entered his body and tore it, and they pierced also the flesh of Rostam, and steed and rider were impaled upon the irons that had been hidden by the King.

Rakush managed to struggle out of the pit, only to land in the next one and the next, until horse and rider had fallen into all seven of the traps and were mortally wounded. The king and Shugdad came to gloat. Rostam begged Shugdad to hand him his bow and arrows so the wild animals would not eat him alive before he died. Shugdad did so, but when he saw Rostam grab the weapon he was afraid and went to hide in a hollow tree. However, Rostam found the strength to fire an arrow through the tree and kill Shugdad.

And Zal caused a noble tomb to be built for Rostam, his son, and he laid him therein, and there was placed beside him also Rakush, the steed that had served him unto the end.

Rakush and Rostam figure also in a Simurgh story in the Other Beasts section. See back cover for a 25,000-year-old cave painting of horses like Rakush: "*in colour it was as rose leaves that have been scattered upon a saffron ground*".

Cúchulainn's Grey of Macha and Black Sainglenn

Ireland

On the night Cúchulainn, one of Ireland's greatest heroes, was born, the two horses that were to power his chariot until the day he died were foaled: the Grey of Macha and the Black Sainglenn. Cúchulainn was so handsome and attractive to women that the men of Ulster urged King Conor to encourage him to find a wife. Ostensibly, this was to ensure that he produced a son to carry on his heroic deeds in case he died young, but really to safeguard their wives and daughters. So Cúchulainn dressed in his finest array and groomed his horses to show them at their best and went to woo Emer, who was the only woman he knew of who possessed all six gifts of the ideal mate: beauty, voice, sweet speech, needle-work, wisdom and chastity. As he approached her father's house, she was teaching her sisters and friends needle-work in the garden. They heard the clatter of hooves.

"One of you go and find out who is coming," Emer said.

Her sister Fiall reported:

"I see two big, bold, beautiful horses, fast, fiery, formidable and fearless, high-headed, hard-driving, slim-flanked, solid-shouldered, with plaited forelocks and wavy manes and tails. One is a vigorously prancing spirited fierce wild grey with a broad chest and haunches and arched neck.

His hooves strike sparks from the road, and he breathes out flames.

"The other one is a mighty jet-black: sturdy, slender-shanked, nimble-footed, agile, alert, with a many-locked mane and a long, curly, sweeping tail. This warrior stallion bounds gracefully along the road, bold and impervious to obstacles, champion steed of the world."

They got married, and Emer revealed three more valuable virtues: patience, loyalty, and an uncommon lack of jealousy – famously celebrated in the tale The Only Jealousy of Emer. But back to those magnificent horses.

In the longest tale of the Ulster Cycle, the eighth-century Bricriu's Feast, Cúchulainn, Conall Cernach and Laoighaire Buadach were in competition for the Champion's Portion. Their wives trumpeted the men's accomplishments. After Emer's vehement speech boasting of her husband's abilities, Conall Cernach said with a sneer, "If what you say is true, let that crafty lad come forward and show us some of his warrior feats."

(These feats were tricks and stunts that showed off a warrior's skill in handling weapons, meant to impress fellow warriors and enemies: the apple feat, the lying-on-the-back feat, the sword-edge feat, the javelin feat, etc.)

"I won't," said Cúchulainn. "I'm tired today. I won't fight until I've had food and drink."

He was tired because it was on that day that he fought and subdued both the Grey of Macha and the Black Sainglenn. He had lain in wait for the Grey to emerge from the Grey Lake at Slieve Fuait, and when the horse came out he grabbed him around the neck and wrestled him to the ground. Then he did the same with the Black when he came out of Lake Black Sainglenn. Cúchulainn passed it off modestly as a sight-seeing canter:

"Today the Grey and I ranged over the plains of Ireland from Meath to Mayo. All I want now is food and sleep, and then I'll take on any man."

Cúchulainn was the acknowledged champion of Ulster. He had been awarded the Champion's Portion for life, and at the age of 17 he single-handedly held off the massed armies of Queen Maeve of Connacht when she invaded Ulster in pursuit of the Brown Bull in the epic Táin Bó Cuailnge – the Cattle Raid of Cooley. When he was 27, Queen Maeve, still smarting from her humiliation, gathered the sons and daughters of the many warriors he had killed during his career. She invaded Ulster again, this time using deception and magic spells.

As Cúchulainn prepared for battle, several omens foretold his death. When he was fastening his brooch to his cloak, the brooch fell and the pin pierced his foot, drawing blood. His charioteer complained that the Grey of Macha refused to be harnessed. Cúchulainn scolded the horse, and the Grey relented, but a bloody teardrop fell from his eye and splashed on Cúchulainn's foot. Then he stopped to visit his mother on the way to the battlefield in County Louth. She poured him a cup of white wine, but when he tried to drink it turned to red. A crone offered him a piece of cooked dog meat. It was *geis* (taboo) for him to refuse food but also geis to eat dog meat, since dog (*cú*) was his totem animal. He took the meat with his left hand, which withered immediately. He came across a woman washing bloody clothes at the ford of a stream. They were the same as his own clothes. It was clear that his death was imminent.

In the battle, Cúchulainn threw his spear three times, and each time before it was thrown back at him the magic-wielding daughters of Calatin predicted that a king would fall. The first time, his charioteer, the king of charioteers, was killed. The second time, the Grey of Macha, the king of the steeds of Ireland, received a fatal wound. Cúchulainn cut him out of the traces, they bade each other farewell, and the horse ran to his home, the Grey Lake. In the third charge, Cúchulainn received six mortal wounds from Lugaid son of Cú Roí. The Black Sainglenn ran off still in harness, leaving the chariot behind him and Cúchulainn lying on the ground.

He got up and tied himself to a standing stone so he would die facing his enemies. The Grey returned to the battlefield to defend the dying Cúchulainn and killed fifty with his teeth and thirty with his hooves. In the play *The*

Death of Cuchulain by W. B. Yeats, Aoife, the mother of his only son, appears at his side and says:

> The grey of Macha, that great horse of yours
> Killed in the battle, came out of the pool
> As though it were alive, and went three times
> In a great circle round you and that stone,
> Then leaped into the pool; and not a man
> Of all that terrified army dare approach.

Only when the hero light on Cúchulainn's forehead went dark, and the battle goddess the Mórrígan perched on his shoulder in the form of a raven, did the Grey accept that his master was dead, and he set off again for the Grey Lake.

Lugaid cut off Cúchulainn's head, but when he did, Cúchulainn's sword fell on his hand, cutting it off. In retaliation, Lugaid cut off Cúchulainn's right hand. His head and hand are buried on the Hill of Tara.

Conall Cernach's Dewy Red
Ireland

Cúchulainn and Conall Cernach had an agreement: whichever was killed first, the other would avenge his death before sunset. Conall was on his way to the battlefield when he came across the Grey dripping with blood as he was returning to the Grey Lake, and he understood that Cú was dead. The Grey led him back to the battlefield – which is still known locally as the Field of Slaughter – and Cú's body tied to the standing stone, commemorated today as Clochafarmore, the Stone of the Big Man. The Grey laid his head on Cúchulainn's chest in mourning.

Conall set off to find Lugaid, who was on his way to Dublin, knowing that Conall would be looking for him. Conall caught up with him on the north border of Dublin.

Lugaid's charioteer saw a horseman approaching furiously and said, "You'd think that all the ravens of Ireland are flying above him, and it's snowing in front of him."

Lugaid replied, "It's Conall on the Dewy Red. What look like birds are the pieces of sod thrown up by his hooves, and the flakes of snow are the flecks of foam spouting from his mouth."

"You have to give me fair play," said Lugaid when Conall faced him. "I'm missing my right hand, and so you have to tie your right hand to your side to make us evenly matched."

Conall did so. They fought long and hard with neither prevailing. When the Dewy Red saw that Conall was in trouble, he charged Lugaid and bit a chunk out of his side.

"That's cheating, Conall," said Lugaid. "You promised you'd give me fair play."

"I promised fair play on my behalf," Conall replied. "I'm not responsible for the horse's behaviour."

(*Fir fer*, a gentlemen's agreement, literally "truth of men", is one of the Irish terms for "fair play".)

Weakened by the Dewy Red's attack, Lugaid was quickly defeated.

"I know," said Lugaid, "that you'll cut off my head for my cutting off Cúchulainn's head. But I'm going to do you a favour. Place my head on your head so that all my skill and experience will be added to yours."

Conall didn't trust him. He cut off his head and set it on a stone, and the stone melted.

Conall Cernach and Sualtam, Cúchulainn's father, were the first in Ireland to break horses to saddle. Previously, they had only been used to pull chariots, carts and ploughs.

Nart Horses
North Caucasus

"A man without a horse is like a bird without wings."
(Colarusso, *Tales*)

"Nart" means "hero/strong man" and is thought to be cognate with Irish *neart*, meaning "strength". The Narts are the heroes of the mythology of the peoples of the North Caucasus on the northeast coast of the Black Sea. They are human-like with the characteristics of demi-gods, a class between gods – "heavenly beings" – and mortals; they recognise a supreme God of gods. Their superhuman powers and the magical abilities of their horses are similar to those of characters in Irish hero tales and later medieval Indo-European legends of mounted warriors – Rinaldo, Rostam, and knights of the Arthurian cycle – which scholars say are derived from, or at least strongly influenced by, the Caucasian mythological sagas.

According to the stories, the Narts were the first horse riders. Historians, archaeologists, linguists and geneticists agree. There is evidence that horse riding began in the North Caucasus during the Maikop Period, 3700-3000 BC (Ivanova). Groups of riders, apparently Scythians and Cimmerians, passed from the east through the North Caucasus between 850 and 750 BC (Raftery). Horses had been used as draught animals in Europe since the Bronze Age or earlier, and archaeological evidence shows herds of horses in the Colne Valley west of London in the Mesolithic period of 11,000-8000 BC, but suddenly about the seventh century BC horse riders appeared in Central Europe. They became known as the Celts. Raiding and trading their way across Europe, they quickly spread in all directions, including back to the east, and by the sixth century BC had become the dominant power in Europe north of the Alps, as well as in Ireland and Britain and most of Spain.

Celtic DNA is widespread among Europeans and people of European descent, especially British and Irish. "Some [pre-Celtic] 'Iberian' blood, possibly, runs through the veins of every modern Englishman, more in the Scots, and in a higher degree in the Welsh and Irish." (Sainero, *Huella*; Trevelyan) Memories of those pre-Celtic horse riders are embodied in the Narts, who are culture heroes of not only the North Caucasians but all of us with European heritage. Curiously, a horse in one Nart story is named "Gee-gee", which is a term of disputed origin used by British and Irish bettors for a race horse.

The Narts are not nomads, but their lifestyle reflects the influence of the cattle-raiding Scythian and Cimmerian horsemen of the Steppes. They enjoy a symbiotic relationship with their horses, who also have magic powers – a *durdul* is a winged horse – and can understand and speak human, like the Hungarian táltos horse. The following episodes derived from two books by John Colarusso, one by David Hunt, and Amjad Jaimoukha's website show how the horses work with their two-legged partners. They are not pets. They serve as both transport and fighting comrades and are often treated like machines in ways that modern horse lovers would identify as abuse.

However, what else is a hero to do when his horse instructs him how to survive a dash between two mountains that continually crash together, back away, and crash again, like wild rams in perpetual combat?

"Whip me as hard as you can! Beat me so that the skin flies from your hands, and bits of my hide fly from my side, big enough to make a sole for a pair of boots!" (Colarusso, *Tales*)

Names and spellings vary widely in versions of these stories, of which more than 700 have been collected in verse and prose from the several ethnic groups of the North Caucasus. The simplest ones are used here, for example "Sosruko" for all variants of "СосрыкъуапцIэ".

Cúchulainn was inserted into the Irish national epic The Cattle Raid of Cooley in the seventh century AD. Striking parallels between him and Sosruko suggest that he is a literary reincarnation of the Nart hero: both are described as short and dark; both had superhuman powers; Sosruko's horse was foaled on the night Sosruko was born; likewise

Cú's chariot horses; Sosruko's "midwife" was a smith; Cúchulainn was apprenticed to a smith.

Sosruko is the most popular of the Nart heroes and is the protagonist of one of the oldest tales, "Sosruko Fetches Fire" (front cover), which was found on the third century BC Maikop slab but is probably a thousand years older. Sosruko needed to steal fire from a sleeping giant to bring to his companions before they froze to death. This is my verse version of the advice his horse, Thozhey, gave him, based on Jaimoukha's English translation of a Kabardian language text. The full ballad is in my book *A World of Tricksters*.

"Leap on my back, and I will make my hooves like canine paws,
And when we near the giant, change to cat pads without claws.
You can snatch a burning brand, and we will then escape
And be afar and out of danger when the giant wakes."

In another story, Sosruko had to acquire a certain horse from a woman in order to kill a giant and save a captive daughter of the Narts. On his way he rescued three animals in trouble: a wolf, an eagle and a fish. The woman promised him his choice of her stock of cattle if he looked after her valuable three horses successfully for three nights. They disappeared each night, and the three animals brought them back. Following the advice of the fish, Sosruko requested and received a colt that had been born on one of the nights. It was the brother of the giant's horse.

Sosruko led the colt away, but while his own mount, Thozhey, was galloping, the colt was keeping up just by walking. When they stopped to rest after travelling two days and two nights, he commented, "That colt will probably grow into a good horse."

"I'm already a good horse, Sosruko," the colt said. "But my brother, the mount of the giant you're going to fight, suckled on our mother only three times before the giant took him. I have also suckled three times, so we are equal in strength. If I go back and suckle once more, no horse in the world will be my equal."

Sosruko objected: "I don't have time to spend four days and four nights taking you back there and returning here."

"I'll go and come back while you rest."

Sosruko went to hobble Thozhey, and when he turned around he saw the colt.

"I thought you were going back to suckle your mother a fourth time."

"I did, so now I'm ready and we can go."

They set off again, but Thozhey was not able to match the pace of the ambling colt no matter how hard he galloped.

"Thozhey," said Sosruko, "you're too slow. I can't wait for you. If I leave you here, the wolves will eat you. I want you to know that I have been very pleased with you."

He took his bow and arrow and shot the horse dead.

The giant saw Sosruko and the colt as soon as they entered his land, and he saddled his horse and began to chase after them. He beat his horse trying to catch them until he almost killed him. When he finally drew close – only because Sosruko's colt slowed down – the giant's horse recognised his brother.

"Young brother, my rider is killing me. Let me overtake you. Don't let him kill me."

"Brother," said the colt, "why are you carrying him? Fly up and turn upside-down and throw him off your back."

The horse did that, and when the giant fell he kicked him in the head and killed him. Then he galloped away to return to his mother.

(Colarusso, *Sagas*)

When Sosruko's horse, Bzow, died, he refused to mount another horse out of respect. But one day as he was walking through the woods, he came to a river that was too wide and turbulent for him to cross so he could join his comrades. A wild horse – not a Nart steed – was grazing on the near side. Only the Narts could ride horses, and only the Nart steeds would allow the Narts to ride them. Sosruko went to the wild horse and asked him if he could possibly take him across, but the horse didn't understand human speech. So he made a rough hackamore and bit from mulberry-bark twine and mounted the horse. The horse jumped into the river, which was what Sosruko wanted, and when they reached the middle he turned the horse's head into the current and urged it on until it was too tired to resist.

Then he rode the horse to the far side where his fellow Narts were gathered. The Narts mocked him for not borrowing a Nart horse, but there were non-Narts among them, and they were amazed to see a wild horse tamed and ridden. They asked Sosruko how he had managed it, and he explained his method. And that is how non-Narts learned to tame and ride wild horses.

(Colarusso, *Sagas*)

Sosruko's enemies discovered that the only way to defeat him was to kill his horse first by attacking the only vulnerable parts – the lower legs. So they heated an iron bridge that Sosruko would have to cross. When they approached the bridge, the horse refused to step on to it, but Sosruko forced him to go, and so they both were killed.

In another version of Sosruko's end, it was beach shingle that weakened the horse's legs. When the horse fell, he told Sosruko, "I'm no good to you now. Kill me and wrap my skin around yourself so you can continue to fight." Sosruko did that and managed to battle his enemies for three days. They couldn't kill him, so they buried him alive. He remains under the earth, not exactly dead, but inactive.

(Colarusso, *Sagas*)

Seska Solsa (Sosruko) asked his horse if there was any man in the world stronger and more virile than himself.

"I wouldn't say Byatar is stronger and more manly than you, but I wouldn't say he is weaker either," replied the horse.

Seska Solsa knew that his horse wouldn't lie, but he asked, "How do you know that?"

"His horse is a friend of mine, and he told me so."

(Hunt, David)

Psabida's wife, Quaydukh, looked after his horse so well that the horse loved her more than he loved Psabida. One day, the horse observed Psabida and Quaydukh quarrelling. Psabida set off on the horse to steal cattle. Normally, when they arrived at a crossroads, he would let the horse decide which direction was best, and the horse was usually right. But this time, the horse refused to cooperate because of the quarrel. Psabida beat him and pulled the reins to one side, so the horse went in that direction. It was the wrong way.

Out of spite because of the quarrel, Quaydukh used her magic to make the weather alternately freezing and frying, but Psabida eventually came across some horses, buffalo and cows. Psabida wanted to take them home, but the horse refused to move. He beat him all day and night until the horse was bleeding and all of his ribs were broken.

He finally figured out what the problem was.

"Look, Quaydukh and I may have had a disagreement, but her heart is with us."

At the sound of her name, the horse ended his protest and moved on.

(Colarusso, *Sagas*)

Bataraz wanted to rescue his father-in-law, Wazarmis, who had long been in captivity, and he followed his mother's instructions about how to tame Wazarmis's horse so it would cooperate. He hid in a tree over a path the horse used, and when the horse was beneath him he leapt onto its back. The horse reared and tried to throw him, but he squeezed it so hard the horse calmed down and said, "I'll serve you if you stop squeezing my ribs." They went on until they met a bedraggled old man. The horse then refused to obey Bataraz and placed its head on the old man's shoulder, recognising him as Wazarmis.

(Colarusso, *Sagas*)

Kanz was too old to ride his horse in a race, and his son, Shauwai, offered to take his place. But he had to convince the horse that he was really Kanz's son. He went to the cellar where the horse was kept. The horse kicked out at him but missed. Shauwai picked him up by the hind legs and swung him against the ground several times. Then the horse grabbed Shauwai with his teeth and slammed him to the ground. Shauwai took the horse by the ears and pounded the ground with his head, saying, "Don't you recognise me as the son of Kanz?"

"How can I not?" said the horse. "You are the only one besides Kanz who has ever dared to touch me. I acknowledge you as my master."

(Colarusso, *Tales*)

Prince Shainag was dying, and only a magic apple from a faraway land could save him. He offered the use of his horse to Aishana, who saddled and mounted him. The horse bucked Aishana off. He shape-shifted into a swallow and remounted. The horse bucked him off again. He became a tack and stuck himself into the saddle but was unseated. Then he shifted into a saddle towel between the saddle and the horse, and this time he stayed on.

"I accept you as my rider," said the horse.

"And I accept you as my mount until I find a better one."

(Colarusso, *Tales*)

Zili's son needed to go on a quest but didn't have a suitable horse. A wise old woman gave him the dried hide of a horse that had belonged to Washtirji, one of the heavenly beings.

"All you have to do," she instructed, "is shake it and pray facing the east: 'God of gods, make this hide what it used to be.'"

When he did that, the hide changed into a horse that was seven times more powerful than it had been in its previous life.

(Colarusso, *Tales*)

The Narts called a meeting to select a new leader. Every family had to send a son. If they didn't have a son, they had to send a daughter, who would work as a slave. Alimbeg, one of the most respected of the elders, died leaving only a baby daughter. When she heard the family lamenting about having to send her to the meeting as a slave, she told them to bake bread and feed it to her. They did, and she reached her full growth immediately. She took her father's horse and gave him a thorough wash, shod him with iron shoes, saddled him and "tugged at the girth-strap so hard that his eyes nearly popped out." Then she cut her hair short, donned her father's armour and mounted the horse.

The family praised her appearance, but the horse complained, "I've always been ridden by the best of the Nart men, but now my rider is a girl."

That made Alimbeg's daughter angry. She beat the horse with her whip and made him jump over a high wall.

"What do you think of that?" she said.

"I like it," replied the horse. "Your father never made me jump over a wall like that."

She went to the meeting pretending to be Alimbeg's son, and she was quickly appointed as advisor-in-chief to the Nart Council. Their affairs began to run more smoothly, and their battles were more successful, so they were contented with their new leader. However, a notorious mischief-maker discovered that she was a girl and told everyone. The Narts didn't know whether to believe that or not, so as a test they sent her off to find a bride. With the help of Alimbeg's horse and Washtirji and another heavenly being, Wasilla, she abducted the daughter of wealthy Adil.

Washtirji, in his divine wisdom, knew Alimbeg's "son" was a girl, and he had a solution to the problem. He presented an apple to the two girls and told Alimbeg's daughter to eat the core and the seeds, and Adil's daughter to eat the rest.

They did so, and Alimbeg's daughter changed into a man and Adil's daughter fell in love with him. They were married, Alimberg's son remained the leader of the Narts for the rest of his life, and they contributed enough young Narts to the community that their family name continued long after their deaths.

(Colarusso, *Tales*)

The Horse Lurja
Georgia

The king and the queen have abandoned their beautiful daughter in a tower. She has never seen them. A witch convinces the queen that she can recover her youthful looks and reignite the king's interest in her by killing her daughter and eating her heart and liver. The king approves.

They send for the girl, but her horse, Lurja, warns her of her parents' plan. Following his advice, she asks to be allowed to ride her horse out and see the world dressed as a man before they kill her. They agree. When she is ready to leave, the horse says: "Seat yourself, hit me three times, hard enough to make three strips of skin fly from me and three from your hand, and just make sure that you sit very firmly and hold tight."

The princess survives several adventures with the help of the horse, including another incident that requires skin-flaying, and she marries a king's son. She is reunited with her parents but sensibly keeps them at arm's length.

(Condensed from Berman)

Mongolian Talking Horses

Mongolian horsemen also engaged in dialogue with their horses. The khan has ordered the son of Êlsuin the aged to capture the monster Manguis.

> The hero rode further; all at once his horse stopped.
>
> "Why hast thou stopped?" said the son of Êlsuin the aged.
>
> "See that black spot; what is it, in your opinion?" asked the horse.
>
> "I think it is far, far away – some mountain-ridge."
>
> "No; that is Manguis!"
>
> The horse told the hero to tie himself to her by a rope eighty-eight fathoms long, and himself to sit in a well,

and that when Manguis fell upon his horse, to catch him while he was fleeing and spurring the steed. The son of Êlsuin the aged seized him (Manguis) and led him to the khan.

(Verbatim, Gardner, 1886)

In the Mongolian folktale "Soning Tsetseg (Remarkable Flower)," an evil "black monster mangus" wants to marry the eponymous princess; the princess, however, has a magical talking bay horse and escapes with its help.

(Verbatim, Muskheli)

The Táltos Horse

Hungary

Some claim that a táltos is a shaman or a type of shaman; others deny that, saying that although their powers seem to be similar, a táltos is not a shaman. A shaman studies and learns and earns his or her abilities; the knowledge and abilities of the táltos are innate. A shaman is made with acquired knowledge; a táltos is born with inner knowledge.

A táltos horse is the steed, helper and advisor of a person, usually a táltos, with whom it is intimately bonded in a symbiotic relationship – the horse is the person's alter ego. The táltos horse is a táltos himself – it's always a male – and can shape-shift. Shamans in the stories can have a táltos horse. Typically, the táltos horse first appears as a weak and useless-looking nag, but if the hero treats it well, it asks to be fed hot cinders and then transforms into a mighty steed. There are strong similarities with the Nart horses.

I've seen references to this story elsewhere, but the only text I've found in English is Csenge Zalka's translation from the Hungarian in her *Tales of Superhuman Powers*. It's not clear whether János is a shaman or a táltos.

János was on a quest to meet and marry the Diamond Princess, but first he had to survive passage through the

Copper, Silver and Gold Kingdoms. The Silver Princess fell in love with him and gave him a mare that foaled two colts. One was strong, but the other was so feeble he had to carry it. Suddenly, the colt said, "Put me down. I can carry you now." It turned into a full-sized horse that could outrun any other.

The following is from "The Way of the Táltos: A Critical Reassessment of a Religious-Magical Specialist" by László Kürti.

> In a wonderful fairy-tale from Transylvania, the heroic Miklós Küs fights an old hag in order to find his sweetheart. He rides on his talking magic (*táltos*) horse, a pattern common in fairy-tales in many cultures. However, in the Hungarian version, before each magic flight, the horse "skips" and "stomps" a number of times and, only by so doing, are the horse and rider able to be airborne. [Note:] Actually, the stomping and the jumping occur three times but differently on every occasion: first as ... one jump, two stomps, then ... two stomps, one jump, and finally ... one stomp, one half-jump. ... as the power of the hero increases, (his transformation from copper and silver to gold), the number of stomps and the jumps decreases.

(See Appendix for a modern "talking horse" incident.)

Pardallo, Íñigo Ezquerra's Horse

Basque Country

Diego López, Lord of Bizkaia, was a fine horseman, and one day when he was boar-hunting he heard the sweet voice of a woman singing from the top of a mountain. He followed the sound and discovered a beautiful, well-dressed lady, well shaped in every way except that she had one foot that was cleft like a goat's foot. She told Don Diego that she was of high birth, but her name is not mentioned. He immediately fell in love with her, and he told her that he was lord of all the land and asked her to marry him. She accepted his proposal on condition that he would never make the Sign of the Cross in her presence, to which he agreed.

They lived happily and had a son named Íñigo Ezquerra and a daughter whose name is given simply as Doña. They used to sit at dinner together with Íñigo next to Don Diego and Doña next to her mother. One day Don Diego went to the mountains and killed a large pig and brought it home for dinner. As they were eating, he threw a bone on the floor. Suddenly, two dogs appeared, a Great Dane-greyhound crossbreed called an *alano* and a smaller hound called a *podenco*, and they began to fight over the bone. The lighter podenco grabbed the alano by the throat and killed it. When Don Diego saw this he took it for a miracle and made the Sign of the Cross, saying, "Who ever saw such a thing? Holy Mary, save us!"

His wife took hold of the boy and the girl and started to run off, but Don Diego held his son so that she couldn't take him. The woman grabbed the girl and fled through the garden and went to the mountains. The story says that they were never seen again, but that is not completely true.

Years later, Don Diego was fighting against the Moors and was captured and taken prisoner to Toledo. His son, Íñigo, grieved at this, and he asked the people for advice on how to free him. They told him that the only way was to go to the mountains and find his mother, and she would tell him how to rescue his father. He mounted his horse and went alone to the mountains. When he reached the summit, he heard a voice: "Son Íñigo Ezquerra, come to me, for I am the one you seek."

He went to her, and she said, "You have come to ask how to get your father out of prison."

Then she summoned a horse that roamed wild on the mountain, calling it by its name, Pardallo, and she said to her son:

"Pardallo is yours for the rest of your life. He does not need a saddle or bridle or shoes, nor does he have to be fed or watered. Whenever you ride him into battle you will win.

Now mount, and Pardallo will take you to Toledo, and he will stop at the door of the place where your father is being held. When you find your father, grasp him by the hand as if you are greeting him, and quickly pull him onto the horse and hold him in front of you. You will be back in Bizkaia before nightfall."

And that is exactly what happened. After some years, Don Diego López died and left his land to his son Don Íñigo Ezquerra.

(Close translation from Barcelos. Íñigo I López Ezquerra was Lord of Bizkaia 920-924.)

The Spirit Horse and Ku-suk-seia

Pawnee, United States

Ku-suk-seia lived with his grandmother because his parents were dead. They were poor, so poor that the tribe despised them and refused to help them in any way. They didn't even have a horse, so the boy couldn't ride with the bison hunters, and when the tribe moved they had to carry their few possessions on their shoulders: outcasts trudging behind the rest of their people.

One day when they were searching for leftover food after the tribe had left the village, they saw an old lame, starving and half-blind bay horse also foraging for scraps. After a snort and a near-sighted stare, the horse approached them in a friendly manner. As the boy and the grandmother began to put their bags on their shoulders, the horse whickered and knelt.

"The poor thing wants to help," said Ku-suk-seia, so they loaded their bags on him, and he limped along with his new human friends.

The tribe had already made camp when the three stragglers arrived. Scouts had reported a herd of bison nearby with a white female. The hide of a white bison was highly prized, and the chief declared that the hunter who brought him that hide could marry his daughter.

Ku-suk-seia wanted to join the hunt, if only to watch the action, so he grabbed his spear and carefully mounted the old bay to see if he would carry him. The warriors laughed more than usual at the idea that the boy could be a hunter with such a horse. He rode well behind the main party to avoid their jeers and to spare his steed.

As they passed through the long grass, the horse said, "Take me to that valley," head-pointing to a small stream. The boy did so, and the horse said, "Now cover me completely in mud and then mount me again." Ku-suk-seia did that.

The warriors spotted the herd, and they scattered to surround it. To the boy's surprise, the old bay launched himself into the chase and quickly caught up with the white bison. Ku-suk-seia hurled his spear, and the bison fell, to the triumphant bugle of the horse.

Ku-suk-seia butchered the animal and loaded the pieces onto the horse and mounted, wrapped in the white hide. He rode past the chief, who asked him for the hide, but the boy said that he had to take the meat to his grandmother first. This was disrespectful, but the chief said nothing. As soon as he had delivered the meat to his grandmother, the boy obeyed the first rule of a horseman: he fed and watered the horse.

After dinner, he visited the horse, who told him that the Sioux, the arch-enemies of the Pawnee, were going to attack at dawn.

"Ride me straight at them," he said, "and kill their chief. Then attack three times more. They won't be able to hit you. But only three times, or else one of us will be killed."

It happened just as the horse predicted, but the boy forgot the last part of the instructions, and he attacked a fourth time. The horse was killed under him, pierced with arrows. The Sioux retreated, but not before cutting the horse's body into small pieces and scattering them.

Ku-suk-seia went to the battlefield and gathered up the pieces and bones of the horse and took them to the top of a hill. Then he sat next to the heap wrapped in the white bison hide, crying and praying to the Great Spirit and all the other gods.

Suddenly, lightning flashed and thunder rolled to announce the coming of a raging storm that lasted for three days and nights. Ku-suk-seia didn't move. When the storm was over, the horse stood sound and vigorous where the heap of bones had been.

"The Great Spirit brought me back to life," he told the boy. "Why did you disobey me?"

"I forgot. I'm sorry."

"You should follow my advice. It comes from the Great Spirit."

Ku-suk-seia promised. He gave the bison hide to the chief and married his daughter, and when the chief died, he became chief, loved and respected by the people. When he died, they went to look for the horse to send him to the Afterlife with his master, but they never found him.

(Retold from Ya-Native online)

Bucephalus and Alexander the Great
Macedonia

Bucephalus (Ox-head) was named for the ox-head brand on his haunch. He really existed, so it would seem that he is not eligible to be included among beasts of myth and legend. However, Plutarch makes it clear in the "Life of Alexander" chapter in his second-century *Parallel Lives* that "it is not history that I am writing, but lives," devoting himself to the soul and character of his subjects and leaving the deeds to other writers. That inner truth is the nature of legend; some historians suggest that the following story may not be factual.

Alexander (356–323 BC) was the son of Philip II of Macedonia. One day, when Alexander was about ten years old, Philonicus the Thessalian brought a stallion to Philip for his inspection with an offer to sell. The horses of Thessaly had the reputation of being the finest in the region, and this was a magnificent specimen of the breed: huge compared to other war horses and spirited. At the age of five, he had never been ridden.

Philip's soldiers tried to mount the horse to test his abilities, but he reared up and shied away from them, and they were careful to stay clear of his flashing hooves. Alexander had already demonstrated his broad learning and proud criticism of his inferiors, and he had made known his frustration that his father was earning all the glory and was not likely to leave him anything to accomplish to build a reputation for himself. He was a bit spoiled and more outspoken than would be expected for one so young.

He watched the farcical spectacle of the so-called experts' failure to subdue the horse, and voiced his disapproval loudly as the attendants started to lead Bucephalus away as being unmanageable and useless.

"What a waste of a good horse just because they can't handle him."

"Do you think you can tame this horse when those more experienced than you have given up?" Philip said sharply.

"I can manage the horse better than they can," Alexander replied.

"What would you wager that you can?"

"The price of the horse."

The asking price was thirteen talents, three times the going rate.

Philip accepted the bet. They all laughed at the boy's audacity.

Like many a side-line spectator, Alexander had noticed something that escaped the supposed experts: the horse was shying at his shadow, which seemed to be following him closely and was therefore a potential threat. Alexander simply turned Bucephalus so he faced the sun so he couldn't see his shadow and spoke to him softly and stroked him. He saw that the flapping of his cloak was also spooking the horse, and he let it slide slowly to the ground, allowing him to inspect it. Once Bucephalus had calmed and regained his confidence, Alexander leapt on his back and controlled his movements with gentle but firm pressure on the reins.

When the horse had settled, Alexander encouraged him to run by voice and heel pressure. Philip watched anxiously as they galloped off, and all were relieved to see them return with the partnership intact.

Whether or not it was Alexander's intention, he had accomplished one of his goals. Philip greeted him by saying, "My son, you will have to find a kingdom of your own, because Macedonia is too small for you."

There was another lesson in it for Philip. Plutarch explains:

> After this, considering him to be of a temper easy to be led to his duty by reason, but by no means to be compelled, [Philip] always endeavoured to persuade rather than to command or force him to anything; and now looking upon the instruction and tuition of his youth to be of greater difficulty and importance than to be wholly trusted to the ordinary masters in music and poetry, and the common school subjects, and to require, as Sophocles says, "The bridle and the rudder too," he sent for Aristotle.
>
> (John Dryden's translation)

Alexander was the only one Bucephalus allowed to ride him, and their active lives were spent together with one brief interruption. Someone stole the horse, and Alexander threatened to flatten the countryside and slaughter all the inhabitants. He was quickly returned. When Bucephalus died of old age in 326, Alexander named a city after him: Bucephala, on the Hydaspes River in India.

King Alfonso's Horse and the Hidden Chapel

Spain

Next to the magnificent 14th-century mudéjar (Christian-Islamic art style) Puerta del Sol in Toledo is a smaller, older gate, the Puerta de Valmardón. Next to this gate on Calle

Cristo de la Luz (Street of Christ of the Light) stands the tenth-century former Muslim sanctuary now called the Mezquita del Cristo de la Luz.

When El Cid liberated Toledo in 1085 after nearly four centuries of Moorish occupation of Spain, King Alfonso VI ceremoniously entered the city through the Puerta de Valmardón. His horse stopped suddenly in front of the Mezquita, knelt down reverently on a white stone in the pavement, and refused to move on. Respecting his horse's instinct, Alfonso ordered that the wall of the Mezquita be breached. When this was done and a hidden chamber revealed, the king entered and found a lamp burning in front of a crucifix.

Some accounts say an ancient monk greeted the king with relief that he could now die in peace after his nearly century-long vigil. Others say there was no sign of human presence, but it is agreed that the chamber appeared to have been sealed and that the lamp had been burning miraculously since the Mezquita was built in 999. Alfonso ordered all the Muslim inscriptions removed from the sanctuary, had a Mass celebrated immediately, and converted the Mezquita into a Christian chapel.

A variant of this story has El Cid entering the city, and it is his horse, Babieca, who kneels.

Babieca, the Mount of El Cid
Spain

Rodrigo (Ruy) Díaz de Vivar, El Cid Campeador, was born in the village of Vivar near Burgos about 1040 and died in Valencia in 1099. He was largely responsible for the middle stages of the Reconquista, the reconquest of Spain from the Moors, who invaded the peninsula in 711 and dominated it until they were pushed into the south in the 13th century and finally expelled in 1492.

El Cid's long-lived horse, Babieca, was with him from his youth. Rodrigo's godfather gave him his choice of colts, and he selected one that was rough and unruly. His godfather called him an idiot – *babieca* – for his decision, and Rodrigo transferred the name to the horse. In one version of the story of King Alfonso's discovery of the Mezquita del Cristo de la Luz in Toledo, it is Babieca, bearing Rodrigo, who genuflects at the white stone.

Babieca died in 1102 at the age of about 45 and is buried in the grounds of the monastery of San Pedro de Cardeña, where Rodrigo was originally interred. The inscription on the horse's tombstone refers to the time Alfonso asked Rodrigo to give a demonstration of Babieca's speed, and, the king having admired the horse, Rodrigo evidently felt obligated to offer Babieca to him:

> "King, I give you Babieca, my swift horse."
> Then the king answered, "I do not wish that.
> If I take the horse he will not have such a fine master.
> A horse like that is for someone such as you
> To conquer the Moors and be their pursuer,
> For because of you and the horse we are well honoured."

Buraq and Muhammad's Night Journey

Middle East

> Bounty and happiness are ever on horseback; horses are gold that one may hold.
> (Attributed to Muhammad)

This story comes from hadith literature: a collection of oral traditions compiled after Muhammad's death.

> I was brought al-Buraq, who is an animal white and long, larger than a donkey but smaller than a mule, with two wings in its thighs, which came up to its hoofs and were set in them, who would place his hoof a distance equal to the range of vision. I mounted it and came to the Temple (Bait Maqdis in Jerusalem), then tethered it to the ring

> used by the prophets. ... When I went near it to ride, it became restive. Thereupon [the angel] Gabriel placed his hand on its head and said: "O Buraq! Are you not ashamed of what you are doing? By Allah no servant of Allah has ridden you before Muhammad, more honoured in the sight of Allah." It felt ashamed till it was covered with sweat and became calm; then I mounted it. It moved its ears, and the earth shrank to such an extent that its hoofs seemed to touch its surface at the end of the range of our sight. It had a long back and long ears.
> (Attributed to Muhammad)

The name is said to come from a generic Persian word for a riding animal; alternatively, from the Arabic meaning "lightning". Buraq (or "the Buraq") is variously described as either male or female, and often depicted as a winged white horse with the face of a woman. One source says that when he went uphill he extended his hind legs, and when he went downhill he extended his front legs.

Buraq was a regular mode of transport for the prophets, and it was he who took Muhammad on his Night Journey. The Prophet was in the Great Mosque in Mecca when Gabriel brought the steed to him.

Accompanied by Gabriel, they went to the "farthest mosque", which is believed to have been at the site of the present Temple Mount in Jerusalem. There Muhammad tethered Buraq – probably at the al-Buraq mosque near the Western Wall – dismounted and prayed, then remounted, and the three carried on to a tour of the heavens, where they met with the earlier prophets.

When Muhammad died, Buraq carried him to heaven.

The Pursuit of the Gilla Decair and his Horse
Ireland

The Celtic sea-god figure, Manannán mac Lir, is also a trickster and a tester. One of his favourite manifestations in Ireland is the Gilla Decair (Difficult Servant). In his role as a humbler of the high and mighty, it is not surprising that the Gilla Decair would target the elite warrior band of the Fianna and their leader, Fionn mac Cumhaill, one of the two greatest Irish heroes along with Cúchulainn. However, in this case Ábhartach, a warrior-wizard of the Tuatha Dé Danann, borrowed the Gilla Decair persona to play a trick.

The Fianna's responsibility was to defend Ireland from invasion and punish crime, as a combined national police force and standing army. During the summer, from the First of May to the First of November, they roamed the country and supported themselves by hunting. During the other six months, they were quartered on the people as the price for their role as defenders.

One November Eve (Halloween), when the gates between this world and the Otherworld are especially open, they held a feast, and they decided to have one last hunt before retiring for the season. They went to Munster, and when they reached the plain around Knockany (Cnoc Áine, the Hill of Áine, the regional goddess) in County Limerick they stopped for a rest on the side of a mound.

Fionn mac Cumhaill asked who would climb to the top and watch for any mischievous members of the Tuatha Dé Danann or fierce Fomors who might take advantage of the open gateways to intrude into this world. Fionn Bán mac Bresail volunteered. He took his weapons and went to the top of the hill and looked north, south, east and west.

He had not long been there when he saw coming from the east a menacing, malevolent, misshapen, dreadful, devilish, disgusting, lusty lunk of an ill-favoured formidable Fomor. He carried a hideous-hued solid shield sloped across his back and a broad-grooved, smart-smiting sword on his grimy left thigh. He bore on his shoulder a brace of broad-bladed battered javelins long left unbloodied in battle. A threadbare cloak covered his armour and harness and his coal-black body.

The sad and surly horse he hauled behind him with a crude iron halter sulked and shambled, sluggish, shaky-legged and scrawny-arsed. It was a great wonder he didn't pull the horse's head from its shrivelled, swaybacked body with every jerk he gave of the halter to make it move. But it was even more marvellous that the man's arms weren't torn from his body with each balk, check, stop and backward step of the horse. Meanwhile, the man kept bashing the beast with thunderous thumps of an iron club.

It wasn't easy to frighten Fionn Bán mac Bresail, but when he saw this strange and unexpected sight, and the big man looked straight at him, he thought it best to inform Fionn and the Fianna without delay, and he hastened down the hill to report the news.

The Fianna watched the Fomor approach. It was a short journey that took a long time before the determination of the big man triumphed over the resistance of the cantankerous beast, and he stood before Fionn mac Cumhaill and bowed his head and bent the knee to him.

"Who are you and who are your people?" Fionn asked him.

"I never knew my family. I only know that I'm a Fomor in search of a master to serve."

"Why do you not have a horse servant?"

"A good reason. I require the food of three hundred men a day to satisfy my appetite, and I would begrudge any of that to a servant."

"And your name?"

"I'm called the Gilla Decair."

"Why 'Decair'?"

"Because I find nothing in the world more difficult than to do anything to satisfy my master. Conán mac Morna," he said to one of the Fianna, "which gets the higher wages – a horseman or a foot soldier?"

"A horseman is paid twice as much as a foot soldier," said Conán.

"I call you as witness, Conán, that I am a horseman because I have a horse. And now, Fionn mac Cumhaill, I will let my horse out among the horses of the Fianna under your protection and that of the Fianna."

"You may do that," said Fionn.

The Gilla Decair removed the iron halter from the horse, which galloped off to the herd and quickly began biting and kicking and killing them.

"Take your horse away," Conán said. "If it wasn't under the protection of Fionn and the Fianna, I'd make its brain flow out of its mouth, ears and nose."

"I won't do that," said the Gilla Decair. "Remember I'm a horseman, and it's not my responsibility to lead a horse. That's the job of a horse-boy."

So Conán went and put the iron halter on the horse and led it to where the Fianna were standing.

"To all your accomplishments as a warrior, Conán," said Fionn with a chuckle, "you can now add experience as a horse-boy. I suggest you mount that horse and ride it over hill and dale and flat flowery plains until its heart bursts out of its chest in payment for the killing of the Fianna's horses."

Conán leapt onto the horse and dug it in the ribs with his heels, but never an inch did it budge.

"I know what the problem is," said Fionn. "It won't move until it has as many men as will equal the weight of the Fomor on its back."

So thirteen of the Fianna jumped up behind Conán on the horse, and it sagged under them and then straightened up.

"I see that you're mocking me and my steed," said the Gilla Decair, "and woe to me if I put in the rest of the year of service to you if this is how I'm treated on the first day after all the good reports I've heard about you, and so I'm leaving."

He set off, and it wasn't long before his lanky legs put a hill between him and the Fianna. When the horse saw its master leaving, it took off at a fast gallop after him. The Fianna howled with laughter at the sight of the fourteen men abducted by the nag. When Conán found that he wasn't able to dismount, he let out a string of imaginative curses on Fionn and the Fianna if they didn't follow the horse and the Gilla Decair and release them. So they pursued the horse over hills and glens until the Gilla Decair reached the sea.

Then Liagan Luath grabbed the horse's tail with his two hands, thinking to bring it to a halt before it entered the water, but the Gilla Decair continued into the sea, and the horse with its unwilling passengers followed, dragging Liagan Luath behind it.

The horse doesn't re-enter the narrative until the end, so here is a brief summary of the rest of the story.

Fionn and fifteen of the Fianna pursued the Gilla Decair in a ship magically made available to them and endured a welter of magic and mayhem in a world of wizards and winsome women. They fought the army of the King of Greece, whose daughter, Taise, had fallen in love with Fionn, sight unseen, after hearing about his reputation as a warrior. When he killed her brother in battle, her love increased seven times. She ran off with Fionn, was kidnapped by her father, and then recovered by Fionn. They were aided by the Wizard of Chivalry, who informed them that it was Ábhartach who had carried off the fifteen Fianna.

At the end of their adventures, they encountered Ábhartach in the Land of Promise, who supplied them with a ship to take them home. He asked Fionn to name the price of indemnity for the trick he had played on them, and Fionn said that the wages he had promised for a year's service and the indemnity would cancel each other. But Conán demanded compensation: that the fourteen most beautiful women of the Land of Promise should be made to ride the horse, and Ábhartach's own wife to be stuck to the horse's tail as Liagan Luath had been, until they reached Ireland.

Ábhartach agreed, but when they arrived in Ireland, he said, "Here are your people, Fionn," and when Fionn looked around, all the Fianna were accounted for, but Ábhartach and the horse and the women had disappeared, except Taise, who Fionn married.

Standish Hayes O'Grady translated this late 16th-century tale from an 18th-century manuscript and published the Irish original and the translation in *Silva Gadelica* (1892). My rendition is based on both, with some input from P. W. Joyce's translation in *Old Celtic Romances* (1894). There may also be an echo of seanchaí Eddie Lenihan's telling of this story, which I heard many years ago. In the older tales, Fionn and the Fianna never rode horses or used chariots, suggesting that the Fionn Cycle predates the domestication of the horse.

Ancient authors ardently admired accumulated alliteration and assonance, adding adjectives and adverbs as appeared appropriate. I have replicated the result in a few places, without overdoing it too much. For example, I loosely translated "fomor ferrda fírghránda, ocus in dúil diablaide dodelba, ocus in mogh modarda mísciamach" as "a menacing, malevolent, misshapen, dreadful, devilish, disgusting, lusty lunk of an ill-favoured formidable Fomor".

The Strange Colt
Ireland

There was a very rich man once who lived near Brandon Bay, and his name was Breogan. This Breogan had a deal of fine land and was well liked by all people who knew him.

One morning as he was walking on the strand for himself, he found, above the highest tide, a little colt, barely the size of a goat, and a very nice colt he was.

"Oh, what a beautiful little beast!" said Breogan. "He doesn't belong to any one in this country. He is not mine, but still and all I'll take him. If an owner comes the way, sure he can prove his claim if he is able."

Breogan carried the colt to the stable and fed him as well as any beast that he had. The colt was thriving well, and when twelve months were passed, it was a pleasure to look at him. Breogan put him in a stable by himself after that and kept him three years. At the end of the third year, it isn't a little colt he was, but a grand, fiery steed. Breogan invited all his friends and neighbours to a feast and a great merrymaking.

"This will be a good time," thought he, "to find a man to ride the strange colt."

There was a splendid race-course on the seashore. The appointed day came, and all the people were assembled. The horse was brought out, bridled and saddled, and led to the strand. The place was so crowded that a pin falling from the sky would not fall on any place but the head of some person old or young, some man, woman, or child that was there at the festival. For three days the women of the village were cooking food for all that would come. There was enough ready and to spare. Breogan strove to come at a man who would ride the horse, but not a man could he find. The horse was so fiery that all were in dread of him.

Not to spoil sport for the people, Breogan made up his mind to ride himself. As soon as the man mounted and was firm in the saddle, the horse stood on his hind-legs, rose with a leap in the air, and away with him faster than any wind, first over the land, and then over the sea. The horse never stopped till he came down on his fore-feet in Breasil, which is a part of Tir nan Og (the Land of the Young).

(Verbatim, Curtin)

The Crazy Horse
Galicia, Spain

In the ski country of the highest mountain range in Galicia, the Serra (Sierra) de Queixa (1778m) near A Pobra de Trives, tales are told round the fire in the winter evenings of a majestic pure white horse with a streaming mane that is so long that it merges with its tail. At night, the mane glows with a golden luminescence that turns dark into daylight. It can run like the wind, passing from here to there without ever stopping, and it is so fast that it seems to be everywhere at once.

Just before it appears, there is a deafening sound that announces its imminent arrival – a noise so loud that a deaf man in Celeiro had to plug his ears. When it approaches a church, the bells ring out as if enchanted. Because of their keen hearing, dogs can sense its coming long before humans, whose first intimation of the horse's approach is the complete absence of the barking of the dogs. No obstacle is too high to leap.

No one can explain where it comes from. Some say it's a witch's familiar; others believe that it's a neighbour who failed to shape-shift into a wolf and became a horse instead. They say its home is in the river, because they see lights running under the surface, but no one has tried to confirm that: they are all too terrified to step into its path.

(Loose translation from Mosquera Paans)

The Horse of the Lake

Spain

A widow and her son lived next to an enchanted lake. A herd of horses came out of the lake at night and trampled the crops whenever they were ready to be harvested. One night, the people drove the horses off, except one, which they captured and put in a stable. The horse seemed to be tame, and the son one day took him out and rode him with no problem until the horse saw the lake. Then it made one mighty leap and plunged into the water, killing the son.

Since then, no one goes near the lake at harvest time, when they can hear strange sounds coming from the lake, and at midnight they hear the sound of one horse galloping toward the lake and the screams of agony of the rider.

(Loose translation from Sainero, *Huella*)

The Phantom White Stallion of Skull Valley
Tex Ritter, 1945 recording based on a traditional story
United States

Our family always included at least one dog, and we grew up together as quasi-brothers and sisters. Dogs were familiar, but I was fascinated by the majesty and mystery of horses. When I was seven, I was given Tex Ritter's recording of "The Phantom White Stallion of Skull Valley" – "as wild as the north wind and as fast as a speeding arrow". I played it so often that I never forgot the images and some of the lines and the sound of Tex's voice, and I never forgave my younger brother for sitting on the fragile 78-rpm disc and shattering it. As compensation, my parents gave me riding lessons.

About twenty years later, I met Tex and asked him if the record had ever been re-released. He said he had forgotten he had made it, and no, no re-release. Finally, after years of fruitless searching, I find it's now on the internet, so I'm able to include my long-time horse hero the Phantom White Stallion in this book.

> Skull Valley is in Arizona not many miles south of the Grand Canyon. One of the favourite stories of the cowboys is a strange tale handed down by the Navajo Indians, the story of a great white stallion, as wild as the north wind and as fast as a speeding arrow.
>
> The Indians claim he had roamed this land hundreds of years. The white rangers didn't believe it until many of their horses began to disappear. At first, horse thieves were suspected, but there were no clues, no footprints, no hoofmarks. Finally the rangers became desperate. They formed posses and searched the countryside.
>
> Then one day they sighted their missing horses far, far in the distance, headed for Granite Mountain. As they looked they could hardly believe their eyes, for leading the herd was the phantom white horse of Skull Valley. Later that night, stunned by the spectacle they'd witnessed, the rangers called a meeting. They agreed

upon a plan to completely encircle the great white stallion. He must be captured.

The sky was dark and cloudy as the determined rangers started the drive that would bring them to the very brink of the Grand Canyon. All day they pushed forward – in vain. As night fell, the black sky began to close in upon them. The thunder roared and the lightning slashed and tore the sky and earth. Then suddenly a cry went up, for there on a high plateau, their heads high in the excitement of the storm stood the missing herd. The great white stallion stood proudly in their midst.

In a flash the storm was forgotten and the race for the capture was on. The phantom horse was not to be taken so easily. Like the flashing lightning he was away, and the faithful herd followed, as if drawn by some strange power. They were not able to keep pace with the swift stallion, whose very life was freedom. The ropes of the rangers were ready, as they spurred their horses on to what seemed certain capture. Escape was impossible. The canyon would stop this phantom horse. On and on the stallion raced. Then suddenly there yawned before him the deep, dangerous chasm of the Grand Canyon.

A flash of lightning illuminated the sky and seemed to hang overhead. Then, with what seemed like a last farewell to the herd and defiance to his pursuers, the white stallion made a mighty screaming leap into space and disappeared.

But was the white stallion really gone? Was he dead? Even to this day, boys and girls, when thunder rocks the earth and lightning splits the sky, the Indians tell of having seen a great white beast standing atop some mesa, racing across the grassy slopes, his mane and tail streaming behind him like the lacy froth from a wind-tossed wave. Is the Phantom White Stallion of Skull Valley dead? I wonder.

(Verbatim from Tex's recording)

Léim an Eich: The Leap of Máire Rua's Stallion

Ireland

The History

Mary MacMahon (1615-1686) was born into the aristocracy of County Clare. She was married three times. Her first husband died of natural causes, the second died in battle in 1651, and she was accused of murdering the third but acquitted. The very wealthy and relatively young widow attracted many suitors and a sinister reputation under the nickname of Máire Rua – Red-headed Mary – probably fuelled by lingering doubt about the acquittal and envy of an independent-minded and powerful woman.

The Legend

Her second husband had a nasty accident while shaving. The third fell from the roof of her home, Leamaneh Castle, shortly after the wedding while inspecting his newly acquired property. The fourth was riding Máire's prize stallion near the Cliffs of Moher when she gave a whistle, and the horse reared up and threw the man over the cliff. She had 25 male servant-lovers who she had dressed in women's clothes in an attempt to forestall rumours. A tour guide told me that she married 25 men in all, and killed them the morning after the wedding.

She owned a fierce and untamed stallion (probably the aforementioned prize steed) that was so wild that niches were cut into each side of a gateway so that servants leading the horse through the gate to let him loose could take refuge in them when the horse bolted, to avoid being trampled.

While she may have enjoyed the attentions of her many suitors, it's possible that she had had enough of married life, or maybe she suspected they were only after her money, but in any case she devised a rigid test for them. They were required to ride a spirited stallion – presumably that same one – 15 miles (25 km) from Leamaneh Castle to the Cliffs of Moher and back. The horse was trained to rear and throw them off when he reached the Cliffs, and so they were all eliminated.

Then young Turlough O'Loughlin decided to try his luck with a bit of special help. One story says that, knowing the fate of the previous suitors, a wise man gave him a charm to prevent the horse rearing; another says his father advised him to use his own saddle and bridle, and perhaps he took both precautions. As a result, Turlough was not thrown over the cliff. When Máire saw him galloping back to the castle safe and sound, she closed the gate against him. But he spurred the horse on and leapt over the gate. The stallion fell and was killed, but Turlough survived.

The story doesn't tell us if he married the widow, but the incident is said to be the origin of the name of the castle, Leamaneh, from the Irish *léim an eich*, which means "leap of the horse". However, this is a back-derivation: the district and the castle were called Leamaneh long before Mary MacMahon's time.

The legendary Máire Rua had a suitably legendary death – or three, all involving trees.

One: she was riding her horse on a stormy night when her long red tresses got tangled in the low branches of a tree as she passed under it, and she was hanged by her hair.

Two: she had ordered the destruction of the house of a widow, who laid a curse on her in retaliation. It's well known that the most powerful curses are those made by a poet or a priest or a widow. The widow's curse resulted in Máire being killed by a falling tree.

Three: after she had slain 25 husbands, someone – perhaps the 26th? – fastened her in a hollow tree and left her to starve to death.

Sleipnir, Odin's Horse
Scandinavia

The origin of the eight-legged Sleipnir (Slider or Slipper) is usually glossed over quickly in children's versions of the Norse myths for a good reason: it would be awkward to explain how a male god gave birth to a horse.

During a war with the Vanir, the walls surrounding Asgard were destroyed, and none of the Aesir were willing to do the heavy work required to rebuild it. An imposing mason arrived at the gods' home and offered to complete the job, with the aid of his stallion, Svadilfari, in 18 months for a fee: the beautiful Freyja and the sun and the moon.

"Six months," said Odin, "and without the horse."

He thought the task was impossible: they would have their wall, and Freyja was safe.

The man reluctantly accepted the six-month deadline but stood firm about the horse. Finally, at the urging of mischief-maker Loki, the Aesir agreed to his terms. At the end of six months minus three days of night and day labour the wall was nearly finished, with the horse doing most of the heavy hauling, and it seemed the Aesir would lose Freyja and the sun and the moon. Belatedly realising that the mason was a Frost Giant, they blamed Loki and forced him on pain of death to come up with a plan to prevent the completion of the wall in the contracted time.

That night, and for the next two nights, the stallion Svadilfari heard the urgent neighing of a mare in heat coming from the woods. He burst out of the harness and ran off to satisfy the call of nature. This so disrupted the mason's schedule that the wall was left unfinished at the end of the six-month period, and when Thor the giant-killer arrived, the mason himself came to an end.

However, there were consequences that might have been foreseen. Loki discovered that he was in foal, and eleven months later he dropped an eight-legged grey colt, Sleipnir.

The eleventh-century Ramsund rock carving near Stockholm depicts the Volsunga Saga hero Sigurd with Grani, son of Sleipnir. Sigurd had been seeking a suitable steed when he met an old man, who suggested that they drive a herd of horses into the river Busiltjörn. They did this, and all of the horses with the exception of a large and untamed grey returned to the river bank. That one, the old man said, was of the seed of Sleipnir and would grow with good feeding to be the best of horses. The old man was Odin.

In her book *Gods and Myths of Northern Europe*, H. R. Ellis Davidson suggests an explanation for the horse's eight legs. It is Sleipnir who takes Odin and others to visit the domain of Loki's daughter Hel, who reigned over the abode of the dead not slain in battle. There are traditionally four pallbearers to carry a coffin, and they have a total of eight legs.

The White Horse and the Healing Well
England

Saint Milburga (d. 715), daughter of the king of Mercia, was the abbess of Wenlock Abbey in Shropshire. Stoke St. Milborough is named after her, and St. Milburga's Well, said to have healing powers especially for eye ailments, is located on the east side of the village. At some point, the well was used for washing clothes, and its water is now piped to local houses for general use, both of which usually mean that the well long ago lost its curative function. However, researcher Chris Jenkins visited the village in the 1990s and reported that a workman told him that the flow from the well could not be stopped, and that a cut on his finger had healed quickly after he immersed it in the water.

This is the story of the origin of the well.

A gang of evil-doers was chasing Milburga, who was mounted on a white horse. As she passed a field being sown with barley, she caused the barley to suddenly become full grown, and she told the workers to tell her pursuers, if they were questioned, that, yes, they had seen her, but that was when the barley had just been sown.

When she reached the village now called Stoke St. Milborough, she fell off the horse and her head hit a rock. There was no water nearby to bathe her wound, so she asked the horse to strike the ground three times, and the spring that is now the source of St. Milburga's Well burst forth.

Tam O'Shanter and Meg the Mare
Scotland

Robert Burns sent a prose synopsis of one of his most famous poems to a publisher in 1790. "Tam O'Shanter" was published the following year.

Tam has been drinking with his cronies until past the witching hour of midnight. Riding home on his grey mare, Meg – "A better never lifted leg" – he passes a haunted church where scantily dressed witches and warlocks are dancing to the music Satan plays on the bagpipe. His attention is drawn to an unusually beautiful young woman wearing nothing but a "cutty sark": a very short chemise that she had long outgrown. This is Burns's prose version.

> He involuntarily burst out, with a loud laugh, "Weel luppen, Maggy wi' the short sark!" and recollecting himself, instantly spurred his horse to the top of his speed. I need not mention the universally known fact, that no diabolical power can pursue you beyond the middle of a running stream. Lucky it was for the poor farmer that the river Doon was so near, for notwithstanding the speed of his horse, which was a good one, against he reached the middle of the arch of the bridge and consequently the middle of the stream, the pursuing, vengeful hags were so close at his heels, that one of them actually sprung to seize him. But it was too late; nothing was on her side of the stream but the horse's tail, which immediately gave way to her infernal grip, as if blasted by a stroke of lightning; but the farmer was beyond her reach. However, the unsightly, tailless condition of the vigorous steed was to the last hours of the noble creature's life, an awful warning to the Carrick farmers, not to stay too late in Ayr markets.

In the poem, Tam's encouragement to the ill-clad dancer is: "Weel done, Cutty-sark!" The name was bestowed on the Cutty Sark, a British clipper ship built in 1869 and now on display at Greenwich. The figurehead is an artist's impression of the bare-breasted young dancer with Meg's tail in her hand. A Scotch whisky takes its name from the famous ship.

Kelpies and Other Water Steeds

Widespread

I have been all my life fond of horses, so I feel loth to quit the subject, and will therefore say a few words of the enchanted horses of flesh and blood, or water-steeds as I may call them, from their connexion with that element.

Everyone knows the classic steeds Pegasus and Arion, both the offspring of the god of the sea; the latter by Mother Earth. I need therefore only allude to them.

It was foretold to Yezdejird king of Persia, that he would come to the spring of Soo, and there find his death. He resolved that he would never approach that fount and so live forever. But a disorder seized him, and by the advice of a priest he had himself carried to that fount, where, on praying to God, and sprinkling a few drops of its water on his head, he was cured of his disease. But his pride returned when he found himself restored to health and vigour. Then suddenly rose out of the spring a black horse, strong and wild as a lion. Yezdejird commanded his nobles to take the noose and catch the horse. They tried, but in vain. The Shah, full of anger, pursued the horse himself, but when he came up with him, the water-steed smote him with his hoof on the breast, so that he fell down and died. The horse then plunged into the spring and vanished.

When King Gradasso [he's in the Bayardo story] had cut down the tree in the enchanted wood, there issued from it a stately horse. The undaunted hero mounts him, and the steed rises into the air, and then plunges with his burden into the River of Laughter. This may remind one of the horse in the tale of Prince Agib, or the Third Calendar, who carries the prince away from the castle, where he had lived in such "great joy and solace" with the fifty fair princesses, and leaves him, wanting an eye, on the roof of the Castle of Repentance; a tale, by the way, not without its moral. To these may be added the horse which Sindbad saw come out of the sea to King Mihrage's mares.

> According to Gervase of Tilbury, a Catalonian nobleman of his time, whom he calls Giraldus de Cabreriis, had a very extraordinary horse, by whose advice he was always guided. Gervase cannot say in what manner the steed conveyed his sentiments to his master, but he knew that he ate wheaten bread out of a silver dish or trough and lay on a feather-bed instead of straw; and further, that when, after his master's death, he was seduced to solace himself with some young females, he dashed out his brains with vexation. The good marshal is sadly puzzled what to make of him.
>
> "If he was an ordinary horse," says he, "whence did he get sense and reason? If he was enchanted, why did he eat?"
>
> Whence we may learn that enchanted horses eat not.
>
> I cannot expect everyone to take the same interest in horses that I do myself. I must therefore conclude, passing over that very suspicious steed who carried our great Robert Grosthed (who was afterwards bishop of Lincoln) through the air and among the planets, from England to Rome and back again, in less than a day. This however, and steeds of the sort, I suspect were not real horses, but daemons, who had taken that form for the nonce.
>
> (Verbatim, Keightley, *Tales*)

"Enchanted horses eat not." Also, Rinaldo encountered a horse "which disdained to share the diet of his fellow-steeds – corn or grass – and fed only on air." And Pardallo does not "have to be fed or watered". Fuentelapeña considers this question about duendes, invisible beings that can take physical form: "If the duendes are purely corporeal, they will inevitably need food, because food is simply necessary for every living thing. So if we can't see what it is that they eat, how do they sustain themselves?"

One of his suggestions is that they live off noxious vapours. To support the notion that a being can live on vapours alone, he cites an anecdote about the fourth- and third-century BC philosopher Democritus. At the age of 109, he was on his deathbed. His sister was looking after him and crying because she was not able to fulfil her vows and attend the festival of Ceres. He told her to have hot bread brought to him every day and applied to his nostrils. She did so, and he lived for three more days until the end of the festival.

(Fuentelapeña §§839, 854)

See also Appendix: Extracts from *The Fairy Faith in Celtic Countries* for more theories on this subject.

> Seven little boys, regardless of the warnings of their old grandmother, would go out at night on various affairs. As they went along a pretty little black horse came up to them, and they all were induced to mount on his back. When they met any of their playmates they invited them also to mount, and the back of the little horse stretched so that at last he had on him not less than thirty little boys. He then made with all speed for the sea, and plunging into it with them they were all drowned. ...
>
> At other times [the lutin] appears under the form of a horse ready bridled and saddled. If any peasant, weary after his day's work, is induced to mount him in order to ride home, he begins to kick and fling and rear and bound, and ends by jerking him into a marsh or a ditch full of water. When he takes this form he is called Le Cheval Bayard, probably after the famous steed of the Paladin Rinaldo.
>
> (Verbatim, Keightley, *The Fairy Mythology*)

Kelpies
Scotland

Kelpie as Useful

A man in carting home his peats for winter fuel was in the habit of seeing a big black horse grazing on the banks of the Ugie, at Inverugie Castle, near Peterhead, each morning as he passed to the "moss." He told some of his neighbours. They suspected what the horse was and advised the man to get a "waith-horse" [ownerless or stray horse] bridle, approach the animal with all care and caution, and cast the bridle over his head. The man now knew the nature of the creature and followed the advice. Kelpie was secured, and did good work in carrying stones to build the bridge over the Ugie at Inverugie. When his services were no longer needed he was set at liberty. As he left he said:

Sehr back an sehr behns
Cairryt a' the Brig o' Innerugie's stehns.
[Sore back and sore bones
Carried all the Bridge of Inverugie's stones.]

The old man, who handed down this story to his children, from one of whom I have now got it, used to say to any of them that complained of being tired after a hard day's work: "Oh, aye, ye're like the kelpie that cairryt the stehns to big the brig o' Innerugie, 'sehr back an sehr behns.'" ["sore back and sore bones"]

[Waith-horse: "a horse that wanders in pursuit of mares." *Scottish National Dictionary*]

Kelpie as Hurtful

A miller was annoyed by a kelpie entering his mill during night and playing havoc among the grain and meal. One night he shut up in the mill his boar, for a miller generally kept a good many pigs and a breeding sow or two. As usual kelpie entered the mill. The boar stood on his defence, and fought the kelpie. Next night the creature appeared at the miller's window, and called to him, "Is there a chattie i' the mill the nicht?" "Aye, there is a chattie i' the mill, an will be forever mair," was the answer. Kelpie returned no more to the mill.

"A lad and a lass" were taking a journey together. They came to a stream, which they had to cross by a ford. Seeing a white horse grazing on the bank they thought it would be easier to cross on horseback, if they could but catch the animal, than by wading. They found no difficulty in getting hold of the horse. They mounted and entered the ford. Everything seemed to be going well, till they reached the middle of the ford. Then the animal started off at full gallop down the stream. He rushed along with loud haw-hawing, and kept shouting now and again:

> Sit sicker, Jenny Milne; ride fest Davie,
> Till we win t' the pots o' Balrehvie.

Kelpie is commonly spoken of as a black horse.

There is a deep pool in the Burn of Strichen, near the farm of Braco, Aberdeenshire. It was the home of a kelpie. One evening, a man, on his journey home, had to cross the stream. It was in flood, and the man was brought to a standstill. He saw a horse grazing on the bank. He conceived the idea of mounting him, and thus crossing the flooded waters. He went up to the animal, that submitted quite gently, and mounted. No sooner was he seated than off the creature ran, plunging along to the deepest part of the pool, and dragging his victim with him below the water.

Kelpie in Human Form

Kelpie sometimes takes the form of a grey wrinkled old man.

A man was crossing the Burn of Strichen, at the same place, the farm of Braco. On approaching a dyke he had to pass over, he heard, as he thought, someone speaking. He walked quietly towards the spot from which the sound of words came, and peeped over the dyke. He saw an old man mending his trowsers, and, as he was mending, he kept saying, "That clout 'ill dee here; and this ane 'ill dee there." The man looked and listened for a little. At last he inflicted a blow on the old man's head, saying, "An this clout 'ill dee there." In a moment the kelpie was in his true form, and off with loud neighing to his deep pool.

Kelpie Seeking Human Companionship

A young woman was on a journey. Night came down, and she lost her way. After wandering a little, she came to a place which seemed likely to give her shelter for the night. She entered and composed herself to such rest as she could draw out of her resting-place. By-and-bye a little dog came and lay down by her side. Shortly after kelpie made his appearance, and said to her, "Mack bed, bonnie lass, a'll lie wi' you the nicht." She was at a loss what to say or do to keep kelpie away. The doggie came to her help and told her to say she had no blankets wherewith to make a bed. She said, "I hive nithing t' mack a bed wi'."

Kelpie disappeared, but returned after a little, and threw into the place where the woman and the dog were, a quantity of bedding, and repeated his former words: "Mack bed, bonnie lass, for a'll lie wi' you the nicht." What was now to be done? The doggie again came to the rescue. "Tell him y're thirsty, an bid him fess a drink in sieve an rivven dish," said the cunning animal. She did so, and kelpie set off to fetch the water. He soon came back with the complaint: "They winna baud in." "Then stop them wi' fog." Away went kelpie to gather fog (mosses), and to stop up the meshes of the riddle, and the crack in "te rivven dish." Hard did kelpie toil, but still the water escaped. By the time he came back, day had dawned, and the maiden was free.

(All the above "Kelpies" section verbatim from Gregor, "Kelpie Stories from the North of Scotland")

Kelpie Stories
Scotland

It was before carts were much in use, and when everything had to be carried on the backs of horses. One dark night a man named M'Hardy set out from Brochroy to Garchory mill to fetch home some meal. On arrival at the mill he left his horse at the door and entered to fetch out the bags of meal. No sooner was the animal left alone than he started for home. The farmer, on coming out to load his horse, found no horse. He was in much distress, as there was no meal at home; and he gave vent to his feelings in woeful words: "Ma wife an bairns 'ill be a' stervt for wint o' mehl afore I win hame. I wis (wish) I hed ony kyne (kind) o' a behst, although it war (were) a water kelpie." Hardly were the words spoken when a horse having a halter over his head appeared. The farmer approached him, and the horse allowed himself to be handled, and showed himself quite gentle, putting his head right on the man's breast. The man's distress was turned into joy, and the gentle horse was loaded, and led quietly to the farm-house. On arriving, the farmer tied him to an old harrow, till he should unload him, and carry the meal into the house. When he came out of the house to stable the animal that had done him the good turn, horse and old harrow were gone, and he heard the plunging of the beast in a big pool of the Don, not far from his house. He went to examine the stable, and found his own horse quietly standing in it.

A kelpie in Braemar, on Deeside, had taken a liking for a woman that dwelt not far from the mill of Quoich. This woman fell out of meal, and had not very good means of supplying her want. Kelpie resolved to come to her help. So one night, on which he knew corn was being ground at the mill, he went to it after the miller had left it. In those old days mills ground very slowly, and it was not unusual for the miller to put as much grain into the hopper as would keep the mill at work till he got up next morning. So it was in this case. Kelpie entered the mill and patiently waited till the sack that received the ground grain was full. He then lifted the sack on his back and left the mill. It was "the grey o' the morning," and the miller had left his bed, and was coming to the mill to see that all was going on well. He spied a tall man coming round the corner of the mill, carrying a sackful of meal on his back. Seizing the "fairy-whorl,"* that was lying at one of the mill-corners, he hurled it at the man with the oath and threat, "Kelpie, or nae kelpie, G—d d— you, a'll brack your leg." The stone took effect and broke the leg. The kelpie made for the "mill-lead" (mill-race), tumbled into it, was carried by it into the river Dee, and drowned. This was the last kelpie that lived in the Braes o' Mar.

Told by D. McHardy in Ardjerige to my informant, Mr. J. Farquharson, a mason, Corgarff, on the river Don. He is a man of great intelligence, and a mine of Folklore.

* A stone whorl was kept at each mill, which was fixed at night, when the mill was not in use, on the spindle, to prevent the fairies from setting the mill a-going.

(All the above "Kelpie Stories" section verbatim from Gregor, "Kelpie Stories")

The Diañu Burlón

Asturias

The type of trasgu known as the Diañu Burlón or Diablo Burllón (mocking devil) is a prankster, more mischievous than malicious. It delights in ruining the day for line fishermen by throwing stones at them or into the water to scatter the fish, or tangling the nets of commercial fishermen. In spite of its name, it is an earth-bound elemental or *genius loci* unconnected with Satan and the infernal regions. Appearance can be human-like above the waist and goat-like below, but it is often encountered by the unwary traveller at night in the form of a water horse. This story is typical of its behaviour, with the burning britches trick seemingly unique to the diañu.

A young man who had a lover in every village went out one night to court a girl in Alava. As he started to cross the River Narcea, he suddenly felt tired and said, "If only God or the Diañu would send me a horse!"

A graceful white steed appeared, and he mounted it. As the horse was crossing the river, it began bucking, but the man was a good rider and didn't fall off. Suddenly, he smelled the odour of burning cloth, but being brave he wasn't frightened. What scared him, though, was the horse saying, "Don't you smell burning cloth?"

"Yes," said the man.

"Well, it's your trousers that are burning."

The horse launched the man into the air back where he started, and he didn't go courting.

(Loose translation from Canellada)

"I believe in the diablo burllón because my mother told me that she had seen it in Corao or some place, and that it took children up the chimney. My brother truly believed that there was a strange creature in a certain scary wood, because he saw a light at night. And one day [speaking to his brother] we were sitting under a cherry tree and you said, 'Look! There's the devil!' And I said, 'Well, let's go and have a look.' And you lied because we went there and I said the Our Father and I didn't see it. But I still truly believe in it."

(Loose translation from Canellada)

The Horse and the Fairy Tune

Isle of Man

About 1725 in the Isle of Man, in an incident similar to "The Cailín Deas Curse" (Frightening or Dangerous Black Dogs section), an English gentleman was crossing a river on his horse when both he and his mount heard "the finest symphony" of unearthly music. The horse stood in the middle of the river for at least 45 minutes, the man said, judging by the amount of time he arrived late to his destination. He had been sceptical of Manx fairy stories before, but the experience made him a believer.

(Moore)

A Proud Horse
France

Clovis, King of the Franks 481-511, wanted to reclaim a horse that he had given to a church, offering a hundred pieces of gold. But the horse, feeling that this was too cheap for him, refused to move from the church until Clovis doubled the price, and then he allowed himself to be led out without objection.

(Fuentelapeña §770)

The Pope's Horse
Greece

Pope John I (d. 526) was in ill health when he was sent by Theodoric, ruler of Italy, to negotiate a decree with Emperor Justin in Constantinople. When he reached Corinth, he required a fresh mount that was both reliable and gentle, and a noble citizen loaned him his wife's horse. At the end of the next stage of the journey, the Pope sent the steed back to the owner. Later, when the owner's wife tried to mount the horse, it was not possible through art or threat or pleading to make the horse consent, because "the horse, having carried so great a Bishop, would not suffer a woman to come any more upon his back, and therefore he began with monstrous snorting, neighing, and continual stirring, as it were in scorn, to shew that he could not bear any woman" after the Pope himself had ridden him.

So the prudent owner presented the horse to His Holiness, begging that he would do him the honour of accepting the gift, "which by riding he had dedicated to his own service."

(Fuentelapeña §771 and Gregory, with quotes from Gregory)

Trick Horses

Italy

The Sybarites, a people of Italy much given to pleasure, taught horses to dance to the music of hurdy-gurdies or bagpipes, to their eventual regret. When they went to war with their neighbours, the enemy took advantage of the trick. In the midst of battle, instead of sounding trumpets they began to play on hurdy-gurdies the dance tunes that the Sybarites' horses were accustomed to. The horses responded to their training and began to dance and leap joyfully, disrupting the order of the squadrons and giving victory to the enemy.

(Fuentelapeña §774)

CATS

Cats were special objects of dread, if not of some kind of veneration, among the ancient Irish.
(O'Kearney)

On entering a house the usual salutation is, "God save all here, except the cat."
(Wilde)

A Monstrous White Cat
Isle of Man

One night in the back-end of the year, when the dim was coming on middling early, my father was going to shut the door, when he noticed a thing like a big white cat sitting out in the street. He went to "sthoo" it away and gave it a hoist with his foot, when, all at once, the thing stood up and began to grow and grow until it seemed to reach up nearly to the sky, and then it went away. When my father came in he was all white and shaking and he was bad all night, but he would never say whether it spoke to him or not.
(Verbatim: Mona Douglas via "As Manx as the Hills" website by Bernadette Weyde.)

The King of the Cats of Cnoghbha
Ireland

The notoriously arrogant and demanding chief poet of Ireland, Seanchán Torpéist (d. AD 647), decided to honour the famously open-handed King Guaire of Connacht with his company for a year, in order to test his generosity. Custom entitled him to a retinue of 30, but his entourage included

150 each of poets, students, hounds, male attendants, and female relatives, and 27 of each type of craftsperson.

Seanchán's wife and daughter and others made impossible demands: a cuckoo during the Christmas season, a garment made of spider silk, and blackberries and strawberries in January, among other things, not the least of which was the fat from the pet white boar of Guaire's half-brother, Marbán. Seanchán complained about the food and refused to eat for three days. One of his company finally persuaded him to eat an egg she had left over from her meal, but when he went to take it, he found that the mice had eaten it.

Poets had the power to curse, and Seanchán cursed the mice, killing ten of them. But then he had second thoughts. It was really the fault of the cats, because they had not fulfilled their responsibility of keeping the mice away, so he cursed them, starting with Írusán mac Arasáin, King of the Cats, and naming specific members of his family.

In his cave at Cnoghbha, the passage tomb of Knowth in County Meath, Írusán felt the curse, and he said to his daughter Reng Sharptooth, "Seanchán has cursed me, and I'm going to get revenge."

"We would prefer," said Reng, "that you bring Seanchán here alive so we ourselves can take revenge on him for the curse."

"I'm on my way," said Írusán, and he set off like a fire in full blaze.

Seanchán got word that Írusán was coming to kill him, and he asked Guaire to call on the nobles of Connacht to protect him against the cat. They surrounded Seanchán, but when the beast the size of a bullock arrived – bare-nosed, vigorous, snorting, powerful, crop-eared, broad-framed, impetuous, sharp-clawed, sleek, long-fanged, wide-mouthed, quick, violent, foul, wrathful, demented, avenging – he passed easily through them and grabbed Seanchán by the arm, flung him onto his back, and started back the way he had come.

Now, instead of cursing Írusán, Seanchán began to praise him – how skilful his leaps, how powerful his running – and begged him for God's sake to set him down, which Írusán refused to do. As they were passing through Clonmacnoise, Saint Ciarán happened to glance out of the forge where he was working a rod of red-hot iron.

"What a story!" said Ciarán: "the chief poet of Ireland on the back of a cat in violation of the hospitality of Guaire."

He flung the glowing rod at the cat, and it went into his side and through him and out the other side and killed him.

(Wilde)

The King of the Cats of Cruachan

Ireland

When Saint Patrick expelled the demons from Ireland with the sound of his bell, all the animals that had the power of foretelling the future or revealing the location of lost or stolen property fell mute.

But there was another reason for the silence of the oracle of Clogh-magh-righ-cat, the Stone of the Plain of the Royal Cat. Speaking stones in Ireland set down rigid conditions for imparting their knowledge; for example, no question could be asked twice. If the petitioner forgot the answer and returned to repeat the question, the stone would fall silent, in some cases forever.

The stipulation made by Clogh-magh-righ-cat was harsher: if anyone gave a false description of the property he wished to recover, the consequences would be fatal. A man named O'Cathalain lost a mare that wasn't in foal, but he believed she was, and that was how he described the animal to the oracle. The oracle knew the truth, and the response was instant and angry:

> Snotty nosed and bare of tooth,
> Follow your foalless mare to Doom.

Then the Stone split in two with a crash, and a large cat emerged. Incensed by the insulting reply, and perhaps a bit frightened, the man dealt the cat a mortal blow. As the cat lay dying, he told O'Cathalain to tell his two cats at home, the Firedog and the Wheedler of the Ashes, that O'Cathalain had killed the King of the Cats of Cruachan.

He did that, and when the cats heard the news they immediately leapt at his throat and chewed it until he was dead.

The Cave of the Cat
Ireland

Uaimh na gCat, the Cave of the Cat, anglicised as Oweynagat and also known as the Cave of Cruachan, is a cave next to Cruachan, the royal residence of Queen Maeve of Connacht in County Roscommon near Tulsk. It is an entrance to the Otherworld, from which demon birds, pigs, cats and other animals frequently emanated. In the eighth-century tale of Bricriu's Feast, Maeve tested the three greatest heroes of Ulster by requiring them to stand guard in the palace overnight. Three demon cats from Oweynagat attacked them, sending two of the heroes scurrying for the rafters, while Cúchulainn whacked one over its stone-hard head with his sword and out-stared it until dawn.

The same cave was the temporary home of "The Swine of Drebrenn". See that story in the Shape-changers section.

The King of the Cats
Scotland

Many years ago, long before shooting in Scotland was a fashion as it is now, two young men spent the autumn in the very far north, living in a lodge far from other houses, with an old woman to cook for them. Her cat and their own dogs formed all the rest of the household.

One afternoon the elder of the two young men said he would not go out, and the younger one went alone, to follow the path of the previous day's sport looking for missing birds, and intending to return home before the early sunset. However, he did not do so, and the elder man became very uneasy as he watched and waited in vain till long after their usual supper-time. At last the young man returned, wet and exhausted, nor did he explain his unusual lateness until, after supper, they were seated by the fire with their pipes, the dogs lying at their feet, and the old woman's black cat sitting gravely with half-shut eyes on the hearth between them. Then the young man began as follows.

"You must be wondering what made me so late. I have had a curious adventure to-day. I hardly know what to say about it. I went, as I told you I should, along our yesterday's route. A mountain fog came on just as I was about to turn homewards, and I completely lost my way. I wandered about for a long time, not knowing where I was, till at last I saw a light, and made for it, hoping to get help. As I came near it, it disappeared, and I found myself close to a large old oak-tree. I climbed into the branches the better to look for the light, and, behold! it was beneath me, inside the hollow trunk of the tree. I seemed to be looking down into a church, where a funeral was in the act of taking place. I heard singing, and saw a coffin, surrounded by torches, all carried by ... But I know you won't believe me if I tell you!"

His friend eagerly begged him to go on, and laid down his pipe to listen. The dogs were sleeping quietly, but the cat was sitting up apparently listening as attentively as the man, and both young men involuntarily turned their eyes towards him. "Yes," proceeded the absentee, "it is perfectly true. The coffin and the torches were both borne by cats, and upon the coffin were marked a crown and sceptre!"

He got no further; the cat started up shrieking, "By Jove! old Peter's dead! and I'm the King o' the Cats!" rushed up the chimney and was seen no more.

(Verbatim from Burne. Told by a Herefordshire squire, 1845-6, who had heard it from his nurse, and written by the squire's daughter in 1882.)

Beware the Cat

England and Ireland

Versions of this story, first published in 1553, are widespread as international folk tales. The lightly edited excerpt below is from the 1584 third edition by "G. B." (William [Gulielmus] Baldwin). A group of men in London are discussing whether animals have reason and understanding, and the topic of cats comes up.

> "There was in my country," said one, "a man from Staffordshire who had a young cat that he had raised from a kitten and would nightly dally and play with it. One time as he rode through Kank Wood, a cat leaped out of a bush before him and called him twice or thrice by his name, but because he made no answer, nor spoke (for he was so afraid that he could not) she spoke to him: 'Commend me unto Titton Tatton, and to Pus thy Catton, and tell her that Grimmalkin is dead.'
>
> "This done she went her way, and the man went about his business. And after he returned home, in an evening sitting by the fire with his wife and his household, he told of his adventure in the wood, and when he had told them all the cat's message, his cat, which had listened to the tale, looked upon him sadly and said, 'And is Grimmalkin dead? Then farewell, Dame,' and went her way and was never seen after."
>
> When this tale was done, another of the company, who had been in Ireland, asked this fellow when this thing which he had told happened. He answered that he could not tell well, but he guessed not past forty years, for his mother knew both the man and the woman who owned the cat that the message was sent to.

"Sure," said the other, "then it may well be, for about the same time as I heard a like thing happened in Ireland where, if I guess correctly, Grimmalkin of whom you spoke was slain."

"Yea, sir," said I, "I pray you how so?"

"I will tell you," said he, "what was told me in Ireland and which I have till now so little credited that I was ashamed to report it, but hearing what I hear now, I do so little doubt it, that I think I never told, nor you ever heard a more likely tale.

"While I was in Ireland in the time that Mac Morrow and all the rest of the wild lords were the king's enemies [12th century], all the country became a vast wilderness and is scarce recovered until this day.

"In this time, as I was one night at Coshery with one of Filzberie's farmers, we fell in talk as we have done now of strange adventures and of cats, and there among other things the farmer told me as you shall hear.

"There was, not seven years past, a soldier called Patrick Apore, who minding to make a raid in the night upon Cayer Mac Art, his master's enemy, went with his horseboy into Mac Art's territory, and in the night time entered into a town of two houses and broke in and slew the people, and then took such cattle as they found, which was a cow and a sheep, and departed homeward. But worried that they would be pursued, they hid in a church, thinking to lurk there till midnight was past.

"And while this soldier was in the church, he thought it best to dine, for he had eaten little that day, so he made his boy go gather sticks and made a fire in the church and killed the sheep and roasted it. But when it was ready and that he was about to eat it there came in a cat and sat beside him, and said, "Give me some meat." He, amazed at this, gave her the quarter that was in his hand, which immediately she ate up, and asked more till she had consumed all the sheep, and asked for more.

"So they supposed it was the Devil, and thinking it wise to please him killed the cow which they had stolen, and when they had flayed it, gave the cat a quarter which she immediately devoured. Then they gave her two other quarters, and in the meanwhile after the country fashion they cut a piece of the hide and pricked it upon four stakes which they set about the fire, and they set a piece of the cow for themselves, and with the rest of the hide they each made shoes, both to keep their feet from hurt all the next day, and also to serve for meat the next night if they could get none other, by broiling them upon coals.

"By this time the cat had eaten three quarters and called for more, so they gave her the rest of the meat, and afraid that when she had eaten that, she would eat them too because they had no more for her, they left the church and the soldier took his horse and away he rode as fast as he could.

"When he was a mile or two from the church, the moon began to shine, and his boy espied the cat upon his master's horse behind him, told him, so the soldier took his dart and turning his face toward her flung it, and struck her through with it, but immediately there came to her such a sight of cats, that after a long fight with them his boy was killed and eaten up, and he himself, as good and as swift as his horse was, had much to do to escape.

"When he had come home he sat down by his wife and told her his adventure, which when a kitten which his wife kept scarce half a year had heard, up she started and said, 'Hast thou killed Grimmalkin?' And then she plunged in his face, and with her teeth took him by the throat, and before she could be taken away, she had strangled him.

"This the farmer told me, now about thirty-four winters past, and it was done, as he and several other credible men informed me not seven years before, so I gather that it was this Grimmalkin that the cat in Kank Wood sent news of to the cat which we heard of even now."

"Tush," said another that sat nearby. "It's reasonable to admit that cats have reason, and that they do in their own language understand one another, yet how should a cat in Kank Wood know what is done in Ireland?"

"The same way we know what is done in France, Flanders & Spain, and the rest of the world. There are few ships but have cats belonging to them, which bring news to their fellows from other parts."

The Kilkenny Cats
Ireland

There once were two cats of Kilkenny.
Each thought there was one cat too many.
So they fought and they fit,
And they scratched and they bit,
Till excepting their nails and the tips of their tails
Instead of two cats there weren't any.

The origin of this old rhyme is said to have been an occasion when occupying British soldiers tied two cats' tails together – or all the cats in the city in pairs – and slung them over a washing line to watch them fight. It's also reported that the tale is a political allegory.

The people of County Kilkenny and their sports teams are called the Kilkenny Cats. With the black and amber uniforms the players resemble tortoiseshell cats. The county insect is the black and amber bumblebee.

The Troll Turned Cat
Zealand, Denmark

About a quarter of a mile from Soröe lies Pedersborg, and a little farther on is the town of Lyng. Just between these towns is a hill called Bröndhöi (*Spring-hill*), said to be inhabited by the Troll-people.

There goes a story that there was once among these Troll people of Bröndhöi an old cross-grained curmudgeon of a Troll, whom the rest nicknamed Knurremurre (*Rumble-grumble*), because he was evermore the cause of noise and uproar within the hill. This Knurremurre having discovered what he thought to be too great a degree of intimacy between his young wife and a young Troll of the society, took this in such ill part, that he vowed vengeance, swearing he would have the life of the young one.

The latter, accordingly, thought it would be his best course to be off out of the hill till better times; so, turning himself into a noble tortoise shell tom-cat, he one fine morning quitted his old residence, and journeyed down to the neighbouring town of Lyng, where he established himself in the house of an honest poor man named Plat.

Here he lived for a long time comfortable and easy, with nothing to annoy him, and was as happy as any tom-cat or Troll crossed in love well could be. He got every day plenty of milk and good groute [porridge] to eat, and lay the whole day long at his ease in a warm arm-chair behind the stove.

Plat happened one evening to come home rather late, and as he entered the room the cat was sitting in his usual place, scraping meal-groute out of a pot, and licking the pot itself carefully.

"Harkye, dame," said Plat, as he came in at the door, "till I tell you what happened to me on the road. Just as I was coming past Bröndhöi, there came out a Troll, and he called out to me, and said,

"Harkye Plat,
Tell your cat,
That Knurremurre is dead."

The moment the cat heard these words, he tumbled the pot down on the floor, sprang out of the chair, and stood up on his hind-legs. Then, as he hurried out of the door, he cried out with exultation, "What! is Knurremurre dead? Then I may go home as fast as I please."

And so saying he scampered off to the hill, to the amazement of honest Plat; and it is likely lost no time in making his advances to the young widow.

(Verbatim, Keightley, *The Fairy Mythology*)

BIRDS

Cranes as Guardians
Ireland

The Common or Eurasian Crane (*Grus grus*) is one of the largest birds in Europe at 100 to 130 cm (39-51 in) in length with a wingspan of 180 to 240 cm (71-94 in), slate grey with red, white and black markings. The spectacular dancing Japanese or Red-crowned Crane is similar in appearance, except that it is white instead of grey, but with the same colour markings. Pairs mate for life, which can last 30 to 40 years, and their chicks take three months to become fully mobile. That is one reason they are notorious for aggressive defence of their nest, attacking even herbivores that graze too close. The Roman naturalist Pliny observed: "They maintain a Watch all the Night long, and the Sentinels hold a little Stone in their Foot, which by falling down from it, if they sleep, reproves them for their Negligence." (Pliny, Book X, Chapter XXIII)

Although cranes have been extinct in Ireland for some 300 years, largely because of agrarian development, their former prominence is reflected in surviving legends and folktales. They are associated with magic and the Otherworld, and in many cultures are regarded as messengers between this world and heaven like angels in Christianity. Some Chinese exercises and kung fu styles take their forms and names from the movements of cranes.

Psychologists, advertising/branding consultants and occultists substantially agree that the crane markings symbolise certain qualities and evoke predictable subconscious reactions: red for power and protection, white for cleansing and perfection, black for banishment and secrecy. The colours are frequently encountered in international fairy tales. Snow White is the best-known example: the queen pricks her finger and notices the blood in the snow on the black windowsill and says, "How I wish that I had a daughter that had skin as white as snow, lips as red as blood, and hair as black as ebony." In the Irish tale, Deirdre dreams of a man of the same description and wakes up to see a raven picking at a bloody rabbit in the snow. Note the association with wounding and violence. Many of the 6000-year-old passage tombs in the Iberian Peninsula still retain traces of red, white and black paint in their interior – an association with death. One reason for the popularity of those colours is probably that they are among the most convenient to extract from abundant and accessible natural materials. They are prominent in Stone Age cave paintings dating back to 25,000 BC.

Cranes' ferocious hostility, diametrically opposed to the long tradition of generosity and welcome in Ireland, is relevant to the following two stories, and their seemingly playful habit of picking up wisps of vegetation and throwing them into the air strikes a sinister resonance with one of the curses in the second.

Cranes and the Curse of Saint Colmcille

File (plural: *filí*) is usually translated as "poet", but the *filí* of Ireland were not mere rhymers – low-class illiterate bards and ballad-makers, whose songs ironically survive in popular tradition to this day, while the exquisite works of the *filí* are known only to scholars. These poets were highly educated historians, genealogists, lawyers, judges, scholars, reciters of legendary history, healers, and druids, as well as composers of arcane and highly structured poetry. It took twelve years of study to reach the seventh and top rank of ollamh. In their final years they studied magic spells. They had a reputation for arrogance.

Saint Colmcille (Dove of the Church), one of the three most important Irish saints next to Patrick and Brigit, and a poet-druid before he converted to Christianity, once gave shelter to a lost and exhausted crane. He was famously short-tempered and had been exiled to Scotland for instigating three battles. When his cousin Aed Ainmire, the king of

Ireland, convened the nobles in 575 to expel the poets for their gross abuse of power, the poets called on Colm to return and defend them. He had vowed never to set foot on Irish soil again, so he filled his shoes with Scottish soil (and/or he had been ordered never to set eyes on Ireland again and wore a blindfold) and attended the Convention of Drum Ceat. When he arrived, he learned that Aed's wife had given orders to their son Conall not to show honour to "that crane-cleric" or his retinue. ("*Chorrchléireach*" is also given as *choirrchléireach*, "criminal- or outsider-cleric", and it's likely the pun was intentional.)

Colm said, "May the queen and her handmaid be in the form of cranes on that ford over there until Doomsday."

The women immediately vanished and reappeared as two cranes at the ford, one of them, the queen, with a broken wing and only half a tail. Then Conall and his companions threw clods of dirt at Colm and his group. Colm ordered 27 bells to be rung at him, and he laid a curse that Conall would be without a realm, without authority, without sense, without memory and without understanding. For that, the young man earned the epithets Conall of the Bells and Conall the Delirious. He never became king.

So when Colm presented his defence of the poets and two unrelated demands of his own, the king, having seen the results of offending him, graciously granted everything he asked for.

According to Geoffrey Keating, who relates this story in his 1634 *The History of Ireland*, the reason Colm cursed the handmaid as well as the queen was that she was the one who carried the message from the queen to her son. "And I have heard from many people," he adds, "that two cranes have regularly been seen at that ford since then."

Cranes and the Glám Dícenn

Chief Ollamh Ferchertne is one of four authors credited as the creators of the *Auraicept na nÉces*, the Grammar of the Poets. One, Cenn Faelad (d. 679), is well attested historically as a scholar-king. The other two belong to the mists of legendary history. An Ulster poet named Ferchertne turns up frequently and is quoted in legendary history, but it is not clear if it's the same one or even if there was ever a historical personage of that name.

His "son", the equally doubtful ollamh Athirne Ailgessach, was described in the 12th-century *Book of Leinster* as "the most churlish man in Ireland". His cognomen, "Ailgessach", means unaccommodating, inhospitable, contrary, among other negative descriptions, yet he made unreasonable demands on those people unfortunate enough to be the recipients of a visit from him, threatening them with a poet's curse if they didn't comply. He took full advantage of the required deference to an ollamh by inviting himself and his company of poets and assistants to kings' feasts: "A seventh part of the 'eric' fine for [an ollamh's] death is paid for denying him food." (O'Donovan, *Ancient Laws*) He once demanded and received the remaining eye of a one-eyed king.

The *Book of Leinster* reports that Athirne went to the Sídh lord Midir at Brí Léith in County Longford and fasted against him until he gave him the three cranes that stood guard at his door. Athirne brought them home out of sheer meanness and begrudgery, lest any of the men of Ireland come to his own house expecting free food or lodging or entertainment.

"Don't come in," said the first crane.

"Go away," said the second.

"Walk on past, walk on past," said the third.

No one who saw them dared approach.

As a Sídh lord, one of the god-like Tuatha Dé Danann who occupied Ireland before the present race of Celtic humans, Midir possessed a considerable amount of magic ability, augmented by the mystical colour-powers of his cranes. Fasting against someone – a hunger strike – to bend them to one's will, with the prospect of dying publicly on their doorstep, is an effective form of extortion. In Athirne's case, that would be reinforced by the threat of one of the powerful curses in the armoury of a top-ranked ollamh.

The poet's curse on refusal: "He grinds the lobe of the person's ear between his fingers, and the person on whom he performs this operation dies." (*Sanas Cormaic*)

Throwing a hay or straw wisp with a spell into the victim's face caused him to go mad.

The fatal *glám dícenn* was the most feared. It is "one of the three things which are the peculiar right of the ollam of poetry." (McLaughlin, Roisin) The exact meaning of the term (see below) is disputed, but *glám* may be related to the original Scottish sense of "glamour" – enchantment – from Scots "glaum", modern English "glom", meaning to grab with the hand. Also from the Old Norse "shout": in the Robert Graves short story "The Shout", a man learned a shout from Australian natives that could kill a person at short range. *Dícenn* ("from head") could be literally "headless" or refer to a person without a lord or chief; alternatively, "extreme". In the clandestine language of the poets, explained in suitably obscure terms in the *Auraicept*, metaphors can be stacked, and all meanings are valid. So *glám* could describe words or a shout of enchantment accompanied by a magical gesture of the hand, and *dícenn* could be a combination of a virtual beheading of the victim, energy from the poet's head, and the raising of the poet's hand above his own head in the stance described below. Or the term, validated by the stories, could simply mean "the extreme curse".

The connection with cranes, besides the throwing of wisps and their fierce unfriendliness, is the position taken by the person setting the curse. He closes one eye, stands on one foot, and raises one hand above his head, imitating the stance of a crane, while possibly bending the hand to mimic a crane's head and formidable beak. From that, the curse is also called *corrguinech*, which means magician or sorcerer and derives from *corr*, crane (or swelling or both), and *guinech*, fatal wounding. The name of the victim of the curse is required. The formula is typically: "Evil, death, short life to X. Let spears of battle wound him, X. X under earth, under ramparts, under stone." (*Sanas Cormaic*) Death is the eventual, if not necessarily immediate, object. In most cases, three blemishes appear on the victim's face – the crane colours of red, white and black – and they die of shame as a result.

The curse could be double-edged. A young poet, Nede – strangely not an ollamh – made an unjustified *glám dícenn* on Caier that raised three blisters of reproach on his face. Caier ran away, but Nede had second thoughts and followed him to apologise. When Caier saw him he died of mortification, and a stone simultaneously exploded, killing Nede as the unjust curse rebounded on him.

A nasty incident, shrouded in careful euphemisms by the chroniclers, involved Athirne and his two poet sons and Luaine, the fiancée of King Conor of Ulster. The young men expressed their "love" for Luaine, and all three threatened to make a *glám dícenn* on her unless she permitted them to "foregather" with her. She indignantly refused, and each of them cast a spell that left her with three blemishes on her face, which caused her to die of shame.

Although there were set punishments for the making of an undeserved curse, the high ollamh "binds, he is not bound". (O'Donovan, *Ancient Laws*) Fed up with his continual flouting of basic social norms, and with no legal options, the Ulstermen burned down Athirne's house with him and his sons inside.

From the *Oxford English Dictionary*:
glam[1]: (ON glam – noise) – shout
glam[2]: also glaum – hands
glamour (n.): magic, enchantment, spell
glamour (v.): to charm, enchant
glaum (v.): "to snatch at (a thing). Also, to make threatening movements."

(See Appendix for the Lethal Effects of Sound.)

The Cruel Crane Outwitted

A Jataka Tale

India

The monks were discussing a report of a monk in the city who worked as a tailor. He had been cheating his customers by giving them old patched clothes for the new cloth they brought him instead of making new clothes for them. A tailor from the country heard about this fraud, and he came with old clothes dyed to appear brand new and traded them with the monk tailor for new cloth.

The monks' teacher came in and asked them what they were talking about. When they told him, he said, "That monk also cheated in a past life, and he was outwitted then as well." And he told this story. (A bodisat has achieved sainthood and will be a Buddha in his next incarnation.)

Long ago the Bodisat was the spirit of a tree next to a pond. An old, feeble crane landed and stood with his head down looking sorrowful. Although his body was wasted and the lightning speed had gone out of his fishing thrust, his cunning remained intact, and he had worked out a plan to make his meals come to him.

"What are you thinking about that makes you so sad?" asked a curious fish.

"I'm worried about what's going to happen to you fish when the fishermen arrive."

"What fishermen?"

"The ones I heard discussing their next expedition this morning."

"What are they going to do, and how does it concern us?"

"One of them said that they should use a big net and take all the fish in this pond at once, but the other one said it would be better to clear out a certain lake first and then come here next week."

"Oh. What can we do about it?"

"Well, it's more a question of what I can do to help you."

"What can you do?"

“There is a large, deep pond with clean water not far from here where you’ll be safe, and since you fish can’t make the journey yourselves, I will be happy to carry a few of you there every day. I can’t do it more often because of my age.”

“But you’re a crane. You eat fish.”

“We cranes can eat anything, and because of my ill health the grains in the fields are better for me. I promise I won’t eat you. If you don’t trust me, let one of you come with me and I’ll show him the pond.”

The fish assembled to discuss the crane’s proposition and appointed one of their elders to go with him to inspect the pond. The representative was nervous about being in the beak of a natural enemy, but when he saw the pond and was returned safely to the others, he announced his approval of the plan. They all agreed that it was their only chance for survival. So for the next week, the crane transported several satisfying meals each day to the pond, where he landed beside a tree and devoured his unwitting victims.

A crab had been suspiciously watching the gradual disappearance of her neighbours. When they had all gone, the crane looked around the pond and saw that the only remaining resident was the crab. She was large and mature, and the crane thought she might provide two or three days of food.

“Now, madame crab, it’s your turn when you’re ready.”

“But I’m too big and heavy for you to carry in your beak. You might drop me. I’ll feel safer if you let me hold on to your neck with my claws.”

Perhaps because he had an easy time with the gullible fish, the crane didn’t see any danger in the crab’s suggestion, so he let the crab climb on to his back and grip his neck with her claws as securely as a blacksmith’s tongs. When they reached the other pond, which to the crab seemed strangely unpopulated, the crane veered away towards the tree where he had been feasting on the fish. The crab saw the discarded fish bones.

“Ah, so that’s your plan, crane. I expect you intend to eat me now.”

"Of course. Crab meat will be a welcome change from all those fish."

"But for me, crane meat will add variety to my usual diet of algae."

The crab gave the crane's neck a threatening squeeze.

"No, no, I beg you," said the crane. "I was only joking."

"If you want to live, set me down, and then I'll laugh at your joke."

The crane did so, but as soon as his feet touched the ground, the crab put all her strength into her claws and cut the crane's head off.

When the teacher finished the story, he said, "The crane was that monk tailor in the city, and the crab was the country tailor. I was the tree spirit."

The Birds of White Lake
(Adar Llwch Gwyn)
Wales

Drutwas, the son of Trephin, received from his wife three birds of White Lake, and they would do whatsoever their master bid them. A combat was appointed between Arthur and Drutwas, and no one should come to the field but they two. Drutwas sent his birds forth, saying to them, slay the first that comes into the field.

Then as Arthur went into the field, the sister of Drutwas, who was Arthur's friend, came and prevented Arthur going to the field, out of affection to each of them. At last Drutwas came into the field, thinking the birds had slain Arthur, and the birds caught him up and killed him, and when high in the air, they knew him, and fell to the ground with most doleful lamentations, for having slain Drutwas, their master.

The song of the birds of White Lake still exists on the strings [harp], which was made at that time to record the event. And from that Llywarch Hen had the subject, on which he composed the following Englyn:

Drutwas, the son of Trephin, on the day of combat,
With toil and exertion,
A breach of compact committed, formerly,
And was slain by the birds of White Lake.

The above is copied verbatim from the collection of Iolo Morganwg (1747-1826), translated by his son, Taliesin Williams, and published in 1848. Morganwg was a collector of manuscripts but was also a literary forger, though this story seems to be accepted by the experts as genuinely ancient.

For the Welsh title Adar Llwch Gwyn, some use "dust" as an alternative meaning of *llwch* and give *gwyn* ("white") as *gwin*, which is "wine", so "the wine-dust birds". Lewis Morris (*Celtic Remains*, 1884) interpreted the birds as ruffians: "Adar Llwch Gwin are vultures, and vultures is a proper term enough for ruffians." MacKillop says Adar Llwch Gwyn "was a synonym for hawks or falcons and a metaphor for strong, brave men". The birds have also been identified as griffins.

According to Morganwg's suspect *The Triads of Britain*, first published in 1801 and probably reflecting earlier traditions, Drutwas was an orator, one of the Three Golden-tongued Knights of Arthur's Court: "They were the wisest of all the wise of their time; and so fair and gentlemanly was their deportment, and so mellifluous and eloquent in all their addresses, that no one could refuse to grant them what they desired." Drutwas was also said to be the son of the king of Denmark.

Whether Arthur in this story is King Arthur or not is debated, but Llywarch Hen (534-608) was not only one of the four great bards of Britain, but also one of King Arthur's councillors and generals.

The Rooks of Ardfert

Ireland

St Brendan's Cathedral in Ardfert [County Kerry] was originally to be built in a field called the Gallan Field. Construction began but the very first night a large flock of rooks removed the stones and the mortar to the west of Ardfert village where the church was then built, and where its ruins remain to this day.

(Verbatim, O'Sullivan)

The Jackdaw

Dublin, Ireland

Tom Moor was a linen draper in Sackville Street. His father, when he died, left him an affluent fortune and a shop of excellent trade.

As he was standing at his door one day a countryman came up to him with a nest of jackdaws, and accosting him, says, "Master, will you buy a nest of daws?"

"No, I don't want any."

"Master," replied the man, "I will sell them all cheap; you shall have the whole nest for ninepence."

"I don't want them," answered Tom Moor, "so go about your business."

As the man was walking away one of the daws popped out his head and cried, "Mawk, mawk."

"Damn it," says Tom Moor, "that bird knows my name; halloo, countryman, what will you take for the bird?"

"Why, you shall have him for threepence."

Tom Moor bought him, had a cage made, and hung him up in the shop.

The journeymen took much notice of the bird, and would frequently tap at the bottom of the cage, and say, "Who are you? who are you? Tom Moor of Sackville Street."

In a short time the jackdaw learned these words, and if he wanted victuals or water, would strike his bill against the cage, turn up the white of his eyes, cock his head and cry, "Who are you? who are you? Tom Moor of Sackville Street."

Tom Moor was fond of gaming, and often lost large sums of money. Finding his business neglected in his absence, he had a small hazard table set up in one corner of his dining-room and invited a party of friends to play at it.

The jackdaw had by this time become familiar; his cage was left open, and he hopped into every part of the house; sometimes he got into the dining-room, where the gentlemen were at play, and one of them being a constant winner, the others would say, "Damn it, how he nicks them." The bird learned these words also, and adding them to the former, would call, "Who are you? who are you? Tom Moor of Sackville Street. Damn it, how he nicks them."

Tom Moor, from repeated losses and neglect of business, failed in trade and became a prisoner in the Fleet. He took his bird with him and lived on the master's side, supported by friends in a decent manner. They would sometimes ask what brought you here? when he used to lift up his hands and answer, "Bad company, by G--." The bird learned these likewise, and at the end of the former words, would say, "What brought you here? Bad company by G--."

Some of Tom Moor's friends died, others went abroad, and by degrees he was totally deserted, and removed to the common side of the prison, where the jail distemper soon attacked him, and in the last stage of life lying on a straw bed. The poor bird had been for two days without food or water, came to his feet, and striking his bill on the floor, calls out, "Who are you? Tom Moor of Sackville Street; damn it, how he nicks them. What brought you here? bad company, by G--, bad company, by G--."

Tom Moor, who had attended to the bird, was struck with his words, and reflecting on himself, cried out, "Good God, to what a situation am I reduced! My father, when he died, left me a good fortune and an established trade. I have spent my fortune, ruined my business, and am now dying in a loathsome jail; and to complete all, keeping that poor thing confined without support. I will endeavour to do one piece of justice before I die, by setting him at liberty."

He made a struggle to crawl from his straw bed, opened the casement, and out flew the bird. A flight of jackdaws from the Temple were going over the jail, and Tom Moor's bird mixed among them. The gardener was then laying the plats of the Temple gardens, and as often as he placed them in the day the jackdaws pulled them up by night. They got a gun and attempted to shoot some of them, but, being cunning birds, they always placed one as a watch in the stump of a hollow tree, who, as soon as the gun was levelled, cried "Mawk," and away they flew.

The gardeners were advised to get a net, and the first night it was spread they caught fifteen; Tom Moor's bird was amongst them. One of the men took the net into a garret of an uninhabited house, fastens the doors and windows, and turns the birds loose.

"Now," said he, "you black rascals, I will be revenged of you."

Taking hold of the first at hand, he twists her neck, and throwing her down, cries, "There goes one."

Tom Moor's bird, who had hopped up to a beam at one corner of the room unobserved, as the man lays hold of the second, calls out, "Damn it, how he nicks them."

The man, alarmed, cries, "Sure I heard a voice, but the house is uninhabited, and the door is fast; it could only be imagination."

On laying hold of the third, and twisting his neck, Tom's bird again says, "Damn it, how he nicks them."

The man dropped the bird in his hand, and turning to where the voice came from, seeing the other with his mouth open, cries out, “Who are you?” to which the bird answered, “Tom Moor of Sackville Street, Tom Moor of Sackville Street.”

“The devil you are; and what brought you here.” Tom Moor’s bird, lifting up his pinions, answered, “Bad company, by G--, bad company by G--.”

The fellow, frightened almost out of his wits, opened the door, ran down stairs, and out of the house, followed by all the birds, who by this means regained their liberty.

(Verbatim from Yeats. Hazard is a game of chance played with a pair of dice. Craps is the modern version.)

The Magnificent Bridge of Feathers

Asia

Some people in Ireland and Britain believe that if you see one magpie you’ll have bad luck, and if you see two you’ll have good luck. If you’re pregnant and see three, you’ll have a girl, or a boy if you see four, and so on.

One for sorrow, two for joy,
Three for a girl, four for a boy,
(Or: Three for a wedding, four for to die)
Five for silver, six for gold,
Seven for a secret never to be told,
Eight for a wish, nine for a kiss,
Ten for a bird you must not miss.

You never see a magpie anywhere in this world on the seventh of July, unless the weather is stormy. A legend common to Japan, China and Korea explains why.

Every day, all day, Weaver Maid worked at her loom next to the Great River in the sky we call the Milky Way, weaving clothes for the gods so they could look resplendent, even though she herself dressed plainly. Her father, the Sun God, said to her one day, “You shouldn’t spend your whole life working. Go out and meet other young people and enjoy yourself."

"No, Father," she said. "There is a saying: 'Sorrow, age-long sorrow shall come to Weaver Maid if she leaves her loom.'"

But her father pulled her away from her loom, dressed her in fine clothes, and introduced her to Herd Boy, who tended his flocks on the bank of the Great River. Weaver Maid delighted in his company, and soon the gods noticed that they no longer had new clothes to wear, and they went about in rags and tatters. They complained to Weaver Maid's father, and he ordered her to return to her loom.

"No," she said. "You opened the door, and no one, not even a god, can close it again."

So her father banished Herd Boy to the other side of the Great River of the Milky Way, and you can see them both in the sky now. We call them the stars Altair and Vega, and the smaller stars surrounding one of them are their children.

How do they manage to make children when they are separated by the Great River?

When Weaver Maid returned to her loom, the clothes she wove were sometimes grey with her sadness, and other times bright and rosy with her dreams when she thought about her life with Herd Boy. Her father noticed this and took pity on her, and he ordered all the magpies in the world to assemble once a year on the seventh of July on the bank of the Milky Way to form a bridge, so that Weaver Maid can cross that Great River to spend one day with her lover.

And that is why you never see a magpie anywhere in this world on the seventh of July, unless there is a storm, because then the magpies cannot form a bridge over the swift-running waters of the Great River.

A Chinese opera with the title *The Magnificent Bridge of Feathers* is based on this story.

I tell this rhyme and story on my Dublin Walking Tour when we arrive in Merrion Square. The magpies that live in the Square never tire of listening to it, and there are always several in attendance. One July 7th when I was conducting the Tour, no magpies were to be seen in the Square or anywhere else in Dublin, so the story must be true.

A Robin Warns of Danger

Ireland

If a robin perched directly in front of someone, that person might expect some important news. (O'Sullivan)

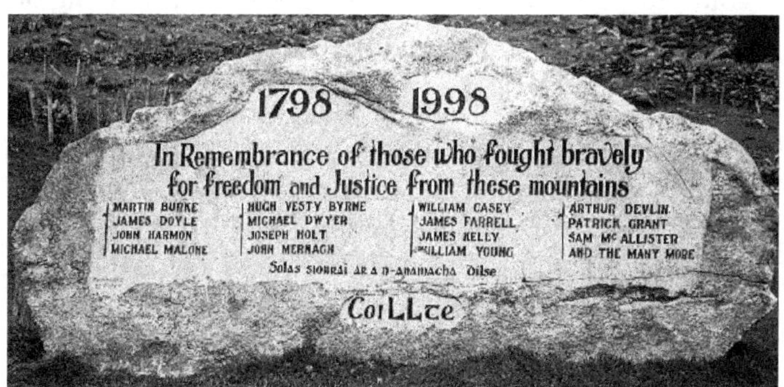

The 1798 Rebellion against British rule in Ireland lasted barely a month before it was swiftly and mercilessly put down. However, in County Wicklow, where it was still risky for British troops because of the hilly terrain ideal for ambush, Michael Dwyer and his band of rebels ran free for another five years in a doomed effort to keep hope alive.

Mrs O'Toole of Ballycumber, Ballinglen, was eight years old when her grandfather, Larry Byrne, one of Dwyer's closest companions, died. She recorded part of her family's oral history on an Ediphone in 1934 for the Irish Folklore Commission, a year before her death at the age of 86. This is her story of one of Dwyer's famous escapes.

> On one occasion Dwyer and my grandfather and Hugh Byrne of Monaseed and poor McAllister – I am troubled to the heart when I think of poor McAllister; he was a true man – well, the four of them were in a cave on Lugnaquilla when the daylight came. ... So the four

awoke, and they began to talk, and they got up and struck their flints and steel 'cause there was no matches. Then they lit their pipes, each of them, and they commenced to smoke and to talk as happy as the day is long, when a robin came in – and a robin is unusual so high up in the mountain, you know – a robin flew in, and she jumped around the quilt over them, and one grabbed at her, and another, and she flew out from the whole of them, and it wasn't two minutes till she came in again, and when she came in she bustled and set herself just as if she was going to jump at them, and she got wicked looking and: "O!" says they, "there is something in this."

The four jumped to their feet, and one of them put his head through the hole and he pulled back excited. "O!" he says, "the hillsides is red with soldiers." "Which will we lie in," says another, "or will we get out? If they have bloodhounds we're found out." "That's right," says they, and they all jumped to their feet, and the bloodhounds came in to the bed, but they dragged on their breeches and put their hat on them, and out they went with their guns. Dwyer whipped his sea-whistle and he whistled, and he could be heard, I suppose, in Arklow, and they fired off their three shots, and the soldiers turned around and they ran for their lives, and they never got time to look back till they fell over Lugnaquilla, and they told when they got below that the hills was full of rebels.

(From Ó Tuathail, "Wicklow Traditions of 1798", *Béaloideas*, Vol 5, No. 2, Nollaig 1935. Used with permission of the Folklore of Ireland Society.)

King Sindbad and his Falcon
Persia

Sindbad, King of Persia, delighted in hunting. He had a falcon that accompanied him day and night, wearing a cup of gold around its neck so it could always have water.

During one hunt, the king was resting under a tree. It was hot and he was thirsty, but he had run out of water. What seemed to be water was dripping from the tree, so Sindbad took the cup from the falcon's neck and filled it. He was just about to drink when the falcon knocked the cup over. He refilled it and offered it to the falcon, thinking it was thirsty, but the bird knocked it over again. Realising that he had neglected the first rule of horsemanship – look after your steed before anything else – he filled the cup again and offered it to the horse, but the bird spilled it.

"Confound you. You won't drink or let me or the horse drink," he said in a rage, and he cut off the falcon's wings with his sword.

The bird looked up meaningfully into the tree before it died, and Sindbad followed its gaze to see a group of snakes dropping the venom that he had been using to fill the cup.

(Condensed and paraphrased from Payne. See "Gelert's Grave" in the Other Dogs section and "The Saviour Gnat" in Other Beasts for similar tales.)

WOLVES

After wolves were exterminated in Britain, bounty hunters killed the last wolf in Ireland in 1786 at Croghan Mountain on the border of Counties Wicklow and Wexford. Both counties claim the honour. During the 17th- and 18th-century Penal Times, the bounty on wolves and priests was five pounds. Wolves do not figure prominently in the consciousness of modern Irish people, and the surviving tales are mainly set in the early medieval period. There is one Irish werewolf story in the Shape-shifters and Shape-changers section, and a few featuring wolves in Saints and Animals.

On the other hand, the wolves of Spain currently number some 2500 and constitute nearly 30% of the population of Europe. They are concentrated in the northwest of the peninsula, so it is not surprising that the animals have a strong presence in the contemporary folklore of the region. The bagpipe (*gaita*) is the most characteristic instrument of Galicia.

The Piper and the Drummer and the Wolf
Galicia, Spain

A piper and a drummer were returning from a religious procession at night, came to a wood and were confronted by a wolf. They ran for their lives. The drummer happened to have a sack of sardines, and he threw them to the wolf, hoping to distract it. But the wolf quickly devoured the sardines and continued chasing the men. As they ran towards an abandoned house, the piper collided with a tree, and the impact caused the pipes to sound. The wolf was so scared that it ran away faster than anyone had ever seen a wolf run.

(Retold from the Spanish in Girgado)

The Wolves and the Pipers
Galicia, Spain

A band of pipers from Requeixo were returning from a fiesta at Rendal de Camba at night, when they heard wolves howling.

"Come on, lads," said the master. "We have to retreat."

"The cottage of Fanado is nearby," said one of the pipers. "It has straw and wood, and we can make a fire."

They went into the cottage, barred the door, and accommodated themselves in the straw, intending to sleep. But the howling of the wolves came closer, and soon they were just outside the door. One wolf jumped on to the roof and began removing the tiles with its paws. They could see its eyes gleaming and hear its growls, desperate to enter. Then another wolf jumped on to the roof, and soon the roof was tumbling down.

"Lads," said the master. "The hour has come. Take out your instruments, and let's play the Muiñeira [a popular dance] de Chantada. At least we'll die happy."

As soon as the pipes and drums began, the howling and growling outside stopped. The wolves had fled, and the musicians made a fire and settled in for the night in comfort and safety.

(Retold from the Spanish in Noia Campos, *Cuentos Gallegos*)

The Piper and the Wolves of Fraga do Eume
Galicia, Spain

One day a piper was travelling to Fraga do Eume between the villages of As Pontes and A Capela in the northeast of Galicia. He was a labourer by day and a piper in the evenings.

Caught out by darkness one night on his way home, he decided to take a shortcut over the mountain, but his way was encumbered by rocks and thick vegetation. Then he heard wolves, and then he saw them – lean and hungry. He instinctively climbed a tree in spite of suffering from vertigo. He grabbed his pipes, intending to use them as a club to fend off the wolves if they tried to climb the tree, but then it occurred to him to play them to attract someone's attention and bring help.

As soon as he started to play a muiñeira, the wolves stopped howling and growling and disappeared. But the people in Fraga do Eume enjoyed the music.

Retold from the Galician in Piñeiro de San Miguel. "Fraga" means "woods". Eume is a river. Google Fraga do Eume to see a photo.

Beltrán and Haro have a couple of recently collected Asturian versions and a French one in which the piper accidentally squeezes or falls on the bag, which makes the pipes squawk, startling the wolf/wolves. In one he says: "Oh, they're afraid of the pipes." So he plays a tune and they leave. There is also a Portuguese version.

A version of this tale, "El buner d'Ordino", is so famous in Andorra that the French postal service issued a stamp depicting it in 2002. (See back cover.) It's on the internet in English, French and Spanish.

An Imprecation against Wolves
France

This prayer or incantation was used in El Rosellón in France, formerly part of Spain, to protect against wolves.

> Wolf, O wolf,
> the beast that you want
> is not yours or mine
> but belongs to the holy Virgin Mary,
> who will tear your throat
> and close your teeth
> with the key of Saint Lawrence.
> (Súarez López, *Fórmulas*)

The Wolf Who Saved a Woman

Native North American

There was a big battle between two tribes, and a young woman from one side was captured and taken back to the camp of the chief on the other side. The chief tied her up and kept her in his tent, and he told his old wife to keep an eye on her.

The wife felt sorry for her – or maybe she just wanted to get rid of the competition – and one night when the chief was asleep she cut the ropes and gave the young woman a pair of moccasins and some food and a flint and told her to run as fast as she could.

She got a long way from the camp before morning, and it snowed after she left, so they couldn't follow her, but she kept going at night and rested during the day. She knew where she was and she knew where her tribe was, so she navigated by the stars, but after four nights she ran out of food.

And besides, there was a wolf following her. No matter how fast she ran, the wolf was right behind her. Finally, she fell down, hungry and exhausted, and waited for the wolf to come and kill her.

But he didn't. He just sat and looked at her. So she told him with sign language that she was hungry, and the wolf went away and came back with a young deer, and she made a fire with the flint and cooked it and ate it and gave some to the wolf.

For the next few days the wolf hunted and got food for her, and she came back to her tribe safe. She brought the wolf into the village with her and told the people how he had saved her.

The people didn't try to drive the wolf away. He stayed on top of a hill where he could watch the woman's house, and she and the people brought food to him. But later, she got sick and died. Her friends still brought food to the wolf, but he went away and they never saw him again.

Mac Cécht and the Wolf

Ireland

Vastly outnumbered by reivers from Britain, King Conaire the Great and most of his defenders were killed in the great battle in County Wicklow called the Destruction of Dá Derga's Hostel in the first century BC. The king's champion, Mac Cécht, so gigantic that his eyes looked like lakes, his nose like a mountain, his knees like hills, his shoes like boats, was one of the few survivors.

He fell down exhausted from his wounds. A woman was passing by, and he hailed her.

"Come here, woman, and see what's in this wound. I don't know whether it's a fly or a midge or an ant that's nibbling me."

She saw that it was in fact a huge hairy wolf that was in the wound up to its shoulders. She grabbed the wolf by the tail and dragged it out of the wound, and it brought the full of its jaws with it.

"It was an ant of the old land," she said.

Mac Cécht took the wolf by the throat and killed it with a blow to the forehead.

The White Wolf and the Shepherd

Galicia, Spain

In the Serra de Coba, in the Highlands of Trives, a she-wolf abandoned a snow-white cub at the foot of an oak tree. A shepherd was taking his flock to pasture when his dogs sensed the presence of a carnivore, but because it was only a cub they began to sniff it instead of killing it. It looked and smelled like a wolf, but since it was as white as a lamb and abandoned, the shepherd picked it up and took it to the village and housed it in the hayshed, where it began to nurse from a ewe as if it were her own baby.

The cub grew up among the sheep and acted as if he were one of them, and he reacted like them when danger approached on the mountain, sheltering among the dogs. As he grew, his coat continued to be pure white, which made him look more like a sheep than a wolf. But when he reached maturity, the sight of him inspired fear in the villagers who saw him, and the dogs of the village paid him no respect, so that he often came home with his fur bloodied in combat with them.

Feeling rejected, the wolf stayed away from the flock and the village. However, the shepherd took food to him every day, and the wolf felt that he had no family but the shepherd and the dogs of his flock. They were the only ones who respected him, and an unbreakable bond grew between him and the shepherd.

One day, the shepherd was attacked by a group of fugitives, but while they were beating him and killing his guard dogs, their horses became nervous, scenting danger. Suddenly, with no time to react, the attackers were assaulted by a huge ferocious white wolf who went straight for their throats.

A villager found the dying shepherd and took him to the village, and others gathered his flock. They found seven of the robbers dead with their throats torn out. The white wolf was never seen again in the neighbourhood, but they say that at night they can hear a howling.

The Wolf of the Chest: How Luarca Was Named

Asturias, Spain

Background

The Chest of Relics, dating from the time of the Apostles, was removed from Jerusalem when the Persians conquered the city in 614 and was taken to Africa, then to Seville for safekeeping. When San Isidoro of Seville was appointed bishop of Toledo, he took it there with him. Then King Don

Pelayo and Archbishop Urbán took the Chest from Toledo to Asturias when the Moors invaded in the eighth century, and deposited it in the Cathedral of San Salvador in Oviedo, where it remains in the Cámara Santa, the Holy Chamber, which was built in the ninth century to house it. It is made of black oak, measures 72 by 119 by 93 cm (28 x 47 x 37 inches) and is covered in silver with depictions of the life of Christ.

King Alfonso the Wise's 13th-century *Primera Crónica General* (Chapter 614) lists the contents of the Chest, which included a glass vial containing the blood that came from the side of Jesus on the Cross, a piece of the Cross, part of the Crown of Thorns, some of the bread miraculously multiplied for 5000 people, bread from the Last Supper, manna that rained on the Israelites in the desert, one of the utensils used in the converting of water to wine at the wedding feast at Cana, milk from the breast of the Mother of Jesus, the hands of Saint Stephen, the right sandal of Saint Peter, hair of the Holy Innocents, hair of Mary Magdalene that she used to wash the feet of Jesus, and bones of prophets and saints too numerous to mention. A 1465 inventory adds the blood-stained cloth that was wrapped around Christ's head after His death.

One account says the Chasuble of Saint Ildefonso, made for him by angels at the order of Mary the mother of Jesus, was in the Chest. When the Chest was opened in the 16th century, "they came upon a very small coffer about the size of the palm of a large man's hand. This bore an inscription that said, 'The Chasuble that Our Lady Gave to San Ildefonso'. Inside they found a sky-blue light silk cloth in the form of a Portuguese cloak big enough to cover the tallest man in Spain, seamless and with no trace of weaving, like an onion-skin, so light and delicate that the men's breath made it swell like a sail in a strong wind."

When the list of contents of the Chest was read out in a speech in 1993 on the occasion of the Feast of Our Lady the Virgin of Covadonga near Oviedo, the Chasuble was not mentioned. After much searching elsewhere in the Cathedral, it has never been found. It seems to have disappeared.

The Chest of Relics Arrives in Luarca

A mighty ship of ancient design with a mountain of sails, much larger than any of the local boats, docked in the small fishing village now known as Luarca to the amazement of the residents. Out stepped a dark man of foreign aspect, imposing and dignified, dressed in flowing robes and an enormous turban. He asked for a priest to be sent to him. The people were confounded: an infidel asking for a priest?

When the priest arrived, he consulted with the stranger, and then two muscular men in bejewelled loincloths carried from the ship a chest the size of a small altar and covered in silver and set it down carefully on the dock. Then the men returned to the ship and sailed away.

The people stared in astonishment. They were awakened from their stupor by the howling of wolves and listened with alarm as the sound drew nearer. The pack approached the dock, headed by the largest wolf anyone had ever seen. Numbed by wonder, the people made way for the wolves, who surrounded the chest. Their leader prostrated himself in front of it in an attitude of reverence. Then the wolves departed, and the chest was removed to the Cathedral in Oviedo.

In memory of the wolf who with such sanctity recognised the importance of the Chest of Relics – El Arca de las Reliquias – the town was named Luarca, a contraction of the Asturian *Llobu del Arca*: the Wolf of the Chest.

(Wolf story mainly from Arrieta Gallastegui)

Fostered by Wolves: Cormac mac Airt

Ireland

In the founding myth of Rome, set about 750 BC, the daughter of the deposed king gave birth to twin boys, Romulus and Remus, whose father was the war god Mars. The usurper king feared that they would try to remove him, and he ordered that they be exposed on a river bank to be killed by wild animals. A she-wolf took them to her den and suckled them along with her own cubs. The boys were eventually discovered by a shepherd and raised by him, unaware of their true identity. As young adults, they were involved in a dispute between their grandfather and the usurper. Remus was imprisoned, Romulus rescued him, the usurper was killed, and the twins founded Rome.

The authors of Irish legendary history were widely educated and well aware of Roman legendary history, including the Romulus and Remus tale.

The dates of Cormac mac Airt's reign are normally given as AD 227-66. He is the most famous of the high kings partly because he was the most prominent of the seven kings under whom the popular hero Fionn mac Cumhaill served, partly because he was the creation of political manoeuvring, and, probably most important, many tales about him have remained in the oral folk tradition.

The night before High King Art, son of High King Conn of the Hundred Battles, went into his final battle, he lay with the daughter of a druid, with the encouragement of the druid, who foresaw that Art would not survive the battle, and it was politically expedient that Art have an heir. The result was Cormac, on whom the druid put five protections: against wounding, fire, drowning, sorcery and wolves.

A pack of wolves snatched the baby while his mother was asleep and adopted him, which seems to defeat the druid's protection, but that may have prevented his discovery by the usurper king who had killed Art. After seven years, a trapper found him playing with the wolf cubs and brought him back to his mother along with the cubs. While a friend of Art was taking mother and child to the north to be safe from the usurper, the wolves tried to take Cormac back, but a herd of wild horses defended him.

The usurper's name was Lugaid mac Con Son of Lugaid. "Mac Con" means Son of the Dog. Why the apparently double patronymic? His father was Lugaid, and when he was a baby he used to suckle from a female dog.

As a child, Cormac disputed a decision made by Lugaid. A woman's sheep had strayed into a man's field and eaten the grass, and the man demanded that the sheep be given to him as compensation. Lugaid ordered the woman to give up the sheep, but Cormac said that the righteous decision would be "one shearing for another"; that is, the woman should give the man one season's shearing of the sheep for their shearing of the man's grass. The people approved, and Lugaid was deposed by popular demand and Cormac installed as king, righteousness being a requisite of kingship.

The wolves that had come with him as a child stayed with him, "and the reason of that great esteem which Cormac bore to wolves was that wolves had fostered him."

(O'Grady)

Cormac's decision about the sheep was cited in court cases as a legal precedent until the early 20th century.

SAINTS AND ANIMALS

Saint Colman mac Duagh (560-632)
Ireland

Colm is the Irish word for "dove". *Colmán* means "little dove" in an affectionate sense.

Colman mac Duagh befriended a rooster and a mouse and a fly.

The rooster would crow at dawn until Colman woke up and went out to visit with it, and then he rang a bell to wake up the rest of the monks. But the monks also wanted to pray at midnight and 3.00 am, when the rooster would be asleep. So he asked his mouse friend, who stayed awake all night, if he could please wake him up at those times. The mouse did so by nibbling his ear.

During the day, Colman often read prayers from a large and cumbersome manuscript. When he was interrupted to perform a task in the community, he had difficulty finding where he had left off in his reading. He asked his pet fly to sit on the last word he had read, so he could find his place when he returned. The fly did so and remained on the spot often for over an hour. The other monks were so amazed that they noted it in their annals.

Saint Colman Elo or Ela (555-611)
Ireland

Colman Elo, whose tutor was Pope Saint Gregory the Great, was probably named for his illustrious uncle, Saint Colmcille (Dove of the Church). Like his uncle, he could be quite short-tempered.

When a neighbouring abbot stole some of the soil Gregory had sent to Colman from Rome, with the special property that anyone buried in it would not go to Hell, he cursed the thief that wolves would eat his body when he died. He also repeatedly beat a pupil who seems to have had learning difficulties through no fault of his own. But he was less assertive when it came to dealing with a "pestilent monster" in Lough Ela.

This was "a small pointed gaping apparition in the shape of a woman" named Lainn, with "short bushy hair, unwashed and unkempt, all over its head". "No man or beast would venture to go near the lake for fear of it." Cuiniugáin, who later became one of Colman's followers, was hostile to him at the time and suggested that Colman be given the task of expelling the monster, saying, "It would be better in our opinion that neither of them should return."

The king of the region, Donnchad, told Colman that he would grant him the lake and the surrounding land for a monastery if he rid it of the beast. Colman prayed successfully that God would bind the monster with reeds, and when it was bound and helpless, he said to his followers, "Now, one of you saints attack the monster and cut off its head."

One of the king's sons and another follower volunteered for the task, and they brought the head to Colman. Perhaps with a view to posterity and the enhancement of his reputation, he boasted:

> The one that opposed me so strongly,
> The monster, ye see that it is headless.

Colman took charge of the land bestowed on him by the king, and he and his community built a house and established a cemetery, whose first interment was that of the lake monster. (It was a widespread practice until recently to make the first burial in a new cemetery that of a fierce beast to deter evil spirits.) They also built a causeway, and while it was under construction a flock of swans would come and sing to them, for which the area was called Lann Ela – the Land or Homestead of the Swan. The ruins of the site are in the parish of Lynally in County Offaly.

(Based on Plummer.)

Colman Son of Luachan (sixth-seventh centuries)

Ireland

Many years ago, two friends, Malachy Coleman and Colm Lankford, separately told me that Saint Colman – they didn't specify which one – was the patron saint of wolves, and anyone threatened by wolves could call on him for protection.

Colman Son of Luachan was one of the three great Colmans of Meath (including Colman Elo) and was present at the Convention of Drum Ceat with Saint Colmcille in 575. He founded a monastery at Lynn, County Westmeath. According to his biographer, he lived for 147 years. These incidents explain why he is the appropriate one to address if you are confronted by a wolf.

While he was strolling around the cemetery after celebrating Mass for royalty, the queen drew Colman's attention to a pack of wolves that was approaching her flock of sheep.

"Colman," she said, "save my sheep and I'll give you a ewe-lamb from the flock every year."

Colman stuck the wolves so they couldn't move.

"Now give me a prayer that I can use to protect them in future."

He gave her this: "May my sheep be under the protection of Colman Son of Luachan so that they will be safe."

Another time, he had just finished saying seven Masses under an oak called Colman's Oak when a pack of wolves came to him, tails wagging amiably, and licked his feet and lay down in front of him.

He told them, "If anyone prays to me for protection, you are not allowed to kill them."

(Source: Meyer, *Betha Colmáin*)

Saint Columbanus (d. 615)

Born in Ireland, travelled widely in Europe

Columbanus ("little white dove") or Columban or Columba (Latin for "dove") – not to be confused with Colmcille, who is called Columba in Scotland and by Protestants in Ireland – is also called Saint Columbanus of Bobbio (in Italy), because he established a monastery there. He is often depicted with a bear – because in need of shelter he once evicted a bear from its cave, and he tamed and yoked another bear to the plough – or encircled by wolves.

He was walking alone through a wild forest near Anegray in eastern France one day, pondering whether he would rather be killed by wild animals or by men. Better by animals, he decided, because if men killed him they would have committed a mortal sin and be consigned to hell.

Just then, a pack of twelve wolves suddenly surrounded him. He stood still, praying for deliverance (possibly to Colman Son of Luachan), while the beasts sniffed at him curiously and tasted his clothes, and they then moved on. Later he discovered that there had been a band of brigands on the road. None of the accounts point it up, but in light of similar incidents with helpful Black Dogs and púcas and Sahagún's coyote (Shapeshifters chapter), it seems possible that the wolves deliberately delayed his journey long enough for him to avoid encountering the brigands.

(Main source: Seventh-century biographer Jonas the Monk and William Hunt.)

Columbanus is the patron saint of motorcyclists, probably owing to his extensive travels and because he was a bit of a rebel, often at loggerheads with both Church and civil authority and briefly imprisoned once when he offended powerful people. In recognition, Harley-Davidson has issued a commemorative coin available in either silver or bronze: "Saint Columbanis [sic] – Patron Saint of Motorcycles [sic]".

The Monk and the Bird

Collected by T. Crofton Croker
Ireland

Many years ago there was a very religious and holy man, one of the monks of a convent, and he was one day kneeling at his prayers in the garden of his monastery, when he heard a little bird singing in one of the rose-trees of the garden, and there never was anything that he had heard in the world so sweet as the song of that little bird.

And the holy man rose up from his knees where he was kneeling at his prayers to listen to its song; for he thought he never in all his life heard anything so heavenly.

And the little bird, after singing for some time longer on the rose-tree, flew away to a grove at some distance from the monastery, and the holy man followed it to listen to its singing, for he felt as if he would never be tired of listening to the sweet song it was singing out of its throat.

And the little bird after that went away to another distant tree, and sung there for a while, and then to another tree, and so on in the same manner, but ever farther and farther away from the monastery, and the holy man still following it farther, and farther, and farther still listening delighted to its enchanting song.

But at last he was obliged to give up, as it was growing late in the day, and he returned to the convent; and as he approached it in the evening, the sun was setting in the west with all the most heavenly colours that were ever seen in the world, and when he came into the convent, it was nightfall.

And he was quite surprised at everything he saw, for they were all strange faces about him in the monastery that he had never seen before, and the very place itself, and everything about it, seemed to be strangely altered; and, altogether, it seemed entirely different from what it was when he had left in the morning; and the garden was not like the garden where he had been kneeling at his devotion when he first heard the singing of the little bird.

And while he was wondering at all he saw, one of the monks of the convent came up to him, and the holy man questioned him, "Brother, what is the cause of all these strange changes that have taken place here since the morning?"

And the monk that he spoke to seemed to wonder greatly at his question, and asked him what he meant by the change since morning? For, sure, there was no change; that all was just as before. And then he said, "Brother, why do you ask these strange questions, and what is your name? For you wear the habit of our order, though we have never seen you before."

So upon this the holy man told his name and said that he had been at mass in the chapel in the morning before he had wandered away from the garden listening to the song of a little bird that was singing among the rose-trees, near where he was kneeling at his prayers.

And the brother, while he was speaking, gazed at him very earnestly, and then told him that there was in the convent a tradition of a brother of his name, who had left it two hundred years before, but that what was become of him was never known.

And while he was speaking, the holy man said, "My hour of death is come; blessed be the name of the Lord for all his mercies to me, through the merits of his only-begotten Son."

And he kneeled down that very moment, and said, "Brother, take my confession, for my soul is departing."

And he made his confession, and received his absolution, and was anointed, and before midnight he died.

The little bird, you see, was an angel, one of the cherubims or seraphims; and that was the way the Almighty was pleased in His mercy to take to Himself the soul of that holy man.

(Verbatim from Yeats as "The Story of the Little Bird".)

Croker wrote this, he says, word for word as he heard it from an old woman at a holy well. It was first published in *The Amulet* in 1827.

Saint Kevin of Glendalough
Ireland

Saint Kevin founded a monastery in Glendalough (the Valley of the Two Lakes), County Wicklow, in the sixth century and died in 618 at the age of 120. The two lakes are called the Upper Lake and the Lower Lake. The latter also carries the name "Lough Péist" – the Lake of the Water Monster – on the maps, and the name also appeared for several years on road signs on the approach to Glendalough. No one can tell me why those signs were removed.

Kevin was raised by Christian parents on the border of Counties Dublin and Wicklow. As a young man, he decided that he didn't like people very much and wanted to live alone with only animals for company, for he loved God's non-human creatures. So he settled by the shore of the Upper Lake in Glendalough as the sole human inhabitant of the picturesque glen. Obviously a strict vegetarian, he lived on nuts and berries and dressed in the skins of animals that had died of old age.

He is often depicted with a bird in his hand. One day, as he stood praying waist-deep with his arms spread in the form of a cross in the cold water of the Upper Lake, a bird brought a twig and placed it in his hand. Then another and another, until she had built a nest. Kevin loved animals so much that he stood there until the bird had laid her eggs, they had hatched, and the babies were old enough to fly away.

At that time, the water monster lived in the Upper Lake, but Kevin and the monster became friends, and the monster didn't try to eat him.

One day a farmer brought his cattle to Glendalough on a grazing tour: grazing in one place and then moving on to fresh pasture. He noticed that one of his cows was giving as much milk as fifty other cows. This was a wonderful thing, and the farmer sent a servant to find out what the cow was eating that caused her to give so much milk. The servant discovered that the cow spent the whole day licking Kevin's feet.

When the farmer heard this, he said, "That must be a very holy man," and he brought Kevin to his home and scrubbed him up and gave him normal clothes to wear. Kevin hated it, but he accepted that it was the will of God that he be among people and preach the gospel. News of the miracle of the cow spread quickly, and soon pilgrims from all over Ireland and Europe gathered at Glendalough to be near the saint.

This made Kevin even more unhappy, and he took to living in a cave in a cliff above the Upper Lake when he wasn't busy preaching. But the water monster was delighted. It no longer had to go out and look for its food. Dinner was delivered in the form of the fans of the new religious superstar.

The ones who were eaten were very annoyed, and those who weren't eaten yet wanted to kill the monster. But Kevin loved animals and didn't want the monster killed, so he asked it to please move to the Lower Lake so the farmers could wash their animals in the Upper Lake, and it could eat the dirt and disease that flowed into the Lower Lake because it was a monster. The monster complied, and that's why the lake is called Loch Péist.

I told that story at the side of the Lower Lake to a group of annoyingly arrogant Spanish army cadets who were studying to be officers. One of them asked me if the monster still inhabited the lake. I said, "I don't know. I've never seen it."

"What will happen if I go into the lake?"

"I don't know. Do you want to try?"

He stripped to his underwear and walked several metres into the water and then returned safe and sound. Either the monster no longer lives there or it doesn't like the taste of Spanish army cadets. There is another lake on top of Turlough Hill on the northwest side of Glendalough called Loch na hOnchon, which means the Lake of the Monster, so it's possible that the beast has moved there.

According to the 11th-century history attributed to the Irish Nennius: "[There is] a stone in Loch na n-Onchon, in a mountain near Glenn-da-Loch; its property is, if it be struck with a wand by way of assault, rain will ensue, and sunshine after. [note] There is a stone called the Deer Stone in the Glen itself, on the south side of the Lower Lake, of which some similar tales are told; but the original traditions are now so much corrupted by the ignorance of the guides and the folly of visitors to the lakes, that no dependence can be placed on them, as representing ancient thought."

(English novelist and poet William Thackeray visited Glendalough and reported in *The Irish Sketch-book*, 1843: "Only fancy can describe the charms of that delightful place." But he added sardonically: "There is an excellent guide on the spot, who, for a shilling or two, will tell all he knows, and a great deal more, too.")

The Deer Stone is a bullaun (a flat stone with a bowl carved in the top surface) just across the Bridge of the Deer from the Monastic City. This is the story as I tell it.

A local king divorced his wife, Dassan, and married a younger woman. Dassan was a witch, and she used her magic arts to kill the first two children he had with his second wife. When their third child, a boy named Fáelán, was born, the king sent him to live with Kevin as his foster son to protect him from Dassan.

The cows went dry one time, and Kevin needed milk to feed the baby, so he asked a doe that had a fawn to please leave half of her milk in the bullaun bowl. She did, but a wolf came and killed the fawn, so the doe stopped producing milk. Kevin said to the wolf, "You caused this problem, now you fix it." The wolf went to the doe and pretended to be a fawn, and she let down her milk again.

Fáelán became king of Leinster and was the progenitor of the Wicklow lords, the O'Byrnes and the O'Tooles.

Saint Ciarán and the Dun Cow

Ireland

Saint Ciarán the Younger, who founded Clonmacnoise in 546, wanted to study at the monastery at Clonard under Saint Finnian, but his family was too poor to afford tuition fees. He asked his parents if he could take one of their cows as payment. "Go through the herds," his father told him, "and whatever follows you, take it." A dun cow followed him to Clonard, and she used to give twelve measures of milk every day, enough for all of the Twelve Apostle of Ireland.

When Ciarán finished his studies and set out on his travels, he ordered that when the cow died her hide should be sent to him. After he founded Clonmacnoise, the hide was preserved there, and Ciarán said, "Every soul that shall go out of its body on the hide of the Dun shall not be punished in hell." Later, the hide was used to make the famous twelfth-century collection of stories, the Lebor na hUidre, the Book of the Dun Cow.

Saint Francis of Assisi (d. 1226)

Italy

A wolf was terrorising the town of Gubbio, devouring animals and people alike, and the citizens were afraid to venture outside the gates. Saint Francis took it upon himself to solve the problem. He found the wolf and threatened it in the name of Christ. He made the Sign of the Cross and commanded it to cease attacking the animals and humans. The wolf submitted tamely and came to Francis and extended a paw to him like a friendly dog. He led it into the town, where the townspeople, once they understood that the beast no longer posed a threat, adopted and fed it as they would any well-behaved stray dog. They mourned when it died of old age two years later.

Artistic impressions of Saint Francis often depict him shaking hand-paw with the wolf or leading him into the town.

King Saint Edmund

England

The Saxon King Edmund (d. 869) refused to submit to Danish invaders, so they tied him to a tree in the forest and shot him full of arrows. Then they cut off his head and hid it among thorns and briars as a final insult.

However, a wolf guarded the head to prevent other animals from eating it. When the Saxons found the body, they went searching for the head. One of them, finding himself separated from his companions, called out to the others, "Where are you?" and the head answered, "Here, here."

They followed the sound of Edmund's voice and found the head resting safely between the paws of the wolf. After they reunited the head with the body, the men carried it to its resting place at Bury St Edmunds in Suffolk, with the wolf following tamely. It stayed there until the burial ceremony was finished, and then returned to the forest.

Saint Gerasimus and the Lion

Palestine

John Moschus (c.550-619)

About a mile away from the Jordan there is a monastery known as Abba Gerasimus' monastery. When we visited it the old men living there told us about Abba Gerasimus.

One day as he was walking by the banks of the Jordan he met a lion in the way, roaring loudly. He was holding in the air one swollen paw covered in bloody matter, caused by a sharp sliver of reed embedded in it. When the lion saw the old man he stood still and held out the wounded paw with the reed in it, as if weeping and asking to be cured. When the old man realised the plight the lion was in he took the lion's paw, probed the wound and drew out the reed along with a quantity of pus, carefully cleaned the wound and bandaged it and sent the lion on his way. But when the lion realised he had been cured he refused to desert the old man but followed him everywhere like a disciple following a master. The old man was amazed at the gratitude which a wild beast was capable of, and looked after it from then on, feeding it on bread and soaked vegetables.

Now this monastery had an ass, which they used for carrying water from the Jordan to supply the brothers' needs. And it became the old man's custom to let the lion guard the ass while it was grazing. The lion would go with the ass down to the banks of the Jordan and watch it while it grazed. One day, however, the lion wandered off for quite a distance, just when a camel driver from Arabia came along, saw the ass, caught it and took it away with him. Finding the ass missing the lion returned to the monastery and hung his head, obviously grief-stricken, before Abba Gerasimus, who thought that the lion must have eaten the ass.

"Where is the ass?" he said.

But the lion, just as a human being might do, looked away and said nothing.

"Well the Lord be blessed if you haven't eaten it!" said the abba. "So everything that the ass used to do you will have to do from now on."

So the lion henceforth had to carry a harness containing four amphorae in which he carried water for the monastery.

One day a soldier came to the old man to ask his blessing. When he saw the lion carrying water and learned the reason for it, he took pity on the lion, and offered the old men three *numismas* to buy another ass for this task, so that there would be no need for the lion to do it.

Soon after this transaction was completed and the lion relieved of his burden, the camel driver who had stolen the ass came back carrying wheat for sale in the holy city and he still had the ass with him. As he was crossing the Jordan he met the lion, and as soon as he had seen it he let the camels go and fled. But the lion recognised the ass, ran up to it and took the ass's halter in his mouth just as he used to do. He joyfully led the ass and three camels back to the old man, roaring loudly, because he had found the ass which was lost. So the old man who had thought that the lion had swallowed the ass now learned that the lion had suffered a great injustice. He called the lion "Jordan", and he never left the old man but continued to live in the monastery with the brothers for more than five years.

In the providence of God the lion was not in the monastery when the old man passed to the Lord and was buried. But a little while after the lion came into the monastery and Abba Sabbatius, Gerasimus' disciple, noticed the lion looking for the old man.

"Jordan," said Sabbatius, "our father has left us both orphans and passed to the Lord. Try and get used to it, and come and take some food."

But the lion would not eat, and kept on looking about this way and that way, searching for the old man, roaring loudly, unable to bear the old man's absence. Abba Sabbatius and the other old men stroked his neck and told him over and over again that the old man had passed to the Lord and had left us, but whatever they said they were unable to lessen his grief or his roaring. The more they tried to cherish and console him by their words, the greater his grief, the louder he roared and lamented, showing in his voice, his face and his eyes his distress at not seeing the old man.

"Come with me, seeing that you don't believe us," said Abba Sabbatius to him at last, "and I will show you where our old man has been laid."

So he led the lion to where the old man was buried, about five paces outside the church.

"This is where our old man is buried," said Abba Sabbatius to the lion, as he stood above Abba Gerasimus' grave. And Abba Sabbatius prostrated himself over the old man's grave.

The lion understood what was said to him, and when he saw Abba Sabbatius prostrate on the grave, weeping, he too lay down, striking his head forcefully on the ground and roaring. And suddenly, there he died, on the old man's grave.

(Verbatim from *The Spiritual Meadow* [c. 620] by John Moschus in *Vitae Patrum: Lives of the Desert Fathers*, 1628. This story has mistakenly become attached to the more famous Saint Jerome, "apparently through the ignorance of Latin-speaking pilgrims", according to Dalrymple, and the error has been compounded by the use of Jerome's name in the popular and influential collection of religious tales, *The Golden Legend*, by Jacobus de Voragine, 1275, and in Andrew Lang's *The Red Book of Animal Stories*, 1899. The Gerasimus original is much warmer and more personable than the Jerome versions.)

Gnats and Mosquitoes
Mesopotamia/Turkey

In AD 338, the Roman-controlled city of Nisibis, now Nusaybin in Turkey, was under siege by the Persian king Shapur II of the Sasanian Empire (where the Simurgh was an important cultural symbol). Siege engines had not managed to breech the walls, and the city was still intact after 70 days. The Persians came up with an ingenious plan.

The river Mygdonius flowed through Nisibis. They dammed it upstream, and when enough water had collected, they opened the dam. The swollen river not only destroyed the near wall, but it took out the one on the far side as well, leaving the city at the mercy of the besiegers. Shapur and his army waited till the following morning for the water to recede and the mud to dry, confident that they could stroll in virtually unimpeded.

But when they mounted the attack they discovered that the walls had been rebuilt overnight. Jacob, the bishop of the city, had so energised the population that they had not only repaired the walls but now took to the battlements and were driving the Persians back. Shapur was astounded, but there was more to come.

The historian Theodoret reports that the Syrian writer Ephraim suggested to Bishop Jacob that he put a curse on the Persians to drive them away from the city. Jacob was merciful. He only summoned clouds of gnats and mosquitoes. Swarms of the tiny beasts invaded the noses and ears and eyes of the soldiers and their horses and elephants, and the panicked animals broke loose and stampeded.

Shapur lifted the siege, acknowledging defeat by a power greater than himself.

(Source: Leo the Deacon, tenth-century historian, and Theodoret.)

Saint Gobnait's Beehive
Ireland

The supposed miracle that connects the name of Gobnait with bees is commemorated by the presence of a "teacair" or beehive, close to her statue at Ballyvourney, near Cork, and which is known to this day as "St Gobnait's Teacair."

The story current in the neighbourhood is that a poor widow, who was unable to pay her rent, had her sole wealth – a few cows, whose milk she sold – seized by bailiffs, and in her distress, invoked the assistance of St Gobnait, whose church she was passing at the moment, whilst police and bailiffs drove her cows before them. Even as she prayed, a tall woman appeared, holding a bee-hive in her hand and clad in a brown cloak.

Looking with compassion at the tearful face of her supplicant, St Gobnait, for it was she, raised the hive in the air, whereupon out flew a swarm of bees that were immediately transformed into a troop of armed soldiers. At a sign from the saint, they fell upon the bailiffs and police, who were driving the cows away, but who, the moment themselves at the mercy of the soldiers, began to scream and howl and scattered in all directions.

They were far too eager to save their lives to give a thought to the poor woman's cows, which she at once took possession of. She would have fallen on her knees at the feet of St Gobnait, but that the vision vanished as suddenly as it had come.

(Verbatim from NFCS 0342:116-117. Collector: Bridie O Riordan, Shanvallyshane, Co. Cork.)

Saint Roch, Patron of Dogs
Italy and France

Roch – also Rocco, Rocke, Roque, etc. – is typically depicted pointing out a plague sore (bubo) on his leg and/or healing people, and is nearly always accompanied by a dog with a loaf of bread in its mouth or at its feet. He is most famous for his miraculous cures of victims of the plague, though exactly which plague is unknown. His dates are given as 1348-1376 or 1295-1327, which suggests that he may be a conflation of two men. He is the patron of dogs and falsely accused people. Most accounts of his career focus on his cures and unjust imprisonment but leave out the dog, which is strange, since it is the dog-with-bread image in sculptures and paintings that makes Roch instantly identifiable.

The following is based on the "Life of Saint Rocke" chapter in Caxton's *The Golden Legend.*

When he caught the plague himself, Roch was exiled from the Italian city of Piacenza because the citizens feared they would be infected by him. He retired to a nearby forest, where he built a rough shelter of tree branches. A cloud from heaven created a healing spring next to his hut. Wounded and sick wild animals sought him out for cures.

A nobleman named Gotard who lived near the forest kept a pack of hounds. On the order of Divine Providence, one of the dogs started taking loaves of bread from the house and delivering them to Roch. Gotard noticed this and followed the dog one day, but when he arrived at the hut Roch told him to go away so he wouldn't catch the plague from him.

At home, Gotard thought, "It must be a sign that the hand of God is on this man, since the dog, which lacks human reason, has been feeding him. So I, a good Christian, should do at least as much." So he returned to Roch and offered to help him in any way he could. Roch told him to follow the way of Christ, preach the Gospel and live as a beggar, which he did.

Roch was cured by God and travelled to his native France, where he was accused of being a spy and imprisoned. He patiently endured this injustice, and at the end of five years an angel appeared to tell him God had sent him to collect his soul, and this was the time to request his most fervent desire. Roch asked that anyone who prayed to him would be immune to the plague. The request was granted and confirmed in gold letters written on a tablet, which was placed under his head after he died. This divine guarantee is probably the main reason for Roch's popularity, although the dog adds the further element of animal compassion.

San Adrián and the Snakes

Galicia, Spain

Detail of cross base depicting a winged serpent.

At Cabo de San Adrián, a peninsula on the northwest tip of Galicia, there is a shrine to the local equivalent of Ireland's Saint Patrick. When San Adrián arrived in the region to preach the Gospel, it was uninhabitable because of an infestation of snakes, so there was no one to preach to. San Adrián stamped his foot on the ground, and the snakes fled under a stone, except for one that he had stepped on, which was turned into stone. As proof that this story is true, the Pedra da Serpe (Stone of the Snake) de Gondomil, a large weathered stone on the base of which is carved a serpent with wings, can still be seen there. The cross on top represents the victory of Christ over the devil. Some say the Stone dates to Roman times, while others believe it is medieval.

According to Antón and Mandianes, in Galicia serpents don't die a natural death. They grow wings and fly away to the Otherworld and so are symbols of immortality. Serpents enter houses where there is a woman nursing a child or a place where a cow has a suckling calf and suck the milk. They suck the woman so slowly that she doesn't know it's happening, but soon the child and the calf languish and sicken until someone notices and guards against the snake or kills it.

Many fishing boats in the area are named “San Adrián” to put them under his protection. His feast day is celebrated with religious ceremonies at the shrine on 16 June if that date falls on a Sunday; otherwise, it is celebrated on the third Sunday of June. Many come long distances, often on their knees, and devotees hold up their domestic animals as the statue of the saint passes in procession, because he is believed to cure illnesses of both man and beast.

The Seven Sleepers of Ephesus and their Dog

> I wonder by my troth, what thou and I
> Did, till we loved? were we not wean’d till then?
> But suck’d on country pleasures, childishly?
> Or snorted we in the Seven Sleepers’ den?
> *From “The Good-Morrow” by John Donne, 1633*

Both Christian and Islamic traditions have this widespread story about seven young men who were being persecuted for their belief in God and sought refuge in a cave, taking their dog with them.

The Koran (Sura 18) says: “They were youths who believed in their Lord ... they stood up and proclaimed: ‘Our only Lord is the Lord of the heavens and the earth. We will never worship any other god beside Him.’ ... [People] will say there were three, the fourth of them being their dog; and they will say there were five, the sixth of them being their dog, guessing at the unseen; and they will say there were seven, and the eighth of them was their dog.”

Some rabbis asked Muhammad how many there really were. Expecting that Allah would reveal the answer to him, he said he would tell them tomorrow. Sura 18 advises: “Never say of anything, ‘Indeed I will do that tomorrow,’ except when adding, ‘If Allah wills.’” But Muhammad neglected to say, "If Allah wills," and so it took him fifteen days to get a result, which was the revelation of Sura 18, known as "The People of the Cave". Most sources say seven plus the dog.

There are many Christian versions, most of which include the dog. The one by Gregory of Tours (538-594) is one of the few that don't. The "Lives of the Seven Sleepers" chapter in *The Golden Legend* is probably the most influential source.

The Seven were from Ephesus. When Emperor Decius (reigned 249-251) commanded that all Christians sacrifice to the pagan gods or be killed, the young men sold all their possessions and gave away most of their money, keeping enough to live on until the persecution ended, and went to hide in a cave on Mount Celion. They were informed on, and Decius, who declined to kill them because it would be wrong to torment such beautiful youths, ordered the mouth of the cave to be closed off with boulders. This was done while the men were in a divinely imposed coma – "God took up their souls." It was hoped that when they ran out of food they would eat each other, presumably starting with the dog.

Centuries later – the Koran says 300 years, *The Golden Legend* 208 – when the Christian Theodosius II was emperor (408-450), God put the idea into the head of a farmer that he should build a sheep fold. His workers found the rocks blocking the entrance to the cave and thought they would make good building material. When the rocks were cleared away, God put the souls back into the sleepers, presumably including the dog.

The Seven are recognised as saints by the Roman and Orthodox Catholic Churches.

SHAPE-SHIFTERS AND SHAPE-CHANGERS

Shape-shifters voluntarily take on other forms using their own power. Shape-changers transform unwilling victims, often by cursing them.

Shape-shifters

Barewalkers

Algonquian Language Group
United States and Canada

There are three types of barewalking or three theories to explain how it works. One: a person telepathically controls an animal. Two: one of the person's three souls inhabits the animal and controls it. Three: the person strips naked and physically shape-shifts into the animal. The "bare" in "barewalking" reflects that last type. The word is often spelled "bearwalking", because the purpose of the operation is usually destruction, and a bear is the animal most frequently employed. Other Native American groups have different names for the practice.

The Barewalker Wolf

A middle-aged Ojibwe man of the Algonquian language group from the Michigan-Ontario Great Lakes region told me this story in the 1960s.

He was born and raised on a reservation in Michigan's Upper Peninsula. One day, when he was about eleven years old, he was walking in the woods and saw a friend his own age standing naked in a tree flapping his arms like wings. He didn't let the boy see him for fear of embarrassing him, for he knew that his friend spent time with a woman suspected of being a barewalker, and he was evidently learning to shape-shift into the form of a bird.

Many years later, the man was making his living as a trapper. He discovered that something was eating the animals in his traps and ruining their pelts. So one day when he set out to check his traps he carried a rifle. Walking along a forest road with snow banks on both sides, he spotted a large wolf standing on one of the banks. It stared at him with a human-like gaze and then leapt across the road to the other bank. As it did, he shot at it, hitting it in the left hip. He followed the trail of blood into the village, where it was obscured by the traffic on the street.

That evening, he heard that the woman rumoured to be a barewalker was in bed with a mysterious injury to her left hip. He concluded that the woman had been that wolf. His traps were never interfered with again.

A Wolf Story

A Literary Folk Tale by Lady Wilde

Ireland

Transformation into wolves is a favourite subject of Irish legend, and many a wild tale is told by the peasants round the turf fire in the winter nights of strange adventures with wolves. Stories that had come down to them from their forefathers in the old times long ago; for there are no wolves existing now in Ireland.

A young farmer named Connor once missed two fine cows from his herd, and no tale or tidings could be heard of them anywhere. So he thought he would set out on a search throughout the country; and he took a stout blackthorn stick in his hand and went his way. All day he travelled miles and miles, but never a sign of the cattle. And the evening began to grow very dark, and he was wearied and hungry, and no place near to rest in; for he was in the midst of a bleak, desolate heath, with never a habitation at all in sight, except a long, low, rude shieling, like the den of a robber or a wild beast. But a gleam of light came from a chink between the boards, and Connor took heart and went up and knocked at the door. It was opened at once by a tall, thin, grey-haired old man, with keen, dark eyes.

"Come in," he said. "You are welcome. We have been waiting for you. This is my wife," and he brought him over to the hearth, where was seated an old, thin, grey woman, with long, sharp teeth and terrible glittering eyes.

"You are welcome," she said. "We have been waiting for you. It is time for supper. Sit down and eat with us."

Now Connor was a brave fellow, but he was a little dazed at first at the sight of this strange creature. However, as he had his stout stick with him, he thought he could make a fight for his life anyway, and, meantime, he would rest and eat, for he was both hungry and weary, and it was now black night, and he would never find his way home even if he tried. So he sat down by the hearth, while the old grey woman stirred the pot on the fire. But Connor felt that she was watching him all the time with her keen, sharp eyes.

Then a knock came to the door. And the old man rose up and opened it. When in walked a slender, young black wolf, who immediately went straight across the floor to an inner room, from which in a few moments came forth a dark, slender, handsome youth, who took his place at the table and looked hard at Connor with his glittering eyes.

"You are welcome," he said. "We have waited for you."

Before Connor could answer another knock was heard, and in came a second wolf, who passed on to the inner room like the first, and soon after, another dark, handsome youth came out and sat down to supper with them, glaring at Connor with his keen eyes, but said no word.

"These are our sons," said the old man. "Tell them what you want, and what brought you here amongst us, for we live alone and don't care to have spies and strangers coming to our place."

Then Connor told his story, how he had lost his two fine cows, and had searched all day and found no trace of them; and he knew nothing of the place he was in, nor of the kindly gentleman who asked him to supper; but if they just told him where to find his cows he would thank them, and make the best of his way home at once.

Then they all laughed and looked at each other, and the old hag looked more frightful than ever when she showed her long, sharp teeth.

On this, Connor grew angry, for he was hot tempered; and he grasped his blackthorn stick firmly in his hand and stood up and bade them open the door for him; for he would go his way, since they would give no heed and only mocked him.

Then the eldest of the young men stood up. "Wait," he said. "We are fierce and evil, but we never forget a kindness. Do you remember, one day down in the glen you found a poor little wolf in great agony and like to die, because a sharp thorn had pierced his side? And you gently extracted the thorn and gave him a drink, and went your way leaving him in peace and rest?"

"Aye, well do I remember it," said Connor, "and how the poor little beast licked my hand in gratitude."

"Well," said the young man, "I am that wolf, and I shall help you if I can, but stay with us to-night and have no fear."

So they sat down again to supper and feasted merrily, and then all fell fast asleep, and Connor knew nothing more till he awoke in the morning and found himself by a large hay-rick in his own field.

"Now surely," thought he, "the adventure of last night was not all a dream, and I shall certainly find my cows when I go home; for that excellent, good young wolf promised his help, and I feel certain he would not deceive me."

But when he arrived home and looked over the yard and the stable and the field, there was no sign nor sight of the cows. So he grew very sad and dispirited. But just then he espied in the field close by three of the most beautiful strange cows he had ever set eyes on.

"These must have strayed in," he said, "from some neighbour's ground."

And he took his big stick to drive them out of the gate off the field. But when he reached the gate, there stood a young black wolf watching; and when the cows tried to pass out at the gate he bit at them and drove them back. Then Connor knew that his friend the wolf had kept his word. So he let the cows go quietly back to the field; and there they remained, and grew to be the finest in the whole country, and their descendants are flourishing to this day, and Connor grew rich and prospered; for a kind deed is never lost, but brings good luck to the doer for evermore, as the old proverb says:

> "Blessings are won,
> By a good deed done."

But never again did Connor find that desolate heath or that lone shieling, though he sought far and wide, to return his thanks, as was due to the friendly wolves; nor did he ever again meet any of the family, though he mourned much whenever a slaughtered wolf was brought into the town for the sake of the reward, fearing his excellent friend might be the victim. At that time the wolves in Ireland had increased to such an extent, owing to the desolation of the country by constant wars, that a reward was offered and a high price paid for every wolf's skin brought into the court of the justiciary; and this was in the time of Queen Elizabeth, when the English troops made ceaseless war against the Irish people, and there were more wolves in Ireland than men; and the dead lay unburied in hundreds on the highways, for there were no hands left to dig them graves.

(Verbatim from Wilde. The mother of Oscar Wilde, she used the pen name "Speranza" in her political writings. The bounty on wolves and priests was five pounds.)

The Crane Wife
Japan

A poor man who lived alone was out hunting one day, when he came across a wounded crane with an arrow in its wing. He took the crane home and removed the arrow and dressed the wound. The crane stayed with him until it was able to fly away. As it left, it circled the house and spoke a farewell in crane language that the man understood meant Thank you.

Some days later, there was a knock on his door. He opened it to find a young woman holding a bag of rice. She said she was homeless and asked if she could stay with him.

"I have enough rice in this bag to feed both of us," she said.

He welcomed her, and they found that they were compatible, and he didn't want her to leave. Compatibility grew into love, and he asked her to marry him. She accepted.

Although they were never hungry because of the inexhaustible bag of rice, they were very poor. The wife said that she could weave cloths that he could sell to make money, so he built a shed next to the house and installed a loom. She told him she liked to work in private and made him promise that he would not disturb her. He promised.

After her first day at the loom, she presented him with a length of cloth that seemed to shine with an inner light. He took it into town and got a good price for it and a request for more. The woman continued to produce fine pieces of cloth, but the man noticed that she seemed to be getting weaker, and he worried that she might be sick.

One day, he was listening to the sound of the shuttle that carried the weft flying across the warp, as he often did, but this time it was slower than usual. He peeked into the weaving shed and saw not his wife but a crane pulling its feathers out to weave them into the cloth.

He gasped in amazement. The crane-woman heard him and said, "This is why I asked you never to disturb me when I was weaving. I fell in love with you while I was recovering from the arrow wound, and I came here to help you in gratitude for your kindness, but now I have to leave."

As she flew away, she circled the house and spoke a sad and loving farewell in crane language.

The Golden Ass by Apuleius
(Lucius the Ass by Lucius of Patrae)
An Accidental Shape-shifter
Greek/Roman

The Golden Ass is the more famous of the two versions of the 2nd-century AD novel and probably derives from *Lucius the Ass*.

On his travels, Lucius found accommodation in a house where the wife was a witch. He wanted to learn how to be a witch himself, so with the help of a maid who he had seduced (with her active encouragement) he spied on her one night when she was shape-shifting. He watched her take ointment from one of several boxes in a cabinet and rub it over her naked body, recite a spell and then shake herself. Feathers sprouted from her body. Her nose went crooked and her nails turned into talons, and then she flew away in the shape of an owl.

Lucius wanted to try it, so he took some ointment from one of the boxes and asked the maid how to change back into human form. The maid told him that the witch drank a tea made of dill and laurel and then washed herself with it to shift back from a bird. Lucius rubbed the ointment over his body. No feathers appeared, but "my hair turned rough and my skin tough and hard, my hands and feet became hooves, out of my arse grew a tail – I was no bird but a plain ass." He had used the wrong ointment. He was left with human understanding but without the ability to speak. To revert from ass to human, now he needed to eat a rose.

Throughout the rest of the picaresque novel, interspersed by mostly bawdy folk tales, Lucius suffers many misadventures and fails to find a remedy until he prays to the goddess Isis, who provides the roses. In gratitude, he joins her cult.

A Woman in Horse Form
Ireland

> I myself, when a boy of ten or eleven [c. 1870], was perfectly convinced that on a fine early dewy morning in summer when people were still in bed, I saw a strange horse run round a seven-acre field of ours and change into a woman, who ran even swifter than the horse, and after a couple of courses round the field disappeared into our haggard. I am sure, whatever I may believe today, no earthly persuasion would, at the time, have convinced me that I did not see this. Yet I never saw it again, and never heard of anyone else seeing the same.
>
> (Douglas Hyde in Evans-Wentz)

A Hare-witch Shape-shift Spell
Scotland

In her apparently voluntary confession during her witchcraft trial in April 1662, Isobel Gowdie related this incident.

> She had been sent by the devil with a message to Auldearne in the form of a hare but had the misfortune to meet Peter Papley and his hounds. The hounds sprung on the disguised witch, "and I," says Isobel, "run a very long time, but being hard pressed, was forced to take to my own house, the door being open, and there took refuge behind a chest."
>
> But the hounds came in and took the other side of the chest, so that Isobel only escaped by getting into another house, and gaining time to say the disenchanting rhyme:

Hare, hare, God send thee care!
I am in a hare's likeness now,
But I shall be a woman even now.
Hare, hare, God send thee care!

(Sir Walter Scott, *Demonology*, lightly edited)

A Protector Coyote
Mexico

The Franciscan friar Bernardino de Sahagún (1499-1590) has been described as the first anthropologist and the father of American ethnology. In his *Historia general de las cosas de Nueva España* [Mexico], he reported in Chapter 13 of Book Five ("auguries and prognostications"):

> [The Aztec god] Tezcatlipoca often transformed himself into an animal that they call coyote, which is like a wolf, which positioned itself in front of travellers as they went along the road, obstructing their way so that they could not proceed. In that way the traveller understood that some danger was ahead – thieves or robbers – or that some other misfortune would befall him if he continued along the road.

This is like the cadejo in the Benevolent Black Dogs section.

The Chullachaqui
Peru

"El Chullachaqui is a duende or demon of the jungle whose name comes from the Quechua term *chulla* (unequal) and *chaqui* (foot), that is, 'unequal feet'. According to popular belief, this jungle duende has the power to transform itself into any person, fooling the jungle inhabitant by presenting itself to him as a family member or friend, leading him through wrong paths and taking him farther into the jungle. The only way to discover that it is a Chullachaqui is by looking at its feet, which it tries to conceal, because when it is recognised it flees through the underbrush of the jungle." Mural in Spanish, Iquitos, Peru

This is my paraphrase of a story by editor Mike Collis that appeared in *Iquitos Times* in 2008.

In September 2007, Juan Maldonado was guiding ten tourists on a jungle trek. When they came to a clearing that had three paths leading out of it, Maldonado, though experienced, was baffled. Suddenly a young boy appeared and offered to lead them to his village, San Andrés, which was the group's destination. Maldonado gratefully accepted the offer. After an hour's walk, they arrived at another clearing from which three paths led. Maldonado turned to ask the boy which path they should take, but he had disappeared. The group blundered through the jungle for more than three hours until they came upon a village just as the light was fading. It was only three miles from San Andrés, which they reached by a river taxi. When Maldonado told the other taxi passengers about their ordeal, they laughed and explained that the boy was actually a Chullachaqui that had led them astray.

The Tue-Tue
Chile

The Tue-Tue (or Tue-Tué) is a wizard who has shape-shifted into the form of a bird of ill augury. It is named for its song – "tue-tue" – which you cannot repeat correctly unless you hear it, and hearing it means you are about to die or at least suffer misfortune. If you dream that the Tue-Tue is looking at someone close to you, that person is probably seriously ill. Some say that you can't see the Tue-Tue, only hear it, but drawings of the bird show it to be mid-sized and black with perhaps red eyes.

The Tue-Tue misleads those who insult it, so if you encounter it you should say, "Accompany me in good faith" or "Go your own way" or "May you go well."

Some people have challenged the Tue-Tue by inviting it for a meal or a cup of tea. A woman did that one morning, and in the afternoon a man dressed in black turned up at her house, drank a cup of tea and went away. A family was visited by a woman in black, who ate and drank water out of a melon rind and left in the middle of the night, warning the family not to invite unknown people.

A man in Quintay was walking one winter day, when he felt that he was being followed. He said, "Who are you?" and heard "Tue-tue-tue." He said, "If you are good, I invite you to take tea at my house tomorrow." The following day, a man dressed in black with gold teeth arrived. They drank tea without speaking until the visitor left. That is why in Quintay they recommend that you do not speak with strange birds.

However, if you do invite a Tue-Tue to your house and he comes, don't ignore him. Near Loncoche, a group of friends were working the land of their employer when they heard "Tue-tue." One of the men called out inviting it to his house for drinks and a roast. After work, the friends gathered for a party at the house of that man. They were eating and drinking when a strange farm hand approached and asked for a bit of meat. They were all well into the drink by then and they ignored him. Soon afterwards, they noticed that the stranger was no longer among them, and then they heard the woman of the house scream in horror. They entered the house and were startled to see a horrible black bird fly away crying, "Tue-tue." The infant of the couple was lying on the floor with its mouth filled with foam and black feathers scattered around its body.

A Tue-Tue appeared to a woman in Nancagua. She was angry and shouted at him that he should help her feed her children instead of going around causing trouble. The following day, a man appeared at her door dressed like a peasant. He said that he had come in response to the request she made the previous day. Realising her error in confronting the Tue-Tue, she slammed the door in his face. A few days later, she was going into the town on some errands, when she met the Tue-Tue again. This time she threw salt and cursed it, and the Tue-Tue shifted into a bird and flew away, never to return.

The Tue-Tue is often confused with the Chonchón. While the Tue-Tue is a shape-shifted wizard, the Chonchón is the head of a wizard that he has removed from his body by applying an ointment around his neck, and the ears act like wings to make it fly.

A Chilean studying English in Dublin introduced me to the Tue-Tue, but most of the details above are paraphrased from the portalparanormal.net website.

Shape-changers

The Black Pig's Dyke
Ireland

This is the way I tell this wide-spread tale in schools, with the introduction: "Do you want to hear a story about a *bad* teacher?" The answer is always a resounding "Yes", with a mischievous-guilty glance at the teacher, who always – so far – takes it in good humour.

There was once a schoolmaster who had the magic power to change people into animals by tapping them on the head with his wand. One day at the break, he changed the boys into hounds and the girls into hares, and the hounds chased the hares around the schoolyard until the end of the break, and then he changed them back into boys and girls.

At least they got a lot of exercise, but the children didn't like being changed into animals, and when they got home and their parents asked them why they were so tired, they told them what the schoolmaster had done. The parents didn't like that, either, and they went to a wise old woman to ask her advice. She told the parents what to do, and the parents told the children.

The following day, when the schoolmaster was about to change the boys and girls into hounds and hares, they asked him, "Master, can you change yourself into an animal?"

"Of course I can. What kind of animal do you want me to change into?"

"A pig."

So he tapped himself on the head with his magic wand and turned into a pig. But when he went to shift himself back into the schoolmaster, he couldn't. He had forgotten that pigs don't have fingers, and so he couldn't pick up the wand to tap himself on the head.

He was so angry that the children had tricked him that he ran all over Ireland, digging trenches with his tusks. So now where you see two ditches side by side, that is when he was running in a straight line with both tusks in the ground, and where you see only one ditch, that is when he was turning and had only one tusk in the ground.

He was running through Athlone, and as he was crossing the bridge over the River Shannon, a woman hit him on the head with a big wooden hammer and killed him.

Variants of the Black Pig's Dyke

These ditches are normally called the Worm's Ditch, the Dane's (or Danes') Cast, the Duncladh, and most often the Black Pig's Dyke. "The Glen of the Black Pig" is the name specific to the earthworks in the Counties Cavan-Monaghan-Meath area, where a great battle is to occur in the future, when, as James Gaynor told his folklore collector son, P. J., in the 1930s, "Old men would be turned three times in their beds, to see if they were fit to serve in the army." (NFC 792:392-95) The prolific Lord Walter Fitzgerald begins this piece by quoting O'Donovan's *Ordnance Survey Letters*:

> "The tradition about 'Gleann na muice duibhe' (ie. the Glen of the Black Pig) is the wildest I ever heard. A schoolmaster lived in Drogheda a long time ago, who used to work the magic art, and so turn his scholars into pigs. One day as they were playing in the field adjoining the schoolhouse, in this shape, O'Neill, who was hunting in that neighbourhood with a pack of hounds, observing the swine in the field, set the pack at them. The pigs immediately fled in various directions through the country, and formed those dykes called 'glen na muck duv,' which are to be seen in various parts of the south of Ulster. One pig made its way towards Lough Neagh, another faced west, and a third, which was being very

closely pursued, swam across Lough Mucshnamba at Castle Blayney, and gave it name, and then proceeded in the direction of Meath."

Not long ago [Fitzgerald continues], I myself heard from the lips of an aged man, named John Lynch (a native of the County Wexford), who was begging along the road, an "enchanted story" very similar to the one given by O'Donovan. His version of it was as follows:

"In the old ancient times there dwelt in a castle down in the north of Ireland a king, who employed a schoolmaster for the education of his two sons. This same king was notorious for his knowledge in witchcraft, whereby he possessed supernatural power.

"On one occasion, during the king's absence at a hurling-match, the schoolmaster and his two pupils entered the king's private room, though they had been forbidden to enter it on any pretext. On a table in it lay a great book: this the schoolmaster opened and commenced to read aloud from its pages, though he could not understand the meaning of what he read. After a short time he happened to look up from the book, and was amazed to see that, in place of his two pupils, two great shaggy hounds were present; in terror he fled from the room.

"On the king's return home in the evening, he was met near the castle by two strange hounds, which fawned on him, and bayed with delight at his arrival. In perplexity the king proceeded hot-foot to his room, and on seeing the open book guessed what had occurred.

"In a rage he sent for the schoolmaster, transformed him into a big black boar, and driving him from the castle with the assistance of his camaun (or hurly), set the two hounds at him. The boar fled for its life. Crossing the Boyne it ran through Meath to Maynooth, on past Kildare into the County Carlow, then away through the country lying between the Barrow and the Slaney, until it reached Priests-haggard in the County Wexford, where the two hounds eventually killed it.

> They then returned home the same way they came and were transformed by the king back again into their human form."
>
> (Verbatim: Fitzgerald, "The Race ...".)

Midir and Étaín
Ireland

This story is found in the 12th-century *Lebor na hUidre* (Book of the Dun Cow), the 14th-century *Yellow Book of Lecan* (YBL) and other manuscripts. The text is in Middle Irish, date range AD 900-1200.

The last of five occupations of Ireland was that of the Iron Age Celtic Milesians from Spain. With their iron weapons, they defeated the resident Bronze Age Tuatha Dé Danann in spite of the Dananns' magic powers, and relegated them to the natural hills and the mounds they constructed for themselves. Such a mound is called a *sídh*, and the Dananns became known as the people of the Sídh (pronounced "shee", often spelled Sidhe) or Sídh people.

Midir was a Sídh lord whose home mound, Brí Léith, was on Slieve Golry west of Ardagh in County Longford. One day he decided to look for a wife, and he searched through all the worlds that were open to him until he found Étaín (pronunciation and alternative spelling: Aideen) daughter of Ailill, the most beautiful woman in all the worlds that he had travelled. "She was surely the fairest, loveliest and best-formed of all the women in the world that eyes had ever seen." (YBL)

They fell in love, he brought her back to Ireland in this world, they were married, and they spent a year-long honeymoon with Midir's foster-son, Angus, at Brú na Bóinne (Newgrange). Then Midir took Étaín home to Brí Léith, and that's when the trouble started. For Midir already had a wife, Fuamnach, who was not pleased with the competition. "She struck Étaín with a wand of purple rowan and turned her into a pool of water, and then she and Midir left the house to go their separate ways. The heat of the fire and air and the boiling of the ground turned the pool into a worm, which became a purple fly the size of a man's head." (YBL) The most beautiful woman in the land was now the most beautiful fly in the land.

"Melodious were the sounds of pipes and harps and horns that emanated from the humming of her wings. Her eyes shone like gems in the dark. The scent and radiance she brought with her would turn away hunger and thirst, and disease and illness and plague sores were healed by the dew that dropped from her wings wherever she went. She accompanied Midir at gatherings, and her presence nourished him and all who were there. Midir knew that the purple fly was Étaín, and he would be lulled to sleep by her melodies." (YBL)

Fuamnach was also aware of the continuing relationship, and one day she came to Midir accompanied by three gods of the Tuatha Dé Danann, Lugh and the Dagda and Ogma, for protection. She called up a magic wind that sent Étaín into the air for seven years, with no place to settle but the rocks of the sea and the stormy waves. At the end of the term, Étaín landed on the chest of Angus, who sheltered her until Fuamnach once again managed to send her away on the air for seven years. Angus tracked down Fuamnach and cut off her head.

Étaín finally landed in the rafters of the house of Étar of Inber Cíchmaine in Ulster and fell into his wife's cup just as she was about to drink. The woman unknowingly swallowed the purple fly, and nine months later she gave birth to a girl who they named Étaín. One thousand and twelve years had passed since the first birth in the Otherworld of the daughter of Ailill who Midir married, but the daughter of Étar in this world had no memory of her past life.

Midir had been searching for Étaín through all the worlds open to him, and he happened to be in this world one day when he spotted the adolescent Étaín playing with friends by a river. Now that he knew who and where she was, he determined to return when she was older so he could reclaim her as his wife.

Eochaid Airem, King of Ireland, was not married. The nobles refused to attend the Feast of Tara with their wives and daughters until he had a queen, so he sent servants out across Ireland until they found the perfect match for a king. They located Étaín daughter of Étar, and Eochaid married her.

Time does not exist in the Otherworld where the people of the Sídh live, and Midir miscalculated Étaín's coming of age, so when he returned to this world it was at the post-wedding party that he found her. He claimed a dance with the bride, and while they were dancing he said, "Étaín, do you remember me?"

"No. I've never seen you before in my life."

"Perhaps not in this life, but …" And he explained about their previous marriage and how Fuamnach had magicked her away.

"Well, I believe you, but I have no memory of that, and I'm sorry for you, but I'm married to Eochaid now."

"What would it take for you to leave Eochaid and come with me?"

That made her angry.

"I would only leave Eochaid and come with you if Eochaid gave me to you."

Midir left it at that.

Also at the party, Eochaid's brother Ailill Ánguba ("Faultless") fell in love with Étaín, but, being a man of honour, he said nothing. However, his longing made him ill. A wise doctor found nothing physically amiss and made a shrewd guess at the cause of the problem. He told Ailill: "There are two fatal illnesses that no physician can cure: the pain of love and the pain of jealousy." Ailill kept his secret and prepared to die, for which he is called "Faultless".

Eochaid had to take a tour of the country to make sure the sub-kings were behaving themselves, and he asked Étaín to watch over Ailill and make the funeral arrangements if necessary. While she was tending him one day, she noticed the way he was staring at her and guessed the cause. Ailill confirmed her diagnosis. Her wifely duties included saving the life of her husband's brother, she decided, "But not in the house, so as not to shame the king."

They arranged to meet in a nearby cottage late that night, but at the agreed hour Ailill suddenly fell asleep. A man with the appearance of Ailill turned up. Étaín challenged him.

"Who are you that comes here in the form of Ailill but isn't Ailill?"

The man gave no reply but walked away. The same thing happened the following night and the next. On the fourth night, Étaín managed to make him answer. It was Midir.

"It would be more fitting for you to lie with me than with Eochaid or Ailill," he said. And he explained again about their being married, and that Ailill wasn't really in love with her but was under Midir's spell to create the opportunity for this meeting, because if he could only get her into bed something might happen to jog her memory.

"I don't remember any of that life, and I'm a different person now and I'm married to Eochaid and I love him and I'm sorry for you, and that's that."

"What would it take for you to leave Eochaid and come with me?"

"As I told you before, I'd only leave Eochaid and go with you if Eochaid gave me to you."

"Very well," said Midir, and he went away. So Étaín kept her honour, and Ailill recovered from his illness and maintained his faultlessness.

Some time later, Eochaid was standing on the ramparts of the Hill of Tara in the royal province of Meath, looking west over the ever-misty central plain of Ireland, when he saw a strange man in a purple tunic approaching.

"Good day to you, Eochaid," said the man.

"Good day to you, sir. You know my name, but I don't know yours."

"It's not famous: Midir of Brí Léith. I've heard that you're a champion fidchell player."

(Fidchell is a board game like chess.)

"I am. Do you play fidchell?"

"I do. That's why I've come here."

"What stakes do you want to play for? I always play for stakes."

"The winner names his prize," said Midir.

"Oh, that's very sporting. I like that."

They played, and Eochaid won.

"What is promised is due," said Midir. "What do you want for your prize?"

"Twelve black horses with silver bridles and gold saddles."

"They will be here in the morning."

Eochaid woke up to see Midir with the twelve horses, silver and gold bridled and saddled.

"Will we play again?" said Midir. "Same stakes: winner names his prize?"

Eochaid agreed, and again he won.

"What is promised is due," said Midir. "What do you want for your prize?"

"I have enough horses now. I would like you to clear the stones from the fields of Meath."

"It will be done," said Midir, "with my people's help. But you must promise that none of your people will watch our work."

Eochaid promised, but he sent servants to spy on Midir. They reported that Midir's people put collars on their horses to drag the stones; Eochaid's people had always tied a rope to the horses' tails to pull the plough. They recommended Midir's more efficient method, so Eochaid taught his people how to use the horse collars, and that is why he is known as Eochaid Airem – Eochaid the Ploughman. The fields of the now-reduced county of Meath are free of stones, so we know that part of the story really happened.

But Midir noticed Eochaid's people spying on him, and he didn't like it.

The following day, Midir came to Eochaid and suggested another match with the same stakes. Eochaid won. He wanted Midir to build a road across a bog in the west of Meath province, Móin Lámraige, that separated two villages. Midir accepted the task, "but no spying this time".

But during the work on the road, Midir noticed Eochaid's spies again. He complained to Eochaid, saying that he felt he had fulfilled the bargain and in protest would leave the road unfinished. Wetlands archaeologist Barry Raftery discovered an unfinished bog road in Móin Lámraige in 1984 called the Corlea Trackway, and both he and folklorist Dáithí Ó hÓgáin told me they were sure that this was the same road in the Midir and Étaín tale.

They played another match. Midir won.

"What is promised is due," said Eochaid. "What do you want for your prize?"

"Your wife, Étaín."

Eochaid wasn't expecting that, but a promise is a promise, and a king can't be seen to break his word or welch on a bet. He thought quickly.

"Come back in a month, and you may take her if you can."

Midir returned a month later to find the king's palace surrounded by warriors and filled by them. They made way as he walked into the palace and up to the dais where Eochaid and Étaín stood.

"What is promised is due. I've come for my prize."

"I believe I said you *may* take her if you *can*," said Eochaid with a triumphant grin.

Midir wrapped one arm around Étaín, and they both rose through the smoke-hole in the roof in the form of two swans linked by a golden chain. Eochaid and the warriors rushed out of the palace to see them fly away to the west, and they followed as fast as they could.

Eochaid now understood that Midir was a Sídh lord, and he ordered his men to begin digging at the first mound they came to. The owner of the mound came out and demanded to know what they were doing. They told him what had happened. He played a popular Irish game known as "Send the Fool Farther" and directed them to the next mound west. And so did the owner of that mound, and the next, until Eochaid and his men had spent nineteen years excavating mounds.

Finally they arrived at Brí Léith, but before they could start digging, Midir came out and said, "I know what you've come for. I'll bring Étaín out, and you may take her back if you can identify her."

The memory of her face had never left Eochaid through the years of searching, she was the most beautiful woman in Ireland, she had been in the Otherworld for the past nineteen years, where the Sídh people never aged – of course he would recognise her.

But then Midir brought out fifty women, all looking exactly like the Étaín who Eochaid remembered. How to pick out the right one? He recalled a certain way she held her little finger aloft when she poured a drink, and he asked each of the women to serve a beverage to him. Only one had that unique habit with the finger.

"This is Étaín," he said with satisfaction.

"That's right, Eochaid," said Midir. "You may take her with you."

They lived happily for nine months, and then Étaín presented Eochaid with a baby girl they named Étaín. Friends and family came to admire the new addition, but what surprised Eochaid was the arrival of Midir to offer his congratulations.

"That's a lovely daughter you have, Eochaid. You must be very proud of yourself."

"I am."

"I have a question: is your mind at ease with me?"

"It is."

"And mine with you. By the way, did you not wonder why your new child's mother was the same age as she was when you lost her to me?"

"No. I assumed that since she had been in your mound for nineteen years, like you Otherworld people she would not have aged."

"Not so. Étaín is human in her present incarnation, and she has aged nineteen years like any human. She was pregnant when I took her. The Étaín who is the mother of your child is your daughter Étaín, and you have lost your wife to me a second time."

With that, Midir disappeared.

For Eochaid's unwitting incest and his destruction of the mounds, people of the Sídh took out their revenge on his son/grandson, King Conaire the Great, whose downfall is recounted in The Destruction of Dá Derga's Hostel.

Because it suits certain agendas, some people insist that Étaín was turned into a butterfly, but the Middle Irish version in the 15th-century *Yellow Book of Lecan*, the oldest one extant, has *cuil corcrai*, "purple fly". "Butterfly" is *etelachán* (literally "a little flying creature": by extension, a butterfly) or *dalán dé*, which could be interpreted as "the image of breath as the principle of life", satisfying the urge for mystical significance. Ref. YBL and eDIL

Bran and Sceolán
Ireland

Tuireann was the younger sister of Muirne, the mother of Fionn mac Cumhaill, leader of the elite band of warriors known as the Fianna. Both women were famed for their beauty. Illann, a member of the Fianna, fell in love with Tuireann and asked Fionn, who was head of the family since his father was dead, for permission to marry her.

"You may," said Fionn, "on this condition: you promise to look after her well and keep her safe. If anything happens to her, I'll cut off your head."

Illann promised, and they were married. But there was a problem. Illann had a lover in the Otherworld, Uchtdealb (Fair Breast), who he had not visited since he met Tuireann. Uchtdealb's friends began teasing her: "We haven't seen your mortal lover, Illann, for a while. Perhaps he's forgotten about you or been unfaithful, as mortal men often are, and he's married a woman of his world."

It made Uchtdealb angry to hear that, mainly because she had been thinking the same thing. So she travelled to this world to see what the story was – and it was true: he had forgotten about his fairy sweetheart and married Tuireann.

Revenge is a dish best tasted hot, she decided, and she quickly gathered several relevant pieces of information.

Fionn loved dogs and often gave some of the finest specimens in his collection to people he favoured.

Fergus Fionnliath, a lord in Galway, hated dogs with a passion and would throw a stone at any dog that ventured within reach. He rewarded his servants when they managed to hit one.

Tuireann was frequently left in the house with only the servants for company when Illann was away on Fianna duties.

So Uchtdealb shape-shifted into the form of Fionn's famously speedy female messenger, Dear Dhubh (Black Streak), and knocked on the door when she saw that Illann was out. Tuireann recognised the familiar face and had no reason to be suspicious.

"Fionn mac Cumhaill has invited you to a feast," Uchtdealb said, "and you have to come with me now."

If Tuireann was surprised at this last-minute invitation, she didn't show it, and she willingly followed Uchtdealb. As soon as they were out of sight of any curious servants, Uchtdealb took out her wand and struck Tuireann on the head. In place of a beautiful woman, there now stood a beautiful wolfhound, eyes wide in fear and astonishment as Uchtdealb put a collar around her neck and fastened a leash to it.

"Bad girl, bad dog," said Uchtdealb, lashing her with the end of the leash. "I'll show you what happens when you steal another woman's man."

Glimmers of comprehension began to peek through the cloud of Tuireann's confusion. Her legs started to tremble.

"Do you know who Fergus Fionnliath is, bad dog?"

Tuireann knew of him.

"And do you know what he thinks of dogs?"

Tuireann had heard.

"So where do you suppose I'm taking you?"

Tuireann was now shaking uncontrollably. She couldn't speak, but the fairy woman's words were perfectly clear.

"Yes, I see you understand, bad girl. I can't think of a better punishment for a man-stealer."

The one-sided conversation continued in this vein until they reached Galway and the house of Fergus.

A servant opened the door to Uchtdealb's knock.

"Come in," he said, "but you have to leave the dog outside."

"I can't do that," Uchtdealb said. "The dog is the reason I've come. It's a gift for Master Fionnliath from Fionn mac Cumhaill."

The servant went into the house, and Fergus Fionnliath came to the door. He scowled when he saw the dog.

"My man was speaking gibberish. What's this about Fionn mac Cumhaill? And what's that thing doing here?"

"Fionn has sent this dog as a gift to you."

"Impossible. Fionn knows – everyone knows – how I hate dogs."

"That's not my affair. I'm only following Fionn's orders."

"Well, I can't afford to insult Fionn by refusing his gift. Bring it in and give it to my servants, but keep it away from me."

Uchtdealb deposited Tuireann with a servant and left, smug and satisfied. Fergus stomped into the house and made sure the staff knew that they were to take care that no harm came to the new resident, or Fionn would be angry. But the malign presence of the dog-hater was even more frightening than the abuse from Uchtdealb, and alarming convulsions of fear took over Tuireann's body.

"What's wrong with that animal?" said Fergus.

"She seems to be nervous," replied a servant who was stroking the dog to calm her.

"Well, pet it or whatever you do with them, or it will shake its legs off, and Fionn won't be pleased."

"I've been doing that, sir, and it makes no difference. Perhaps if you were to stroke her head to reassure her that she's safe."

"Me? Pet a dog? Well, all right, just enough so it doesn't fall apart and make Fionn annoyed with me."

Fergus passed a hand lightly through the fur on Tuireann's head, and the quivering decreased noticeably.

"That seems to help," said the servant encouragingly.

Fergus passed a hand more slowly and firmly through the fur. The quivering decreased. Another stroke, this time on the head and down the neck. Less quivering. The next stroke went over the dog's back, and Fergus, much to his surprise, discovered that the warm, soft fur felt pleasurable to his hand. He did it again and again, and Tuireann stopped quivering and tentatively licked his hand. He jerked it away, but then the meaning behind the lick sank in. The beast liked him, at least a little. With more petting and hand-licking, he had to admit that he was beginning to like the dog – a little.

After this continued for a while, he issued new orders to his staff: no one was to throw stones at dogs, especially this one, or it would mean instant dismissal. Tuireann had become the apple of his eye, the sunrise of his days, the moonlight of his nights.

We are not told if Tuireann knew she was pregnant when she was snatched by Uchtdealb, but it was not long after she arrived at Fergus's house that she gave birth to twin puppies, a female and a male named Bran and Sceolán.

Meanwhile, Fionn noticed that he hadn't seen Tuireann recently, and he asked Illann where she was.

"I don't know."

Fionn looked meaningfully at Illann's head.

"We had an agreement about the risk to your head if Tuireann came to any harm."

"I remember. I think I know where I can find out what happened."

He went to the Otherworld and explained his dilemma to Uchtdealb.

"And I think you might know where she is," he concluded.

"The last time I saw her was when I delivered her to Fergus Fionnliath in the form of a wolfhound, which I put on her. I'm sure she's being well looked after by Fergus," she said with a wicked grin.

"Well, Fionn is going to have my head if I don't bring her back in human form very soon."

"Umm. So, if I save your head, then your head will belong to me?"

"I suppose so."

"And if your head belongs to me, so does the rest of you."

"I suppose so."

"Do you promise that you will leave Tuireann and come to live here with me if I put her proper shape on her?"

"I promise."

"Very well, then."

Uchtdealb went to Fergus's house and changed Tuireann back to human form, but there was nothing she could do about the puppies. So Fionn adopted his four-legged cousins, and they became his favourite hounds, partaking in many of his adventures as heroically as any member of the Fianna.

Fionn only cried three times in his life: at the death of his grandson Oscar, at the re-taking of Sadhbh by the Dark Druid (see next story), and when Bran died. Bran was chasing a deer that Fionn thought might be the transformed Sadhbh, and fearing that Bran didn't recognise Sadhbh and would kill her, Fionn called to the hound. When she passed between his legs he squeezed them together and crushed her. She is said to be buried under Carnawaddy (*carn an mhadaidh*, mound of the dog), on one of the peaks (528m) of Carlingford Mountain on the Cooley Peninsula in County Louth.

Sadhbh
Ireland

Sadhbh in deer form playing with Bran and Sceolán. Illustration by Arthur Rackham from Irish Fairy Tales *by James Stephens, 1920.*

According to the traditional tale, a Dark Druid shape-changed Sadhbh (pronounced "sive") into a deer, because she rejected his offer of love. She found refuge with Fionn mac Cumhaill, which broke the spell, and she appeared in her natural beautiful human form to become the love of his life. Later, the Dark Druid caught her and changed her back into a deer and took her with him to the Otherworld. She was pregnant, and when she gave birth to her and Fionn's son, Oisín (Little Deer), the child was left in this world to be reared by Fionn. Oisín became a poet and the chronicler of the deeds of Fionn and the Fianna. A later tale says that he never died. He managed to find his way to the Otherworld to be with his mother.

Canadian Young Adult author Holly Bennett felt that Sadhbh was not shape-changed, but that she shape-shifted herself to escape the druid. Holly's fast-paced 2010 novel *Shapeshifter* tells her version of the story with a strong and resourceful heroine in place of a victim.

The Children of Lir
One of the Three Sorrowful Tales of Ireland

Bobh Derg, son of the Dagda, was elected chief of the godlike Tuatha Dé Danann. Lir of Sídh Fionnachaidh (Sliab Fuaid) in County Armagh had been a contender for the position, and to console him Bobh Derg offered his foster daughter Aobh for a wife. Aobh bore the twins Fionnuala, a girl, and Aed, a boy, and later died giving birth to the twin boys Fiachra and Conn. Bobh Derg offered Lir his other foster daughter, Aoife, Aobh's sister, for a wife.

Everyone loved the four Children for their engaging personalities and their sweet singing voices. Aoife also loved them and was a good stepmother for a time, but eventually, having no children of her own, she became jealous of their popularity and decided to get rid of them. She didn't have the heart to kill them, but she took them on what she said was a visit to their Great-uncle Bobh Derg. She stopped at Lough Derravaragh in County Westmeath and changed them into swans.

Fionnuala, the eldest, protested at the injustice of this, and Aoife relented so far as to stipulate that they would remain in the form of swans for 300 years on Lough Derravaragh, 300 years on the Sea of Moyle between Ireland and Scotland, and 300 years on the Western Sea off the Mayo coast. They retained their human intelligence and voices.

When Lir discovered what had happened, he complained to Bobh Derg, who ordered Aoife to come before him.

"What is the punishment you dread most?" he asked her.

"To be changed into a demon of the air," she said.

So that's what he did.

Lir and Bobh Derg and all the people of Ireland used to gather on the shores of Lough Derravaragh to listen to the Children sing, but after 300 years the Children were forced by Aoife's spell to move to the stormy Sea of Moyle, and after another 300 years to the wind-swept Western Sea. Inishglora, a small (100 acres; 0.4057 km^2) island off the

Belmullet Peninsula in Mayo, was their home until one day they heard a church bell. Christianity had arrived in Ireland.

They followed the sound of the bell and met with a disciple of Saint Patrick, to whom they told their story. He baptised them, and this broke Aoife's spell. As they changed back into human form, they immediately fell down and died of extreme old age.

That is the image depicted in Oisín Kelly's 1971 massive sculpture in the Garden of Remembrance in Parnell Square in Dublin. Lough Derravaragh is still a popular home for swans.

Deirdre Sullivan's 2020 YA novel *Savage Her Reply* tells this story from Aoife's point of view.

Gulbán
Ireland

Fionn mac Cumhaill and Donn Ó Donnchadha spent a night at the palace of the sun god Angus, which is nowadays called Newgrange. Donn's son, Diarmuid, was the foster son of Angus and lived in the palace. Angus's steward, Roc, had a son named Gulbán. The boys were half-brothers, having the same mother. The people at the palace paid more attention to Gulbán than to Diarmuid, and this offended Donn.

Two of Fionn's hounds began fighting, and as the men stood in a circle watching, the boys tried to escape the commotion by crawling through the men's legs. It happened that Gulbán went in Donn's direction, and as he was crawling between his legs, Donn squeezed them tightly around the boy, killing him.

He tried to blame the dogs, but Angus inspected the body and found no tooth-marks, and he went into a trance and discovered the truth. When he announced that Donn had killed Gulbán, the boy's father, Roc, took out his magic wand and brought Gulbán back to life, but since he couldn't put human life into him again the boy became a wild boar.

Then Roc put geasa (effectively a curse) on both boys: that they would be the death of each other.

Gulbán ran off to live on the mountain Ben Bulben in County Sligo.

That is the prelude to the long, action-packed tale called The Pursuit of Diarmuid and Gráinne. A marriage between Fionn and King Cormac mac Airt's daughter, Gráinne, was arranged, but when Gráinne saw the well-matured Fionn for the first time at the wedding ceremony, she decided that young, handsome Diarmuid would be more suitable for her. She put geasa (in this case an honour-bound injunction) on the reluctant Diarmuid to run away with her. Fionn chased them around Ireland for a year and a day until Angus brokered a peace between them.

But Fionn still brooded over the affair. Many years later, he organised a boar hunt at Ben Bulben in which Diarmuid felt obliged to take part. Fionn well knew what was likely to happen. Roc's curse was fulfilled: Gulbán and Diarmuid encountered and killed each other.

Cursed to Be Wolves
Galicia, Spain

In the lands of Viana do Bolo (Ourense), a man had raised his daughter in the greatest luxury and planned to marry her to a rich and noble cousin. But she was in love with the shepherd of her father's flocks and wanted to marry him.

Her father discovered this and locked her in a dungeon. Her lover rescued her and they fled. When the father found out, he set off in pursuit but failed to catch them. In frustration, he cursed his daughter that she would be turned into a wolf, which happened immediately.

Once she was transformed into a wolf, her first victim was her lover, whose death she lamented pitifully on recovering her human form. Embittered with life and terrible in her ferocity, she killed people and animals for pleasure and relief, bloodying herself with her father's flocks. All the hunters of the kingdom gathered and pursued her for several days, finally managing to surround her. They fired several shots that did her no harm, but from that day forth she disappeared forever.

(Close translation from Prieto.)

A girl in Trives persistently asked her mother for meat. Exasperated, her mother said, "May you turn into a wolf so that you will never be full." She disappeared covered with fur like a wolf and caused much damage. One day she came into a chestnut grove where a young man was working. He was scared and climbed into a tree, then was surprised when she shed her pelt and he saw that underneath was a beautiful girl. He took a long stick and picked up the pelt and threw it into a fire. She tried to retrieve it but was too late, and the pelt burned up. This returned her to her human senses. She told him everything that had happened, and they got married.

(Mosquera Paans)

Variation: He was going to throw it into the fire, but she objected and said that she had to wear it for seven years as a result of her mother's curse. Then she told him what had happened, and that she had to devour a sister and a cousin because of the curse.

(From *Contos Galegos* by Noia Campos. Aquilina Arias Rey, aged 86, from Rubiais-Viana do Bolo, Ourense, told her the story in 1998.)

One autumn, a young man from Sobrado named Ánxel was stripping leaves off a chestnut tree to make fertiliser. A neighbour told him he should go home, because a wolf was attacking people in the vicinity. He went home and barred the door and sat by the fireplace. Soon he heard a scratching at the door, and when the claw of an animal appeared he hid.

A wolf entered and looked around, and when it felt assured that it was alone, it peeled off its skin to reveal a beautiful young woman dressed only in a shirt. Ánxel used a long stick to pick up the skin and throw it in the fire.

The woman told him that his action broke a spell. Her father had died, and her mother remarried. The man abused her, and in defence she stabbed him in the hand with a sickle. Her mother evicted her with a curse that she would be changed into a wolf. Ánxel married her.

(That is a summary of Risco's literary folk tale "O lobo da xente".)

Many years ago in the mountains of Cervantes in Lugo, there lived a rough-natured man who was easily annoyed and never hesitated to curse what he disapproved of. He had a son who was much attracted to women and partying and not fond of work.

One day the father wanted the son to plough up a new field on the mountain, and the son wanted to go to the festival in Pedrafita.

"It's a sin to work on a festival day," said the son. "If the field doesn't get ploughed one day it will get ploughed another day, but if you miss the festival it's gone."

"When there's work to do, you don't go to a festival," insisted the father.

Neither would give in, and finally the father lost his temper and said, "All right, go to the festival, then, and may God grant that just as you follow the women so may you follow the wolves."

In bed that night, the young man lay awake restless, until he finally got up, put on his clothes and went outside. He felt a strange impulse to climb the mountain, and when he reached a meadow he rolled in the dewy grass, not knowing why he did it. When he stood up he found that he was on four legs, not two, and he ran to the summit howling like a wolf and joined the other wolves.

In the village, the people spoke about the disappearance of the man and also of a large wolf that had killed and injured many sheep and lambs. The father recalled his curse and wondered if it could be his son. He explained the situation to an old woman who was said to be a witch.

"Yes," she said. "The curse of a father is the worst. A father should never curse his own blood. But if that wolf is your son, there is a way to change him back to human. However, it's not easy, and one of you could die, since in his wild form he has lost all human sense."

"What do I have to do?"

"Make him bleed, but not enough to kill him or cause serious injury, because he will carry that injury when he regains his human form."

The father decided that he would rather be dead than to leave his son in the form of a wolf. He got a knife and carried a lamb up the mountain and tied it to a gorse bush and hid behind it.

At midnight the lamb became agitated and he guessed that the wolf was nearby. Then the wolf was at the lamb and sinking its teeth into its flesh without noticing that the father was creeping closer. Careful not to wound too much, he stuck the knife into the wolf's back and immediately threw it on the ground. The wolf turned around, showing its teeth. The man wrapped his arms around the wolf's neck and called out sobbing, "Son, son, forgive me."

The wolf's skin began to open at the wound and detached itself from the body, and the son recovered his human form.

(Collected by Carré Alvarellos in 1953.)

Werewolves of Ossory
Ireland

> The descendants of the wolf are in Ossory [modern County Kilkenny and part of County Laois]. They have a wonderful property. They transform themselves into wolves, and go forth in the form of wolves, and if they happen to be killed with flesh in their mouths, it is in the same condition that the bodies out of which they have come will be found; and they command their families not to remove their bodies, because if they were moved, they could never come into them again.
>
> (Nennius, 11th century)

The travel writer Gerald of Wales visited Ireland in 1183 and 1185 and published his anti-Irish *Topography of Ireland* in 1187, based on first-hand observations, written sources, probably including Nennius, and storytellers of varying credibility. But where Nennius said "they transform themselves," which would make them shape-shifters, Gerald reports that they were shape-changed by a saint. This is his account, part quoted and part paraphrased, of "the wolf who spoke with a priest."

Shortly before Gerald's 1183 visit, a priest was travelling through the province of Meath. He camped one night, and as he sat next to his fire a wolf approached and said, "Don't be afraid. There is nothing to fear." The priest asked him to explain what sort of creature he was who in the form of a beast spoke human words.

"My wife and I are natives of Ossory," said the wolf. "Through a curse by Saint Natalis the abbot, a man and a woman of Ossory are made to take the shape of wolves every seven years for a period of seven years. If the couple survives, they are returned to human form, and another couple takes their place. Now my wife lies sick not far from here, and she is close to death. I beseech you to perform your priestly functions for her."

The priest followed the wolf to a nearby tree, where he found a wolf moaning and lamenting. When she saw him, she greeted him and gave thanks to God in human language, and he administered the Last Rites. She asked him to give her Holy Communion, but he said he did not have consecrated hosts with him. The male wolf pointed out the priest's missal in a pouch hanging from his neck, which contained a few unconsecrated hosts. When the priest hesitated, the he-wolf used his claws to peel back the skin of the she-wolf all the way from her head to her navel, exposing her human body. Seeing this, the priest gave her communion more out of fear than reason, and the he-wolf rolled back her skin the way it had been.

In the morning, the man-wolf led the priest to the correct road and thanked him for performing his office for his wife.

The Swine of Drebrenn
Ireland

Drebrenn was a sister of Queen Maeve of Connacht and daughter of Eochaidh Feidlach, first-century BC King of Ireland. She was also the lover of Angus son of the Dagda, who still lives at Brú na Bóinne (Newgrange). She had three foster sisters who were married to three brothers. The girls' mother, Garbhdalbh (Coarse-face), did not approve of the matches, and one day when the three couples were gathering nuts in the woods near Tara, she transformed them into demon pigs.

Their names in pig form were Crainchrin, Coelcheis and Treilech for the women and Fraechan, Banban and Brogarban for the men. Like the Children of Lir, the pigs retained their human reason and speech. They went to live with Buchet, who was a guesthouse-keeper at Kilranelagh Hill in County Wicklow and famed for his hospitality. After a year, Buchet's wife "was seized with longing for a steak off Brogarban's belly". From the *Metrical Dindshenchas*:

> It was a grief to Brogarban of Brega
> when the woman's husband told him of it:
> "Let us slay the white woman,"
> said Buichet to Brogarban.
>
> "No evil hath thy wife deserved of me,"
> said then the white-flanked swine:
> "if she desire a steak of my tender flesh,
> she shall have it for thy sake, brave warrior!"
>
> She mustered – foolish was the woman –
> a hundred warriors, a hundred dogs followed them,
> a hundred spears, a hundred shields sharp-edged,
> it was for the killing of Brogarban.
>
> Brogarban of Borg Brain destroyed them
> by his unaided prowess,
> and he spared the woman
> for the sake of Buichet, whose wife she was.
> (Gwynn)

Brogarban then led the other Swine to Brú na Bóinne, where they stayed under the protection of Angus, and then they were with Drebrenn at Glascarn (possibly near Mullingar) for a year. According to the story of the naming of Mag Mucrame (The Plain of Pig-counting) in County Galway, they broke out of the Cave of Cruachan in County Roscommon, an Otherworld portal from which monsters in various forms regularly issued, to embark on a seven-year rampage that laid waste to Ireland: wherever they went, nothing would grow again behind them.

The Swine could not be caught or killed. If a spear was thrown or a sword swung at them, they disappeared. No one could accurately count them until one day Queen Maeve and her consort, Ailill, came to the plain thenceforth known as Mag Mucrame –

> to hunt them and number them aright:
> and they were found upon the bright sands
> in their lairs in Mag Fráich.
>
> The hunters set to chase them one by one,
> and to count them right heedfully;
> to Maeve at Belach na Fert
> they were brought all together at a marsh.
>
> One pig, deer-like in hue, made a spring,
> and Maeve caught hold of his strong foot,
> and with the haste of danger he left
> his skin in one of her hands.
> (Gwynn)

This broke the pigs' magic power, making it possible to count them. Five were pursued to various parts of the country and killed where place-names commemorate them. And so "they all fell save Brogarban, and their five heads were brought to that mound [near the Cave of Cruachan]. Whence *Dumae Selga* [The Mound of the Hunt]." (Stokes, "The Rennes Dindshenchas")

What became of Brogarban if he was not killed is nowhere mentioned, but alternatively:

> … Glascharn:
> the six trenches thou seest on the hill,
> they are the beds of the warrior-swine.
> (Gwynn)

The Cave of Cruachan is also known as Oweynagat. See "The Cave of the Cat" in the Cats section.

Shape-changed to a Horse
Scotland

Soon after two brothers started working as apprentices to the blacksmith of Yarrowfoot, the younger lad grew pale and lean, lost his appetite, and was constantly tired. Questioned by his brother, he explained that the blacksmith's wife came to him at night, threw a bridle on him, and changed him into a horse.

"She rides me to the moors, where she attends feasts with all sorts of vile creatures, and then she rides me home again, leaving me so weary I can hardly stand."

They were sharing a bed, and they switched sides so that the following night the woman threw the bridle on the older brother and turned him into a horse, which she rode to the home of a neighbouring lord. She left him in a stable, and while she cavorted with her companions in the wine cellar, he rubbed his head against the wall until the bridle fell off. That broke the spell, and he waited in his human form for the woman to return. When she did, he threw the bridle over her head, transforming her into a fine grey mare, which he mounted.

He rode her through hedges and ditches, and when her gait faltered he looked down and saw that the shoe had come off a fore hoof. He found a blacksmith who was open early and had both of her fore hooves shod with iron shoes. Then he galloped her at speed around a ploughed field until she could barely walk and finally took her home just before her husband woke up.

In bed, with the bridle off and returned to human form, she told her husband she felt ill, and he sent for a doctor, who wanted to feel her pulse. She refused to show her hands. The blacksmith pulled the bed covers off, revealing the iron horseshoes nailed to her hands and the bruises and welts on her side where the apprentice had kicked and goaded her during their late-night exercise in the ploughed field.

The brothers told their story, and the woman was tried and condemned to be burned to death. The younger lad was restored to health by eating butter made with milk from cows that grazed in the churchyard, which is the cure for one who has been witch-ridden.

(Henderson)

Nicholas the Fish and Other Amphibians
Spain

Don Quijote and Sancho Panza constitute a joint repository of folk wisdom and general knowledge and the proverbs related to historical events up to the 17th century. A poet asked Don Quijote what science he had studied.

"Knight-errantry," replied the Knight of the Doleful Countenance.

"I don't know what science that is," said the poet.

"It's a science that encompasses all the other sciences in the world. A knight-errant has to [long list of qualifications, including] … know how to swim as well as they say Nicholas the Fish did ..."

Nicholas was a sturdy lad living on the north coast of Majorca with a strong desire to swim in the sea. Those who knew him said he was a better swimmer than the fish. But he gave such free rein to his inclination that his mother, fed up with worrying over his absences, one day said in exasperation, "I hope you turn into a fish."

And so he became a fish from the waist down. This presented the family with two problems. They had to buy a large tank so he could keep his bottom half immersed in water, and when they took him to the sea every day they had to use a cart because he had no legs.

He soon acquired an intimate knowledge of the waters from the beaches to the depths. He learned how to draw navigation maps and made a living by selling them to the fishermen. But there was one area that was especially deep and apparently crossed by a treacherous current that had caused many shipwrecks. He resolved to explore it, partly to make a map and partly to overcome a nagging fear that he felt was unbecoming for a person of his abilities.

His friends and family were aware of the dangers and stood firmly against the venture, but Nicholas gave them the slip and managed to drag himself to the sea. They watched him swim away and kept vigil for the rest of the day and the following day. On the third day they saw a sudden plume of blood well up from the depths and briefly form a red stain on the surface until it disappeared.

A point on the coast is locally known as Sa Nicolaua in memory of the young man.

That and the following stories are a good example of why Juan García Atienza, author of *Magical Legends of Spain*, is an ideal collector and disseminator of legends: taking a well-judged stance between credulity and scepticism, he doesn't completely *dis*believe the tales. After all, a legend is by definition a story based on a real person or a factual event or both.

A woman ran out of patience with her daughter, Serena, for constantly swimming and not helping with the housework, and she cursed her that she would be a fish.

A Galician fisherman fell in love with a woman who was a fish from the waist down. Their twins were like normal humans except that their legs were lightly covered with bright silvery scales.

Atienza cites Fray Benito Jerónimo Feijóo, the famed 18th-century Benedictine monk, scholar, scientist and debunker of myths. Feijóo reported that in 1673, young Francisco went swimming with some friends near Bilbao and didn't return. They called and searched for days, but there was no sign of him dead or alive. Six years later, fishermen at the other end of Spain off the coast of Cádiz caught him in their nets. His skin was partially covered in scales. They restored him to his family, where he lived for several years, though with discomfort on dry land, and was the subject of much interest. Eventually he escaped and returned to the sea and was never seen again.

Atienza emphasises that Feijóo did not in any way appear to doubt the veracity of that story, though he discounted the element of the curse on Nicholas, and he went on to cite several similar “marine beings” mentioned by classical authors, including Pliny and Fuentelapeña. Echoing Fuentelapeña’s musings on invisible beings, Atienza reckons that some things that appear to violate the laws of Nature are subject to the laws of God, which are inscrutable to humans. Looking at it this way, as Feijóo did regarding Francisco, it is entirely natural and logical that a person constantly immersed in water would grow scales; otherwise, his skin would dry out. These events follow rules of a divine science that is unknowable for us – “outside our normal experience”, as Hyde said.

Triple Shape-changing: Gwydion and Gilfaethwy
Wales

In the matriarchal society of the Welsh myth cycle The Mabinogion, the king is the son of the virgin sister of the previous king. This is symbolised by a virgin holding the king’s feet in her lap when he is at home, metaphorically representing the birth process.

King Math never left his palace except when he had to lead a battle. His sister Don was the mother of Gwydion and Gilfaethwy; Gwydion, the elder, would be the future king. Gilfaethwy was enamoured of Math’s foot-holder, Goewin, but he was unable to even try to seduce her since she was always with Math. Gwydion provoked an invasion by stealing a herd of Otherworld pigs from Pryderi in South Wales in order to make Math leave the palace to do battle so Gilfaethwy could take Goewin by force.

On Math’s return, Goewin reported that she was no longer qualified to fulfil her duty and explained why. In compensation, Math married her. Then he sent out an order prohibiting anyone from providing Gwydion and Gilfaethwy with food and drink. Eventually, his starving nephews were forced to come to him to be punished for their insult to him and Goewin.

He took out his wand and struck Gilfaethwy, changing him into a doe, and he struck Gwydion, changing him into a stag.

"Since you are allied together," he said, "I will make you fare together, and be coupled, and of the same nature as the beasts whose guise you are in; and at the time there are offspring to them, that it be to you also. And a year from today come hither to me."

At the end of the year there came to the palace a stag, a doe and a fawn.

"The one of you that has been a hind for the past year, let him this year be a wild boar; and the one of you that has been a stag for the past year, let him this year be a wild sow."

The following year, a wild boar, a wild sow and a well-grown young one arrived.

"The one of you that has been a wild boar for the past year, let him this year be a she-wolf; and the one that has been a wild sow for the past year, let him this year be a wolf."

At the end of the year, the wolf and the she-wolf and a strong wolf-cub came to Math. He changed Gwydion and Gilfaethwy and their three sons into human form and had the children baptised with the names Hyddwn, Hychdwn and Bleiddwn for their original shapes.

(Quotes from Jones)

Saint Patrick's Deer
Ireland

King Laoghaire had promised his father, King Niall of the Nine Hostages, that he would never desert the pagan gods. So when Saint Patrick came to Ireland to spread Christianity, Laoghaire ordered his soldiers to kill him. Patrick invoked the power of God, and the king's army was scattered.

Frightened, Laoghaire invited Patrick to the royal centre at the Hill of Tara so that he could profess his belief in the

Christian God in front of all his people. But it was a sham. He ordered his soldiers to ambush Patrick and his seven followers on their way to Tara. Patrick was suspicious at the king's apparent sudden change of heart, and he transformed himself and his company into deer, with the youngest, Benen, bringing up the rear in the shape of a fawn, and that was what the would-be assassins saw.

OTHER BEASTS

Bees

The bee represents the soul and resurrection or reincarnation. In the rivers is born one of the arcs of the rainbow, and souls climb it to the moon, from where they return in the form of bees. And that is why in Galicia (Spain) there is a proverb:

> Quen mata unha abella
> ten cen anos de pena.
>
> A hundred years of misery
> to anyone who kills a bee.
> (Antón and Mandianes)

The White Butterfly

Japan

Takahama lived alone in a little cottage next to the cemetery. He was old and dying. His nephew came to visit him once a week. One day when he came, his uncle couldn't get out of bed. The nephew offered to call a doctor.

"No," said Takahama. "It's my time."

Just then, a white butterfly flew into the room and alighted on uncle's pillow and then flew out the window. Intrigued, the young man went out and followed the butterfly to the cemetery, where it landed on a well-tended tombstone with the name "Akiko".

When he returned to his uncle's bedroom, the old man was dead. He went home and told his mother what had happened.

"Ah, yes, Akiko. Your uncle and she were very much in love and planned to get married, but she died before they could officially become husband and wife. He built his cottage next to the cemetery where she's buried and looked after her grave for the rest of his life. He never married. That butterfly was Akiko taking his spirit to the Otherworld to be with her."

A Spider Saves King David

Romania

When King Saul heard women singing, "Saul slew his thousands, and David his ten thousands," he became envious of his protégé's popularity with the people, "and Saul did not look on David with a good eye from that day and forward." (1 Kings 18:9) He tried to kill David three times by throwing a spear at him, but each time David dodged, and after the third attempt he went on the run. Then Saul gave orders to kill him, but they were ineffective, largely because most people ignored them, so he set off to do the deed in person.

At one point when he was in hot pursuit, "there was a cave into which Saul went to ease nature. Now David and his men lay hid in the inner part of the cave." (1 Kings 24:4) When Saul removed his robe to facilitate the easing of nature, David cut off the hem and waited until Saul was a safe distance away, and then he showed it to him as evidence that he could have killed him but had refrained out of respect for "the Lord's anointed". That prompted Saul to call a truce. The incident may have been the inspiration for this short tale collected in Romania.

After David hid in the cave, a spider quickly wove a web across the entrance. When Saul came along a few minutes later and saw the web, he assumed that no one could have entered the cave recently, so he passed by without investigating.

When David realised that the spider had saved his life, he prayed, "Lord of the Universe, who can accomplish works like any of thy works? For all thy deeds are beautiful."

(Gaster)

A Spider Inspires Robert the Bruce

A Scottish Legend in Ireland

After Robert Bruce, King of Scotland 1309-1329, had fought and lost six battles against invasions led by the English kings Edward I and II, he was forced to flee for his life. He sought the security of Ulster, where anti-English sentiment was strong.

He was hiding in a cave one day on Rathlin Island, off the North Antrim coast near Ballycastle, idly watching a spider spinning a web, while he pondered whether he should give up trying to oppose the English. As he watched, the spider tried and failed six times to swing from one stone to another to attach a thread, just as Robert had failed six times to prevent the English overrunning his country. Then, on the seventh attempt, the spider was successful.

This inspired Robert to gather his warriors for one more battle, and he defeated the English at Bannockburn in 1314. "Bruce's Cave" is on the northeast corner of Rathlin Island and is so labelled on the 1:50,000 map, proving that the incident happened there and not in Norway, Orkney or the Hebrides, as some historians have speculated. "Bruce's Address to his Troops at Bannockburn" is a popular Scottish song and bagpipe tune.

The Saviour Gnat

Italy

In a poem by Virgil (first century AD), a gnat notices a snake approaching a sleeping shepherd and stings the man to warn him. Awakened by the pain, the shepherd's instinctive reflex is to slap the sore spot, killing the gnat. He sees and kills the snake but then, lamenting the death of his protector, builds a tomb with the inscription:

> Little gnat, to you deservedly the guard of the flock repays his funeral duty for your gift of life.

The tale is classed as Aarne-Thompson-Uther type 178A. See the similar-themed "King Sindbad and his Falcon" in the Birds section and "Gelert's Grave" in Other Dogs.

Origin of the Dragonfly

Romania

We are told that in olden times there was continual strife between God and the devil. God, however, who is peacefully inclined, let the devil play his game as long as possible.

He thought that perhaps after some time the devil might become better behaved. But what can you expect of the devil? He is what he is, and neither good nor bad treatment will change him. And so it proved even to God. He waited a very long time to see him quiet down and become more satisfied. But no sooner had God granted him one thing, than the devil asked for another, and so he went on asking continually. When at last God saw that nothing could be done with Satan, he armed his host of angels and gave each one a beautiful horse to ride on. One morning, at early dawn, they all mounted their horses and, led by St. George, who was riding at the head of the host, they started the fight with the devil.

After a time St. George, who rode a horse which was like unto none of the others, wondrously beautiful, felt suddenly that his horse was backing instead of going ahead. So St. George found himself involved among his own host, and some other horses following his example, started moving backwards and hitting those who were riding behind them. He then suddenly heard the voice of God telling him to dismount, for his horse had been bewitched by the devil.

"If that is the case," said St. George, "then be it the devil's own," and he let it go.

And so it happened. Scarcely had it made three steps when it was changed into a flying insect, which we, upon this earth, call the devil's horse (*Libellula depressa*).

(Verbatim from Gaster. "The Devil's Horse" is a Romanian name for the dragonfly.)

The Alp Luachra
Ireland

There was a farmer in Connacht who was healthy, happy and well-off, with not a bother on him. One warm day while he was watching his workers take in the harvest, he fell asleep next to a stream. When he woke up a few hours later, the workers had left, so he made his way home. He felt a stitch in his side, and when he entered the house his daughter said, "What's wrong with you? You don't look well."

"I feel a bit queer inside. I think a good sleep will set me right."

He slept until the sun was high the following day, and his daughter said, "How are you now?"

"No better," he said. "It feels as if there's something running back and forth inside me."

"That's impossible. Have a rest, and if you're not better by this evening we'll call the doctor."

He was no better in the evening. When the doctor arrived, the farmer told him he could feel something like a bird leaping about inside him. The doctor listened with his stethoscope and heard nothing.

"There it is now," the farmer said. "Can't you hear it?"

The doctor couldn't, and, assuming it was all in the man's mind, he gave him some medicine to make him sleep well, but that did nothing to relieve the man. They called in other doctors to no avail. This went on for six months, while the farmer only got thinner and weaker until he could barely walk. One day he was sitting outside in the sun when a beggarman arrived on his semi-annual rounds.

"What's become of you?" he said. "You're a shade of the man I saw last year."

The farmer told him the whole story – falling asleep, the jumping around inside him, the doctors who could do nothing to help.

"Where was it exactly that you fell asleep?"

"Next to the stream in the meadow where the men were saving the hay."

"Show me."

The farmer hobbled along the best he could and took the beggarman to the field and showed him the place where he had slept. The beggarman stooped down and walked back and forth inspecting the grass, and then he picked up a little green herb and showed it to the farmer.

"You see this? Anywhere you find this herb you'll find an alp luachra [newt], and you've swallowed one. Everything you eat, it eats, and as much as you eat you'll get no nourishment out of it. The doctors are fools. The only man who can cure you is Mac Dermott, the Prince of Coolavin, who lives by Lough Gara up in County Sligo."

The farmer and his daughter and the beggarman set off in the cart, and after three days they arrived at Mac Dermott's house and knocked on the door. The Prince was having a meal, but he listened to the story and said to the farmer, "Sit down and eat some of this."

"Ah, no, thank you anyway. I couldn't eat a thing."

"If you want me to cure you, do as I say."

He placed a big piece of salty meat in front of him. The farmer took a few bites and laid his knife and fork on the table.

"I said Eat," said the Prince sternly.

The farmer managed a few more pieces of the salty meat, and when the Prince saw that he really couldn't take any more, he brought him and the daughter and the beggarman out to a stream running through a meadow.

"Lie down there with your face over the stream and your mouth wide open as close to the water as you can," he commanded. "Don't move till we see what happens."

After fifteen minutes, the man could feel something move inside him and come up into his throat and then back down, up and back again and again, and finally as far as the tip of his tongue, when it got scared and retreated. Then it came up again, stood on his tongue and jumped into the water with a little "plop". The farmer started to get up, but the Prince said, "Don't move. Stay as you are. That's only the first of them."

The farmer took up his position again, and this time it was only a minute before there was another movement up and down, up and down, and finally "plop". Then another and another in rapid succession until the Prince counted twelve. The farmer started to rise.

"Not yet," said the Prince. "Stay where you are. The mother has yet to come out."

They waited for a quarter of an hour, and the farmer, tired, sick and weak, tried to stand in spite of the Prince's protest. So the Prince and the daughter and the beggarman all held him down, until he felt another stirring inside, much stronger this time and painful. It felt as if the mother alp luachra was trying to come out through his side. There was the familiar up and down action until finally the mother, maddened by the smell of the water after eating the salty meat and probably missing her babies, sprang out of his mouth into the stream with a big "PLOP".

The three quickly pulled him away from the stream. He couldn't speak for three hours, and when he did the first thing he said was, "I'm a new man."

They all stayed with the Prince for two weeks until the farmer was strong enough to make the journey home. The Prince refused to accept payment, saying they had spent enough on the doctors already.

"I'm better pleased that the cure worked than I would be with ten pounds in my hand."

The farmer was so grateful to the beggarman that he took him in as a permanent guest. When there was any sickness in the family, it wasn't the doctors they called.

(Rewritten from Hyde)

The Tortoise and the Geese

Widespread. This is the Jataka version.

Once on a time Brahmadatta was king of Benares, and the Bodhisatta, being born to one of the king's court, grew up and became the king's adviser in all things human and divine. But this king was very talkative; and when he talked there was no chance for any other to get in a word. And the Bodhisatta, wishing to put a stop to his much talking, kept watching for an opportunity.

Now there dwelt a Tortoise in a certain pond in the region of Himalaya. Two young wild Geese, searching for food, struck up an acquaintance with him; and by and by they grew close friends together. One day these two said to him: "Friend Tortoise, we have a lovely home in Himalaya, on a plateau of Mount Cittakuta, in a cave of gold! Will you come with us?"

"Why," said he, "how can I get there?"

"Oh, we will take you, if only you can keep your mouth shut, and say not a word to anybody."

"Yes, I can do that," said he. "Take me along!"

So they made the Tortoise hold a stick between his teeth: and themselves taking hold of the two ends, they sprang up into the air.

The village children saw this, and exclaimed, "There are two geese carrying a tortoise by a stick!"

(By this time the geese flying swiftly had arrived at the space above the palace of the king at Benares.) The Tortoise wanted to cry out, "Well, and if my friends do carry me, what is that to you, you caitiffs?" And he let go the stick from between his teeth, and falling into the open courtyard he split in two. What an uproar there was!

"A tortoise has fallen in the courtyard and broken in two!" they cried.

The king, with the Bodhisatta and all his court, came up to the place, and seeing the tortoise asked the Bodhisatta a question.

"Wise Sir, what made this creature fall?"

"O king, they that have too much tongue, that set no limit to their speaking, ever come to such misfortune as this."

"He is speaking of me!" the king thought to himself; and asked the Bodhisatta if it was so.

"Be it you, O great king, or be it another," replied he, "whosoever talks beyond measure comes by some misery of this kind." And thenceforward the king abstained from talking and became a man of few words.

(Lightly edited, from Francis and Thomas, *Jataka Tales*.)

Laelaps and the Teumessian Fox
Greece

The people of Thebes were unwisely disrespectful towards the gods.

Cadmus, founder of Thebes, killed a dragon who was the son of the god Ares. In revenge, Ares sent him constant misfortune. Cadmus complained that if the gods so loved a serpent, he might as well be one himself. So the gods changed him into a serpent.

Pentheus, grandson of Cadmus and his successor as king of Thebes, denied the divinity of his cousin Dionysus (Bacchus), whose mother was Semele, daughter of Cadmus, and whose father was Zeus. Dionysus retaliated by mischievously enticing Pentheus to spy on the frenzied rituals of his female followers the Maenads ("raving ones": Bacchantes), well knowing what would happen. The women discovered him hiding in a tree and with their hands ripped him to pieces.

Niobe was the daughter of Tantalus and wife of Amphion, ruler of Thebes. At a festival honouring Leto (Latona), whose two children by Zeus were Apollo and Artemis, Niobe arrogantly questioned why the people would "prefer beings whom you never saw to those who stand before your eyes." She boasted that she had seven times as many children as Leto. As punishment for her insult, Apollo killed her seven sons, and Artemis killed her seven daughters. Zeus turned her into a stone waterfall at Mount Sipylus (modern Spil Mount) in Turkey, where her face can be seen weeping constantly for her children.

Out of patience with the Thebans' impudence, the gods – some say Dionysus specifically – set the Teumessian Fox on them. This monstrous beast ravaged the countryside, slaughtering the farm animals and people. Hunters and warriors tried to kill it, but it was impervious to weapons and could not be trapped, for it was created to be uncatchable.

Amphitryon arrived in Thebes to request of King Creon the loan of his army to wage a war. Creon agreed on condition that Amphitryon would get rid of the Teumessian Fox. Amphitryon tried and failed with the usual methods, and then remembered the unescapable hound Laelaps. Zeus had given it to Europa, who gave it to her son Minos, who gave it to Procris, who gave it to her husband, Cephalus, the current owner. Amphitryon persuaded Cephalus to bring Laelaps to Thebes to let the unescapable chase the uncatchable.

It went as might have been predicted. Cephalus gives an eye-witness account in Ovid's *Metamorphoses*, which concludes with:

> While to the valley I o'erlooked the wood,
> Before my eyes two marble statues stood.

Zeus had intervened to halt the absurd spectacle, and he cast the images into the sky, where they can still be seen – Laelaps in the form of Canis Major eternally pursuing the Teumessian Fox, Canis Minor, in infinitely slow motion.

The Salamander

Middle East and Greece

If it falls into a well, all those who drink from it will die because of the strength of the poison. "It is known that if you throw the salamander into the middle of the fire it will live without pain and nothing bad will happen to it, and it loves the fire by nature."

(Bruneto Latini)

"Kings ordered clothes made of its skin; when the clothes got dirty, they threw them in the fire to clean them. If someone afflicted with lepra tuberculosis drinks its bile, he will be cured. Rubbing its blood on the penis provides sexual vigour."

(Al-Qazwīnī, *Zoological*. Note: Tuberculoid leprosy is a relatively benign and milder form of the disease and is characterised by a restricted growth and tends to heal spontaneously. Lepromatous leprosy spreads extensively throughout the body.)

Zeus had withdrawn fire from humans because of a trick played on him by Prometheus. Prometheus offered Zeus a choice between two gifts: beef hidden inside the unappetising stomach of an ox, and bones wrapped in scrumptious fat. Zeus chose the latter, and humans took advantage of this precedent to offer bones to Zeus as sacrifice. The god was so angered that he took fire away from humans and chained Prometheus to a rock, where in the form of an eagle Zeus ate Prometheus's liver. Since Prometheus was immortal, that occurred every day.

However, fire was deep inside the earth, and the salamanders, which had been in existence since before even the gods appeared, retrieved it and brought it to the surface for the use of mankind.

(Álvarez, David)

The Goat and the Dog

From *The Jataka*

A goat was in the habit of eating the grass thrown to the elephants beside their stable before they touched it. The elephant-keepers beat it and drove it away, and as it ran away bleating, one man ran quickly after and struck it on the back with a stick. The goat with its back humped in pain went and lay down by the great wall of the palace on a bench.

That same day, a dog stole meat from the royal kitchen. The cook saw the dog and beat it with sticks and stones. The dog dropped the meat from its mouth and ran off yelping, and the cook seeing it run, ran after and struck it full on the back with a stick.

The dog humping its back and holding up one leg came to the place where the goat was lying. Then the goat said, "Friend, why do you hump your back? Are you suffering from colic?"

The dog replied, "You are humping your back too, have you an attack of colic?"

The goat told its tale and added, "Well, can you ever go to the kitchen again?"

"No, it is as much as my life's worth. Can you go to the stable again?"

"No more than you. 'Tis as much as my life's worth."

Well, they began to wonder how they could live. Then the goat said, "If we could manage to live together I have an idea."

"Pray tell it."

"Well, sir, you must go to the stable. The elephant-keepers will take no notice of you, for they know you eat no grass, and you must bring me my grass. I will go to the kitchen, and the cook will take no notice of me, since I eat no meat, so I will bring you your meat."

"That's a good plan," said the other, and they made a bargain of it. The dog went to the stable and brought a bundle of grass in its teeth and laid it beside the great wall. The goat went to the kitchen and brought away a great lump of meat in its mouth to the same place. The dog ate the meat and the goat ate the grass, and so they lived together in harmony by the great wall.

(Lightly edited from Cowell and Rouse, *Jataka*)

The Fox and the Wolf
Mongolia

The wolf and the fox found on the road a skin full of fat.

"Hand it over; let us eat it," said the wolf.

"That won't do here. People are going backwards and forwards. We must carry it to the top of a mountain and eat it there. You carry it."

The wolf carried the fat to a great mountain.

The fox says, "There's not enough fat for us both, it's not worth dividing. Let one of us eat the whole."

"Which of us?" asks the wolf.

"Let the elder eat it," said the fox. "Pray how old art thou?"

The wolf thought a while, and determined to invent a lie, so as to cheat the fox.

"When," says he, "I was a youngster the Mount Sumêru was only a clot of earth in a bog, and the ocean only a puddle."

The fox lay down and wept.

"Why weepest thou?"

"I wept because I once had two cubs, and the younger was just your age."

So the fox cheated the wolf, and the wolf was so ashamed that he ran away.

(Lightly edited from Potanin 1886. Source: Daba, a Khalka man.)

Buddha and the Hare

Ceylon (Sri Lanka)

Buddha was wandering through a wood and met a hare and told it that he was poor and hungry.

"If you're hungry," said the hare, "make a fire and then kill, cook, and eat me."

Buddha made a fire, and the hare leapt into it. Then Buddha exercised his skill as a god, rescued the benevolent hare from the flames, and placed it in the moon.

(Lightly edited from Black.)

The Cat on the Dovrefjell

Norway

Once on a time there was a man up in Finnmark who had caught a great white bear, which he was going to take to the King of Denmark. Now, it so fell out that he came to the Dovrefell just about Christmas Eve, and there he turned into a cottage where a man lived, whose name was Halvor, and asked the man if he could get house-room there for his bear and himself.

"Heaven never help me, if what I say isn't true!" said the man, "but we can't give any one house-room just now, for every Christmas Eve such a pack of Trolls come down upon us that we are forced to flit, and haven't so much as a house over our own heads, to say nothing of lending one to anyone else."

"Oh!" said the man, "if that's all, you can very well lend me your house. My bear can lie under the stove yonder, and I can sleep in the side-room."

Well, he begged so hard, that at last he got leave to stay there; so the people of the house flitted out, and before they went everything was got ready for the Trolls: the tables were laid, and there was rice porridge, and fish boiled in lye, and sausages, and all else that was good, just as for any other grand feast.

So, when everything was ready, down came the Trolls. Some were great, and some were small; some had long tails, and some had no tails at all; some, too, had long, long noses; and they ate and drank, and tasted everything. Just then one of the little Trolls caught sight of the white bear, who lay under the stove; so he took a piece of sausage and stuck it on a fork, and went and poked it up against the bear's nose, screaming out:

"Pussy, will you have some sausage?"

Then the white bear rose up and growled, and hunted the whole pack of them out of doors, both great and small.

Next year Halvor was out in the wood on the afternoon of Christmas Eve, cutting wood before the holidays, for he thought the Trolls would come again; and just as he was hard at work, he heard a voice in the wood calling out:

"Halvor! Halvor!"

"Well," said Halvor, "here I am."

"Have you got your big cat with you still?"

"Yes, that I have," said Halvor. "She's lying at home under the stove, and what's more, she has now got seven kittens, far bigger and fiercer than she is herself."

"Oh, then, we'll never come to see you again," bawled out the Troll away in the wood, and he kept his word; for since that time the Trolls have never eaten their Christmas brose [porridge] with Halvor on the Dovrefell.

(Verbatim, Asbjørnsen. Dovrefjell [correct spelling] is a mountain range in central Norway. AT 1161 "The Bear Trainer and his Cat".)

The Three Cows
Ireland

Once upon a time, three cows walked out of the Atlantic Ocean onto the west shore of Ireland. They were a white cow, a red cow and a black cow. When they saw that there were no roads before them, they started ambling into the woods, and the trees fell in front of them, forming a roadway.

We know that the white cow didn't go far, because an island off the Galway coast is called Inishbofin – Inis Bó Finne in Irish, the Island of the White Cow. The red cow came to Dublin: the notoriously traffic-choked interchange on the west side of the city is known as the Red Cow Roundabout. And the black cow obviously rambled through the tiny community next to the Avonmore River in the Wicklow Hills called Annamoe: Áth na mBó, the Ford of the Cows. The plural "cows" suggests that either the black cow had babies by the time she got there, or the red cow joined her to escape the congestion in Dublin.

And that's how the first roads in Ireland were laid out.

The Riabhach Days
(The Days of the Brindled Cow, The Borrowing Days, The Skinning Days)
Ireland

"Laethanta na Riabhaí – spell of cold weather at end of March (or, variably, at beginning of April)." (Ó Dónaill)

In the past in this part of the country the holdings of land were very small and consequently the winter feeding (fodder) for stock was very limited and in most cases was consumed by the end of March.

The people felt that if their stock survived that month the need for fodder was over.

On one occasion an old cow was so delighted she had survived the cold bitter days of that month, that when the first of April arrived she cocked her tail and started to abuse March and its cold biting winds.

To have revenge on the old cow, March then borrowed three days from April saying "April, April stand to me now and lend me three days to skin this old cow."

And since then the three first days of April are called the Riabhach days.

(Verbatim, Mary Doyle, Tobernaveen, Ballina, County Mayo. NFCS 0150:100)

The Milk-white Milch Cow
Wales

The Milk-white milch cow gave enough of milk to everyone who desired it, and however frequently milked, or by whatever number of persons, she was never found deficient. All persons who drank of her milk were healed of every illness: from fools they became wise, and from being wicked, became happy. This cow went round the world, and wherever she appeared, she filled with milk all the vessels that could be found, leaving calves behind her for all the wise and happy. It was from her that all the milch cows in the world were obtained.

After traversing through the Island of Britain, for the benefit and blessing of country and kindred, she reached the Vale of Towy [in south Wales], where, tempted by her fine appearance and superior condition, the natives sought to kill and eat her. But just as they were proceeding to effect their purpose, she vanished from between their hands, and was never seen again.

A house still remains in the locality, called Y Fuwch Laethwen Lefrith, the Milk-white Milch Cow.

(Verbatim, Morganwg, *Iolo Manuscripts*)

A Cock and Bull Story
Ireland

A few steps down a lane off the square of Donard village in County Wicklow and next to Moat Farm and the ruins of a 15th- or 16th-century church and graveyard is a man-made defensive mound called the Ball Moat. Typical of the many Anglo-Norman mottes (moats) built about 1190 and scattered around the east of Ireland, it is about sixty feet in diameter and twenty feet high (18x6m). There is a six-foot depression in the top caused by treasure hunters, the sort of excavation found in many mottes. Stories similar to this are told about other mottes and burial sites.

In the *Journal of the Royal Society of Antiquaries of Ireland* (1931), Patrick T. Walshe wrote that Mr Allen of Donard told him that:

> a Mr. Cardel, who died many years ago in Donard, related to him that there was always a local belief that gold was hidden in this mound. It was ultimately decided by a number of residents to excavate it, but according to tradition these residents dared not begin their work till "a life was taken" on the spot where they were about to dig. Accordingly they took a cock with them to the summit and killed it there.
>
> They then began to work, but after proceeding to the depth above indicated a "black bull" leaped forth from the opening and the assembled people fled in terror.
>
> (Walshe)

A sceptic to whom I told this tale dismissed it as "a cock and bull story".

The Dragon of West Clandon

England

> I have sent you a drawing of an antient [sic] piece of carving in wood, which has been preserved for many years in the parsonage-house of West Clandon, near Guildford, in Surrey. It is about 4 feet in height.
>
> The account of it I give you verbatim from an old inhabitant of the place.
>
> "A serpent once infested a back lane in the parish of West Clandon for a long time. The inhabitants were much disturbed, and afraid to pass that way. A soldier, who had been condemned for desertion, promised, if his life was spared, he would destroy this serpent. Accordingly he took his dog with him. A fierce battle ensued; the dog fastened him, and the soldier killed it with his bayonet in a field belonging to the glebe, called Deadacre." A. Z.

That report is from *The Gentleman's Magazine, and Historical Chronicle*, Volume 66, Part 2, October 1796, p. 843. "The dog fastened him" probably means that the dog grabbed the dragon. A drawing between pages 840 and 841 shows a lion biting a dragon's head. The editor notes: "This is a *lion* fighting a *dragon*."

The original carving was stolen, but a replica is mounted over the entrance to the church of St Peter and St Paul in the village. The story, first reported in 1776, is current in local tradition as an enhanced version of the bare-bones account above. A 19m by 8m (62x30ft) figure of the fire-breathing dragon was cut into a chalk embankment on the A426 at the village crossroads in 1977 and is maintained by local volunteers. The village sign depicts the dog and the dragon.

Janet Dowling's *Surrey Folk Tales* (2013) includes the tale, and her condensed version is on her surreyhills website.

The Lagarto of La Malena
Jaén, Spain

A *lagarto* (lizard) has been the official symbol of the city of Jaén since 1249, so it was well before that time that a resident of Jaén brought a "lizard" – probably a baby crocodile from Egypt – back from a journey as a present for his daughter. It eventually escaped and found refuge in a cave near a spring in the old quarter of the city called La Magdalena, or La Malena for short. As it grew larger over the years, so did its appetite, and it progressed from eating small beasts of the wild to chickens and other domestic animals. When it started eating children and then adults, the residents of La Malena were afraid to leave their houses. They demanded that something be done.

All attempts to kill the lagarto failed. Either the would-be saviour could not catch it or it killed him when he confronted it. Finally, a prisoner condemned to death offered to rid the city of the menace in exchange for his freedom and a pardon. This was accepted, and he asked for and received a horse, a lance and a sack of gunpowder.

He bought some freshly baked loaves of bread and filled one of them with the powder, leaving a fuse trailing from it. He rode the horse to the monster's lair, and when the lagarto was tempted out by the aroma of the bread, the prisoner threw a loaf to it. The lagarto swallowed the bread with one gulp. From the safety of the horse's back and with the lance for protection, the prisoner continued to throw one loaf after another and thus led the lagarto farther from the cave until it was in front of the church of San Ildefonso. Then he threw the loaf filled with powder. When the lagarto swallowed it, he lit the fuse, and the explosion killed the monster.

The story goes on to state that the lagarto's hide was mounted on a wall inside the church. A friend of a friend has said that he thinks he saw the hide in the church some years ago, though I searched and couldn't find it. The shopkeeper I spoke with in the shop facing the 18th-century neo-classical main entrance to the church of San Ildefonso denied that the monster's hide had ever been in that or any other church in Jaén.

"It's just a legend," he said emphatically.

The event has given rise to a local curse: "May you explode like the lagarto of La Malena."

As I discovered when I visited Jaén on a storytelling tour in November 2000, all the residents of the city know the legend of the lagarto, though they might not agree on some details. In his 1992 book *La Leyenda del Lagarto de la Malena y los Mitos del Dragón*, Juan Eslava Galán describes the results of a survey he carried out in the 1970s. It is curious to note that of the 280 people interviewed, 72% believe that the hide of the beast is in the church of San Ildefonso, while only 65% believe the story to be true. I hold with the 65%: there is no proof that the story *isn't* true.

The Serpent of Orderías

Asturias, Spain

There was a serpent that they had to give a loaf of bread to every day. If they didn't, the serpent would grab a lamb. If they threw a loaf of bread to it, it was satisfied.

One day, instead of throwing it a loaf, a blacksmith heated a ball of iron and threw it to the serpent. The serpent swallowed it and fell down writhing, and that is why this road is called the Road of the Serpent (El Camín de la Culebra).

(From Súarez López, *Folklore*. Informant: Jesús López Galán, 70, from Las Morteras, Somiedo, 1999.)

In another Asturian tale, a monk fed a loaf of bread filled with pins to a dragon with the same result.

The Simurgh and Rostam and Rakush

Greater Iran

From The *Shahnameh* – Book of Kings

This excerpt from the great Persian epic, about the Simurgh (pronounced "si-MURG"), and the one about Rakush in the Horses section, show the two main animal characters in action. Quotes from Helen Zimmern's 1883 translation, some slightly modernised, are in italics.

The Simurgh is a benevolent giant bird with human characteristics that has lived through three destructions of the world. The name comes from the Sanskrit *śyenaḥ* meaning "bird of prey". It can be male or female and is depicted as a composite of peacock, lion, griffin and dog. Its image on the modern Iranian 500 rial coin is a copy of the one on a seventh-century AD gold dish. It also appears on the flag of the Tat ethnic group in the Caucasus. See back cover.

In his 12th-century poem *The Conference of the Birds*, Farid Ud-din Attar of Nishapur fancifully derives "simurgh" from the Persian *sī murğ* to mean "thirty bird", and he relates this story to illustrate.

The birds of the world had no ruler, and they flew across seven valleys, symbolising mystical experiences leading to enlightenment, in search of the Simurgh to ask him to be their king. Only thirty birds arrived at his home in the Mountains of Kaf,* and all they found was a lake in which they saw their own reflections. Those who had endured the challenging journey to the end were themselves the essence of the Simurgh.

*The Mountains of Kaf: emerald mountains surrounding Ocean, which surrounds the Earth. "At the beginning of the centuries God used the mountains as nails to fix the Earth; and washed Earth's face with the water of Ocean." (Attar)

The Hoopoe: "We have a true king, he lives behind the mountains called Kaf. His name is Simurgh and he is the king of birds." (Attar)

The ancient kingdom of Seistan (also called Zabulistan) straddles the modern-day Iran-Afghanistan border. Mount Alberz is Mount Damavand, the highest peak at 5610m in the Alborz mountain range near Tehran. Mubids are astrologers who advise rulers.

Saum was the ruler of Seistan. When his son was born perfectly formed and beautiful but with white hair, Saum was ashamed, and he feared that the nobles would see it as a sign that the boy was cursed. He ordered his servants to take him away and leave him to be killed by the elements or wild animals.

They deposited him at the foot of Mount Alberz, on whose inaccessible peak the marvellous Simurgh had built her nest of ebony and sandal-wood twined with aloes. She spied the naked infant, who was sucking his fingers out of hunger, and she swooped down and grasped him in her talons and carried him up to her nest to feed him to her chicks. But when she set him down, her maternal instincts expanded to include the human, and she raised him as her own.

The years passed, and rumours reached the ears of Saum about a remarkably strong and handsome young man seen at the top of Mount Alberz. In a dream, Saum saw a horseman riding toward him who said, "You disowned your son because his hair is white, though your own is as silver as the poplar. Even a bird saw fit to nurse the child. Will you deny kinship with him forever?"

Saum asked his Mubids to interpret the dream, and on their advice he went to Alberz to beg his son for forgiveness and become reconciled. When he arrived at the foot of the mountain and saw the young man at the top, he had to acknowledge the family resemblance. He tried and failed to climb up, and he prayed to God for help. God heard his prayer and *put it into the heart of the Simurgh to look down and behold the warrior and the army that was with him*. The Simurgh knew why Saum had come, and she said to the boy:

"I sheltered you beneath my wings and raised you like a mother, because your father cast you out, but now he is prepared to receive his son. The time has come for you to return to your people, but I will never be far away. Take this feather, and in time of need throw it into a fire, and I will come and rescue you from danger."

She picked him up and flew down to deposit him in front of Saum, who said as she soared up again, "O, Shah of birds, O bird of God, may you be great forever."

Saum named his son Zal, which means "the aged".

When Zal's wife, Rudabeh, was having a difficult labour, *he cast the feather into the fire as she [the Simurgh] had commanded, and straightway a sound of rushing wings filled the air, and the sky was darkened and the bird of God stood before Zal*. He explained the problem, and she instructed him how to perform a caesarean section, which he did successfully. Rudabeh named the boy Rostam, which means "delivered", because she was delivered of her pains. Later, she embroidered an image of the Simurgh on Rostam's tent.

Rostam grew to be a mighty warrior and the champion of Iran. Four hundred years later, he was feeling his age and looking forward to retirement. The Shah's young son, Isfendiyar, was now the champion and battle leader. He was impatient to succeed to his father's throne. The Shah kept putting him off, promising to abdicate if he accomplished yet one more heroic task, then another, hoping he would be killed. Finally, the Shah commanded Isfendiyar to bring Rostam to him in chains as punishment for not having fought in a battle – which Isfendiyar had won spectacularly – even though the Shah had not summoned Rostam to help in the battle. He knew that Rostam's pride would not allow this indignity, and in the inevitable fight the older warrior would probably kill the younger.

When the two met for the first time, Rostam offered to attend the Shah and give homage to him but refused to be chained. Isfendiyar understood, but he felt obligated to obey his father. Unable to come to an agreement, they reluctantly fought. Isfendiyar's body had been charmed so that it was as hard as brass and impervious to Rostam's weapons. Some say this was the result of a bath in magic water; others say his slaying of a simurgh and/or bathing in its blood was the reason.

Rostam and his horse, Rakush, were seriously wounded by Isfendiyar's sixty rapid-fire arrows, which penetrated both the rider's and the horse's armour, while Isfendiyar remained unscathed. When Zal saw that his son was near death, he cast the Simurgh's *feather into the fire as she had commanded, and straightway a sound of rushing wings filled the air, and the sky was darkened and the bird of God stood before Zal.* She plucked the arrows first out of Rakush and then Rostam and passed her wings over them to close the wounds, and they were immediately healed.

Then she questioned Rostam about the reason he and Isfendiyar were fighting. Rostam explained, and she said, "He has managed to kill one simurgh, and it would be best if you stayed away from him."

Zal said, "If Rostam refuses to fight Isfendiyar, my family and I will be enslaved."

"Try again to reason with him," the Simurgh said. "If that doesn't work, I'll show you how to kill him. But I warn you, *it is written that whosoever sheddeth the blood of Isfendiyar, he also shall perish; and while he liveth he shall not know joy, and in the life to come he shall suffer pains*."

She led him to the sea coast and into a garden where a tall tamarisk grew and told him to break off a branch that was long and slender and use it to make a two-pronged arrow.

She said: "When Zerdusht bathed him in the Water of Invulnerability to make his body like brass, Isfendiyar kept his eyes closed. The only way to kill him is to shoot this arrow into his eyes. The property of an arrow made from this tamarisk is that it will not miss the target."

Rostam killed Isfendiyar. How he met his own death soon afterwards is related in "Rakush – Faithful Steed of Rostam" in the Hero Horses section.

The Simurgh and the Daughter of the King of the East

The King of the East had a daughter and the King of the West had a son on the same day, and it was written that they should be united. The Simurgh stole the girl and took her to her nest and raised her. It happened that the son of the King of the West decided to travel. He stopped near the Simurgh's nest, and the girl saw him and fell in love. She made a plan. The boy wrapped himself in the hide of a dead animal that happened to be nearby. She asked the Simurgh to bring her the hide to relieve her fatigue, and so the two were united and had a child. Then, by order of Sulaiman, the Simurgh brought the hide to his court, and the plot was revealed. The Simurgh disappeared from the company of humans because of her shame.

(Close paraphrase of Al-Qazwīnī, *Bestiario*.)

The Hedley Kow
England

> The Hedley Kow was a bogie, mischievous rather than malignant, which haunted the village of Hedley, near Ebchester. His appearance was never very alarming, and he used to end his frolics with a horse-laugh at the expense of his victims. He would present himself to some old dame gathering sticks, in the form of a truss of straw, which she would be sure to take up and carry away. Then it would become so heavy she would have to lay her burden down, on which the straw would become "quick," rise upright, and shuffle away before her till at last it vanished from her sight with a laugh and shout.
>
> (Verbatim, Hartland)

This is a more detailed example of that behaviour, based on Jacobs.

An old woman who was poor but always cheerful was walking along a road when she saw a large black pot.

"That would be useful for me if I had anything to put in it," she thought. "But maybe there's a hole in it, and that's why someone threw it away."

She looked inside, and to her amazement saw that it was filled with pieces of gold. Well, there was no one around, it was obviously abandoned, so finders keepers. It was much too heavy for her to carry, of course, so she took off her shawl and tied it to the pot and dragged it behind her, dreaming of the house she could now buy where she would live like a queen. Or maybe she would leave it with the priest for safe-keeping, and he could dole out whatever she needed for her new life of luxury.

She stopped to rest and have another look at her treasure. But now in place of the gold coins sat a big lump of silver.

"Oh, my goodness," she thought. "That's even better. I won't have to worry about thieves, because it would be much too difficult to carry away this thing."

She dragged and dreamed about what she would do with the silver lump. When she stopped again to catch her breath and looked in the pot – no silver but a big lump of iron.

"That's wonderful. I can take it into the village and sell it to the blacksmith, and he can make tools with it."

She dragged, stopped, looked: the piece of iron had turned into a big stone.

"Ah, that will be so useful to put against the door so the wind won't blow it shut."

When she reached her cottage and bent down to untie her shawl, there was a wiggle and a jump and a squeal from the pot, and out leapt a long-eared beast the size of a horse that laughed and went galloping off down the road.

"Well, there's a bit of fortune. Fancy that – a personal appearance just for me. All this time I was so close to the Hedley Kow and didn't even know it. What a lucky woman I am!"

Next is an incident typical of the Scottish water horse or the Irish horse-form púca.

Two young men of Newlands, near Ebchester, went out one evening to meet their sweethearts, and arriving at the trysting-place, saw them, as it appeared, a short distance before them. The girls walked on for two or three miles. The lads followed, quite unable to overtake them, till at last they found themselves up to the knees in a bog, and their beguilers vanished, with a loud Ha! ha! The young men got clear of the mire and ran homewards as fast as they could, the bogie at their heels hooting and mocking them. In crossing the Derwent they fell into the water, mistook each other for the sprite, and finally reached home separately, each telling a fearful tale of having been chased by the Hedley Kow, and nearly drowned in the Derwent.

Surely this Northern sprite is closely akin to Robin Good-fellow, whom Ben Jonson introduced to us as speaking thus:

"Sometimes I meete them like a man,
Sometimes an ox, sometimes a hound,
And to a horse I turn me can,
To trip and trot about them round.
But if to ride My backe they stride,
More swift than wind away I go:
O'er the hedge and lands,
Through pools and ponds,
I whirry laughing, Ho ho ho!"

(Hartland, verbatim. Verse in Percy, attributed to Ben Johnson.)

Batcombe Cross

Dorset, England

This story explains the presence of a stone called Cross Hand Stone on Batcombe Down, which stands about three feet high and is apparently the remains of a cross.

A priest on his way to administer the Last Sacrament to a dying man dropped the pyx, the container carrying the consecrated host, on his way across Batcombe Down in a raging storm. He only noticed the loss when he arrived at the man's house, and he retraced his steps with little hope that he would find the pyx.

But on the Down he saw a pillar of fire surrounded by kneeling cows and a black horse that had only one knee to the ground. At the centre of the circle of animals was the pyx. He asked the horse why he knelt with only one knee.

"Wouldn't kneel at all if I could help it."

"Who, then, are you?"

"The devil."

"Why do you take the form of a horse?"

"So that men may steal me, and get hung, and I get hold of them. Got three or four already."

(Paraphrased and quoted from Moule.)

The Buggane of Saint Trinian's
Isle of Man

This religious [14th-century] edifice is said to have been erected in fulfilment of a vow made by a person when in a hurricane at sea, but, according to tradition, it was never finished. This was through the malice of a mischievous *Buggane*, or evil spirit, who, for want of better employment, amused himself with tossing the roof to the ground, as often as it was on the eve of being finished, accompanying his achievement with a loud fiendish laugh of satisfaction. The only attempt to counteract this singular propensity of the evil one, which tradition has conveyed to us, was made by Timothy, a tailor of great pretentions to sanctity of character.

On the occasion alluded to, the roof of Saint Trinian's Church was, as usual, nearly finished, when the valorous tailor undertook to make a pair of breeches under it, before the Buggane could commence his old trick. He accordingly seated himself in the chancel, and began to work in great haste; but ere he had completed his job, the head of the frightful Buggane rose out of the ground before him, and addressed him thus:

"Do you see my great head, large eyes, and long teeth?"

"Hee! Hee!" that is, "Yes! yes!" replied the tailor, at the same time stitching with all his might, and without raising his eyes from his work.

The Buggane, still rising slowly out of the ground, cried in a more angry voice than before, "Do you see my great body, large hands, and long nails?"

"Hee! Hee!" rejoined Tim, as before, but continuing to *pull out* with all his strength. The Buggane having now risen wholly from the ground, inquired in a terrifying voice, "Do you see my great limbs, large feet, and long ------?" but ere he could utter the last word, the tailor put the finishing stitch into the breeches, and jumped out of the Church, just as the roof fell in with a crash.

The fiendish laugh of the Buggane arose behind him, as he bounded off in a flight, to which terror lent its utmost speed. Looking behind, he saw the frightful spectacle close upon his heels, with extended jaws, as if to swallow him alive. To escape its fury Timothy leaped into consecrated ground, where, happily, the Buggane had not power to follow; but, as if determined to punish him for his temerity, the angry sprite lifted its great head from its body, and with great force pitched it to the feet of the tailor, where it exploded like a bomb shell.

Wonderful to relate, the adventurous Timothy was unscathed; but the Church of Saint Trinian remained without a roof.

(Verbatim from A. W. Moore. Wikipedia reports: "The Rev. Phillip Moore, born in 1705, ... got into Bishop Wilson's bad books when one night he masqueraded on the ruins of St Trinian's to scare the country people and to show them how wrong they were in believing in the mythical story of the Buggane.")

Conneelys, the Seal People

Ballyconneely, County Galway
Ireland

Many traditions, connecting these harmless animals [seals] with the marvellous, are related along our western shores. Among these there is one of a curious nature, viz., that at some distant period of time several of the Clan Coneelys, an old family of Iar-Connaught [West Connacht], were, by "Art-magick," metamorphosed into seals! In some places the story has its believers, who would no more kill a seal, or eat of a slaughtered one, than they would of a human Coneely. It is related as a fact, that this ridiculous story has caused several of the clan to change their name to Conolly.

(Verbatim, O'Flaherty. The modern spelling is "Conneely".)

Irish folklorist Bairbre Ní Fhloinn has commented on this seal tradition: "One of the most important things about supernatural beliefs about seals is that the beliefs are ultimately true, or at least that they have a truth of their own, albeit not necessarily a merely literal one; in their own way, they illustrate an infinitely more refined and sophisticated understanding of the delicate balance that exists between man and his natural environment, and of man's place in the overall scheme of nature, than we find in other so-called more advanced systems of belief."

Rat-charmers
Ireland

> Rhime them to death, as they do Irish rats ...
> Ben Jonson, *Poetaster*, 1601

> That our bards could rhyme rats to death was common knowledge among English writers. Ben Jonson and Sir Philip Sidney mentioned it too, while Shakespeare gave the idea to Rosalind in *As You Like It*, when, as the target of an admirer's poetry, she affects to have flashbacks to a past life as an "Irish rat".
> Frank McNally, "An Irishman's Diary", *Irish Times* 11 October 2018

> I was never so be-rhymed since
> Pythagoras' time, that I was an Irish rat, which I
> can hardly remember.
> *As You Like It*, III, 2

In an article with the title "On Rhyming Rats to Death" in *Proceedings of the Royal Irish Academy*, Vol. 5 (1850-1853), the renowned scholar J. H. Todd wrote about "the power said to be possessed by the Irish hereditary bards, of *rhyming rats to death*, or causing them to migrate by the power of rhyme". These bards were the diminished *filí*, the ancient poets featured in the "Cranes" and "The King of the Cats of Cnoghbha" chapters above, whose power and prestige had declined since the reduction in status of their patrons, the Irish lords, under English domination. This "curious superstition", as Todd called it, survives in the folk tradition.

> A man at Herbertstown had his grain collected in the haggard and was troubled with rats and sent for the rat charmer. The charmer ordered all the rats out of the haggard and lined them up in the lane so he could send them off to the haggard of another farmer. They were all lined up and ready to go except one rat, which was still

fumbling around in the haggard. The charmer ordered one of the rats to go back to the haggard and fetch the straggler. The rat went to the fence and got a stick and took it to the lone rat and put one end of it in its mouth. Then the two of them joined the rest. The straggler was blind.

"I heard that story twenty times," James Caffrey of Jamestown, County Meath, age 60, told collector D. F. O'Sullivan in 1938. (NFC 580:97)

The Gormanston Foxes

Ireland

The 1926 *Complete Peerage* sums up the story in the entry for the Preston family of Gormanston Castle in County Meath: "When the head of the house dies, and for some days before, the foxes leave all the neighbouring coverts, and collect at the door of the Castle."

The 12th Viscount Gormanston of County Meath was fox hunting one day. The hounds caught the scent of a fox, chased and had it cornered. When the Viscount went to look at the quarry, he discovered it was a vixen with pups, and he called off the hounds, thereby saving the lives of mother and babies. When he died in 1860, all the foxes in the district gathered on the lawn of the castle and howled with grief. The foxes did not attempt to molest the farmyard fowl, and the dogs of the house left the foxes in peace. This ritual has continued for several generations.

Some foxes attended the house in Dublin where the 14th Viscount died in 1907, but others were already in mourning at Gormanston before the body arrived there. His son reported that when he was keeping vigil in the chapel with his father's body overnight, he heard shuffling and snivelling outside the doors. He opened the doors and saw several foxes in the candlelight. They didn't try to run away; they only moved far enough so that he didn't step on them.

That young man, the 15th Viscount, served in the First World War. His wife was informed that he had been killed in action, but she didn't believe it, as the foxes had not put in an appearance at the house. A few weeks later, she learned there had been a misunderstanding, and her husband was still alive. The foxes gathered at Gormanston for him when he died in 1925, as they did for the 16th Viscount, who was killed at Dunkirk in 1940. The present (17th) Viscount, Jenico Nicholas Dudley Preston, succeeded to the title at the age of seven months.

The Gormanston family crest shows a fox "pleasantly passant", and in the coat of arms is a fox "aggressively rampant".

These events have been documented in *New Ireland Review*, April 1908, and in books written by some of the participants and witnesses, including Eileen Butler Preston's *A Little Kept* (1953) and Elizabeth, Countess of Fingal's *Seventy Years Young* (1937).

The Avoca Non-leprechaun
Ireland

Mick Howlett in Avoca, County Wicklow, told me that when he was about ten years old, he and some friends were out snaring rabbits one day, and they saw a creature running away through the underbrush on two legs. When the boys reported it, people laughed and said, "It must have been a leprechaun."

Mick is adamant that he and his friends never claimed it was a leprechaun. They were familiar with local wildlife, they knew what they saw, they all saw it, it was not a rabbit or a hare, and they had never seen anything like it before or since.

The Coyote and the Snake and the Man
Mexico

This story and illustration are from Sahagún's 16th-century *Historia general, Book Eleven: Natural History.*

One day a man was going across the plain and came across a coyote. He continued on his way, but the coyote was making signs with its paw. The man stared in wonder – what a strange thing! He approached the coyote, and when he was closer he noticed that a corn snake was wrapped around the coyote and was strangling it.

"Which one will I help?" he said to himself.

He picked up a tough and flexible stick and beat the snake, making it loosen its hold so the coyote could go free. The coyote ran to a corn field and brought back two turkeys and set them down in front of the man and made signs with its nose that the man was to take them.

Another time, the coyote delivered a turkey to the man's house, and then it encountered him on the road and gave him a turkey. When the man returned to his house he discovered the turkey the coyote had left.

The Kindness of a Mad Elephant

India

An elephant in Goa during rutting season broke out of his compound and charged furiously down the street. A slave who was carrying a child was so frightened that she dropped the child in the street and ran into a house and closed the door behind her. The elephant approached the boy and recognised him as the son of a fruit seller who would give him and other animals a treat from her stall whenever they passed by. He gently picked up the boy with his trunk and set him down safely on a low rooftop and then checked to see that he was secure. In that way, he repaid the fruit seller for her generosity.

(Fuentelapeña §810 and Huerta/Pliny)

Negotiating with Lions

Africa

In Libya it is taken as fact that lions understand when they are pleaded with and they are pacified. It is said of a slave that when she escaped into the jungles and mountains of Getulia, she mitigated the fury of many lions that she encountered by telling them that it would be beneath the dignity of an animal so generous and noble and the king and prince of the others to take a poor exhausted woman prisoner. So say Pliny and Mayolo [Simeone Maiolo].

(Fuentelapeña §785)

The Chupacabras

The Americas

According to Wikipedia: "The chupacabra or chupacabras is a legendary creature in the folklore of parts of the Americas, with its first purported sightings reported in

Puerto Rico. The name comes from the animal's reported habit of attacking and drinking the blood of livestock, including goats. … Sightings in northern Mexico and the southern United States have been verified as canids afflicted by mange. According to biologists and wildlife management officials, the chupacabra is an urban legend. … First reported March 1995."

"Chupacabras" is the singular and plural, with the literal meaning "(it) sucks goats," like "cuentacuentos" – "(he/she) tells stories." I first heard about the beast in the 1990s through hysterical reports on a Spanish-language television station in Chicago: chupacabras had spread from Puerto Rico to Florida and other southern states and could be heading north.

Benjamin Radford of New Mexico spent five years investigating the sightings and concluded that all dead specimens of supposed chupacabras were dogs, coyotes or raccoons infected with sarcoptic mange, which causes the fur to fall off and make the animal appear like an alien beast.

So the stories are rightly called legends, which by definition are based on fact, and more specifically urban legends, which are current and widely believed but not true as popularly reported.

APPENDIX

Douglas Hyde

Douglas Hyde (1860-1949) was a collector of folk tales and songs before he became the first president of Ireland after independence. He was a major influence in the Irish Literary Renaissance of 1880-1920 and was involved in the promotion of the Irish language, the Abbey Theatre and the recognition of the importance of traditional music and folklore. Dermot MacManus said of him, "With a golden key he opened wide the door to the store of national tradition and culture which had lain hidden for so long."

He wrote the introduction to the Ireland section in Evans-Wentz's *The Fairy Faith in Celtic Countries*, which is online.

Extracts from *The Fairy Faith in Celtic Countries*

"I saw a dog with a white ring around his neck by that hill there, and the oldest men round Galway have seen him, too, for he has been here for one hundred years or more. He is a dog of the good people, and only appears at certain hours of the night." (A Galway piper)

"My private opinion is that in certain places here in Ireland where pagan sacrifices were practised, evil spirits through receiving homage gained control, and still hold control, unless driven out by exorcisms." (A Galway priest)

"Food, after it has been put out at night for the fairies, is not allowed to be eaten afterwards by man or beast, not even by pigs. Such food is said to have no real substance left in it, and to let anything eat it wouldn't be thought of. The underlying idea seems to be that the fairies extract the spiritual essence from food offered to them, leaving behind the grosser elements." (The town clerk of Tuam, County Galway, Mr. John Glynn)

"Apparently the piskies only drank the 'astral' part of the milk (whatever that may be) and then the neighbouring cats drank what was left, and it disagreed with them." (Henry Jenner, in his Introduction to the Cornwall section)

[The fairies] "They are a distinct race between our own and that of spirits, as they have told me." (A man living at the foot of Ben Bulben in Sligo)

"The fairies of any one race are the people of the preceding race – the Fomors for the Fir Bolgs, the Fir Bolgs for the Dananns, and the Dananns for us. The old races died. Where did they go? They became spirits and fairies. Second-sight gave our race power to see the inner world. When Christianity came to Ireland the people had no definite heaven. Before, their ideas about the other world were vague. But the older ideas of a spirit world remained side by side with the Christian ones, and being preserved in a subconscious way gave rise to the fairy world." (A priest who was a professor in a Catholic college in the west of Ireland)

Horses

Equus ferus caballus

The small (11.2 - 12.2 hands, 123 - 125 cm) and sturdy pony-sized Asturcón from Asturias in Spain was favoured by the Roman cavalry for its endurance and manoeuvrability. The breed was imported into Ireland in the fifteenth century, where it became known as the Irish hobby, from the French *haubini*. It's called a palfrey in Britain, where it is typically a woman's mount. Some say "pony" derives from the Celtic horse goddess Epona, who is usually depicted riding a small horse. The slightly larger Galician and Icelandic horses are other examples of *Equus ferus caballus*.

It may seem strange for a horse no larger than a pony to be the mount of a warrior, and I often wondered if medieval paintings and manuscript and book illustrations of heroes riding horses that seemed too small for them were meant to emphasise the size and strength of the man. We tend to think of the Knights of the Round Table encased in steel on their massive armoured chargers like battle tanks, but that seems to have been a late medieval European trend. In the pictorial account of the Norman Conquest on the eleventh-century Bayeux Tapestry, for example, the knights' feet nearly touch the ground, and in a manuscript illustration from 1430 of Isfandiyar in the *Shahnameh* epic the rider is the same size as his mount. Archaeologists have found that men in those earlier times were about the same height as modern men, so the depictions are not just artistic fancy.

Legendary Horse Names Recycled

Some Thoroughbred horse owners familiar with the steeds of myth and legend have named their horses after equine heroes, some of whom are featured in this book.

Bayard (foaled 1928 in Ireland) was in the bloodline of the three major foundation sires of the modern Thoroughbred: the Godolphin Arabian (also called the Godolphin Barb), foaled in 1724 in Syria; the Darley Arabian, 1700; and the Byerley Turk, 1680. Genetic research shows that 95% of today's Thoroughbreds can be traced to the Darley Arabian.

Bayardo (1906 Britain) won 22 of his 25 races, many of them major. Bloodline: Godolphin Arabian, Darley Arabian, and various Turks and Barbs.

Broiefort, a French stallion foaled in 1933, was dam-sire of two winners of the Auckland Cup in New Zealand: Rev in 1952 and Ruato in 1961.

Papillon, an Irish-bred bay gelding, won the British Grand National in 2000 and eight other races out of 39 starts.

The trainer, Ted Walsh, referred to the horse's owner as his "fairy godmother". A previous Papillon, foaled in 1769, was a descendant of the Godolphin Arabian, the Darley Arabian and the Byerley Turk.

Rakush: the First Appaloosa?

Rakush, whose colour is described in the *Shahnameh* as "rose leaves that have been scattered upon a saffron ground," can be called a red roan, or "red corn" in Mustang terminology. Proud Appy fans like to believe he was the progenitor of the spotted Appaloosa horse developed by the Nez Perce Native Americans in the northwestern United States. But Palaeolithic cave paintings from 25,000 years ago depict spotted horses predating Rakush. Colour photos of those in La Grotte de Pech Merle in France are online. See back cover for one of them.

A Modern Talking Horse Incident

With a tenner at 7-1 on Bryony Frost's mount, Frodon, in the Grade 1 Ryanair Chase on 14 March 2019 in the Cheltenham Festival, I was watching the race with intense interest. Jockey and mount moved like one creature as they took the 15 fences with grace and accuracy, and, apart from one soaring showboat leap, economically. Frodon, smaller than most of the others, led nearly the whole way, but he was headed two fences from the end by 33-1 shot Aso.

Frodon took the lead again at the last fence, but Aso was steadily gaining during the run-in. Then something magical occurred: a change in energy, as if Frodon had performed the táltos ritual of three jumps and entered another dimension. He won by a length.

I didn't understand what had happened until Bryony, the first female jockey to win a Grade 1 at Cheltenham, explained afterwards. Dabbing at tears of joy, she accepted the plaudits of the crowd, who recognised that they had witnessed a heroic event, but she kept pointing down to the horse to make sure the credit went to him.

"When he got overtaken two out," she said, "most horses would quit, but he grabbed me by the hands and said, 'Don't you dare give up, don't you dare not send me into the last, I want this more than you, now come on!'"

Even trainer Paul Nichols found his voice cracking in the post-race interview.

Update: Carrying top weight in soft ground, Frodon won a chase on 24 October 2020. "The jumps he did out there were just unbelievable," said Bryony afterwards. "He is just magic to be with."

Simurgh Saxum

Electronically enhanced data from NASA spacecraft OSIRIS-Rex shows details of the asteroid Bennu, including a boulder named "Simurgh Saxum", *saxum* being Latin for "rock".

According to the commentary on the online video: "This prominent boulder defines the asteroid's prime meridian and serves as the basis of its coordinate system. In Persian mythology, the Simurgh is a large and benevolent bird and the possessor of all knowledge."

https://scitechdaily.com/scientists-peer-inside-an-asteroid-is-bennu-in-the-process-of-spinning-itself-into-pieces

Striking the Ground

"Rakush stamped a hoof and swished his tail noisily, waking Rostam."

"The earth shook when [Bayardo] stamped an imperious hoof."

In "Bayardo": "The stranger struck the ground with his spear. The earth opened, and out galloped four fiery steeds drawing a chariot."

In "Toruchaar and Manas", when Toruchaar was born he "leapt three times across the mare / And stamped the earth and grew threefold."

In "The Táltos Horse", the horse jumps three times before taking flight.

In "The White Horse and the Healing Well", "she asked the horse to strike the ground three times, and the spring that is now the source of St. Milburga's Well burst forth."

In "The Piper and the Púca" – "Then the Púca struck three blows with his foot, and a great door opened, and they passed in together, into a fine room." … "One of the old women struck a blow on the ground, and a door opened in the side of the wall …"

Wherever the winged stallion Pegasus stamped on the ground a spring burst forth. The most famous one was the Hippocrene spring on Mount Helicon. The mountain was swelling dangerously because of the music of the Muses, and Pegasus struck a rock – only once – to relieve the pressure.

To rid Galicia of an infestation of snakes, San Adrián stamped his foot on the ground, and the snakes fled under a stone, except for one that he had stepped on, which was turned into stone.

Foot-stamping can be a defensive or aggressive signal, like Bayardo's imperious gesture, or a demand for attention, like Rakush waking Rostam, but the other horse and human ground stampings and strikings seem to be a ritual of tapping into the earth's geomagnetic energy, which is created by Extremely Low Frequency (ELF) electromagnetic waves. The root note of the earth is said to be just above C-sharp or 560Hz, though some have identified it as G. One of the notes on the Scottish bagpipe is just under C-sharp.

Lethal Effects of Sound

Low-frequency sound (20-160Hz: cycles per second), audible to most people, is currently in the public consciousness as Low-frequency Noise (LFN) because of the proliferation of wind turbines. It can have adverse effects on mental and psychological health, causing loss of sleep and depression. Infrasound (below 20Hz), inaudible to humans, can cause serious physical damage and can kill, especially in the range of 3-7Hz.

Russian-born French scientist Vladimir Gavreau (d. c. 1970) reported on an early experiment: "Luckily, we were able to turn [the machine] off quickly. All of us were sick for hours. Everything in us was vibrating: stomach, heart, lungs. All the people in the other laboratories were sick too. They were very angry with us."

(*Sunday Times*, April 16, 1967, "Acoustics," by Frank Dorsey, under the title "Joshua Knew a Thing or Two". That reference is to the well-known story in Josue 6:20, when the combination of people shouting and trumpets blowing destroyed the walls of Jericho.)

"One study has suggested that infrasound may cause feelings of awe or fear in humans. It has also been suggested that since it is not consciously perceived, it may make people feel vaguely that odd or supernatural events are taking place." (Wikipedia, citing "Infrasound linked to spooky effects", MSNBC, 7 September 2007.)

Cranes

Pliny observed: "They maintain a Watch all the Night long, and the Sentinels hold a little Stone in their Foot, which by falling down from it, if they sleep, reproves them for their Negligence." Alexander the Great adapted this trick. When he sat down to rest, he held a silver ball in his hand over a brass basin. Some Spanish people do that with a set of keys when they take a brief siesta after their main midday meal.

An Effective Curse

Whatever entity is in charge of granting curses seems to take its job seriously. José Arandia Rezola, 76, from Amezketa, Gipuzkoa, related this incident to Larrañaga in 1991.

Five agricultural workers who were digging up a field had a jug of a refreshing liquid to make the task run more smoothly. They hung it on a branch of a tree for safe-keeping. When they finished the job and left the field, they forgot to take the jug with them. One of the men noticed that it was missing and thought someone had stolen it. He laid a curse: "May the arm wither on the person who has the jug." The branch of the tree immediately withered.

SOURCES

Alfonso the Wise, King, *Primera Crónica General*, 13th-century.

Al-Qazwīnī, Hamdullāh al-Mustaufī, *Bestiario Medieval*, [same as or included in the below?]

Al-Qazwīnī, Hamdullāh al-Mustaufī, *The Zoological Section of the Nuzhatu-l-Qulūb*, J. Stephenson, ed., The Royal Asiatic Society, London, 1928.

Álvarez, David, blog Naturaleza Cantábrica.

Álvarez Peña, Alberto, *La Güestia y Otros Agüeros de Muerte*, VTP Ediciones, 2006.

Álvarez Peña, Alberto, *Leyendas Asturianas de Difuntos*, 2015.

Álvarez Peña, Alberto, *Un Paseo por la Mitología Asturiana*, Delallama Editorial, Ribadesella, Asturias, 2019.

Antón, Fina María, and Manuel Mandianes, *O Ciclo da Vida,* Ir Indo Edicións, Vigo, Spain, 1998.

Arias Marín de Cubas: see Marín de Cubas.

Arrieta Gallastegui, Miguel I., *Historias y Leyendas de Asturias*, Distribuciones Cimadevilla, Gijón, 1998.

Asbjørnsen, Peter Christen and Moe, Jorgen. *East o' the Sun and West o' the Moon.* Translated by George Webbe Dasent as *Popular Tales from the Norse*. Edinburgh: David Douglass, 1888, 1904. Reprinted as Dasent, *East o' the Sun and West o' the Moon.* New York: Dover, 1970.

Atienza, Juan García, *Leyendas Mágicas de España*, EDAF, Madrid, 1997.

Attar (Farid Ud-din Attar), *The Conference of the Birds*, 1177.

Baldwin, William (Gulielmus), "G. B.", *Beware the Cat*, London, 1570, 1584.

Barcelos, Pedro de, *Livro das Linhagens*, "Book of Lineages", 14th-century.

Behan, Brendan, *After the Wake*, O'Brien Press, Dublin, 1981.

Beltrán, Rafael, and Marta Haro, *El cuento folclórico en la literatura y en la tradición oral*, Universitat de Valencia, Servei de Publicaciones, Valencia, 2006.

Bennett, Holly, *Shapeshifter*, Orca Book Publishers, Victoria, Canada, 2010.

Berman, Michael, *The Shamanic Themes in Georgian Folktales*, Newcastle: Cambridge Scholars Publishing, 2008.

Bernheimer, Richard, *Wild Men in the Middle Ages*, Octagon, New York, 1979.

Bidpay: see North and Thomas Scott.

Black, William George, "The Hare in Folk-lore", *The Folk-Lore Journal*, Volume 1, 1883.

Book of Leinster: see O'Curry.

Breatnach, Deasún, "The Púca: A Multi-Functional Irish Supernatural Entity", *Folklore*, Vol. 104, 1993.

Briggs, Katherine, *A Dictionary of Fairies: Hobgoblins, Brownies, Bogies and Other Supernatural Creatures*, Penguin, 1977.

Brown, Theo, "The Black Dog", *Folklore* Vol. 69, 1958.

Bruneto Latini, *Li Livres dou Tresor*, F. J. Carmody, ed., University of California Press, Berkeley-Los Angeles, 1948.

Bulfinch, Thomas, *Age of Fable: Vol. IV: Legends of Charlemagne*, 1913.

Burne, Charlotte S., "Two Folk-tales", *The Folk-Lore Journal*, Volume 2, 1884.

Byrne, Patrick, *Irish Ghost Stories*, Mercier Press, Cork, Ireland, 1999.

Cabal, Constantino, *La mitología asturiana (Los dioses de la muerte. Los dioses de la vida. El sacerdocio del diablo)*, González y Huici Editores, Gijón, 1987.

Canellada, María Josefa, *Folklore de Asturias: Leyendas, Cuentos y Tradiciones*, Ayalga Editiones, Gijón, 1983.

Carré Alvarellos, Leandro, *Las Leyendas Tradicionales Gallegas*, Collección Austral, Espasa Calpe, Madrid, 1977, 1999.

Carrín, Cristobo, "Monsters of the Underworld and Hell of the Asturians", *Asturies, Memoria Encesa d'Un País*, Issue 35, 2015.

Caxton, William, trans., *The Golden Legend.* Written by Jacobus de Voragine as *Aurea Legenda* c. 1260 with later additions, translated and published by Caxton in 1483. Temple Classics edition 1900, reprinted 1922, 1931. Online: https://sourcebooks.fordham.edu/basis/goldenlegend/index.asp

Colarusso, John, and Tamirlan Salbiev, eds., Walter May, trans., *Tales of the Narts: Ancient Myths and Legends of the Ossetians*, Princeton University Press, 2016.

Colarusso, John, trans., *Nart Sagas from the Caucasus*, Princeton University Press, 2002.

Coren, Stanley, *Gods, Ghosts, and Black Dogs: the Fascinating Folklore and Mythology of Dogs*, Veloce Publishing, Dorchester, UK, 2016.

Cowell, E. B., and W. H. D. Rouse, trans., *The Jataka*, 1907.

Curtin, Jeremiah, *Hero Tales of Ireland*, 1894.

Dalrymple, William, *From the Holy Mountain*, HarperCollins, 1997.

Dasent, George Webbe: see Asbjørnsen.

De Barcelos: see Barcelos.

De Trueba, Antonio, *Cuentos Populares*, 1864.

Depping, G. B.: see Timoneda.

Douglas, Mona, "Folk-Lore Notes. Lezayre Notes", *Mannin* No.7 (1916).

Dowling, Janet, *Surrey Folk Tales*, History Press, Gloucestershire UK, 2013.

eDIL: *Electronic Dictionary of the Irish Language* – Old and Middle Irish c. 700-1700, online at http://www.dil.ie

Elizabeth, Countess of Fingal, *Seventy Years Young*, 1937. (Gormanston Foxes)

Ellis Davidson, H. R., *Gods and Myths of Northern Europe*, Pelican Books, 1964.

Evans-Wentz, W. Y., *The Fairy Faith in Celtic Countries*, Oxford University Press, London, 1911.

Ferdowsi Tusi, Abu 'l-Qasim, *The Shahnama: The Epic of Kings*, Helen Zimmern, trans., 1883.

FitzGerald, Lord Walter, "Customs peculiar to certain days, formerly observed in the County Kildare", *Journal of the County Kildare Archaeological Society*, Vol. V, No. 6, 1908.

Fitzgerald, Lord Walter, "The Race, or Road, of the Black Pig, across the Curragh", *Journal of the County Kildare Archaeological Society*, Vol. II, No. 6, 1898.

Fleming, Abraham, *A straunge and terrible wunder wrought very late in the parish church of Bongay ...* (pamphlet), 1577.

Flor, Fernando R. de la, "El discurso del duende en los momentos inaugurales del periodo novator", *Criticón*, 103-104, 2008.

Foster, Jeanne Cooper, *Ulster Folklore*, H. R. Carter Publications, Belfast, 1951.

Francis, H. T., and E. J. Thomas, selected and edited, *Jataka Tales*, Cambridge University Press, 1916.

Frutos, R., *Leyendas Gallegas*, Breogan, Madrid, 1981.

Fuentelapeña, Antonio de, *El ente dilucidado: discurso único novísimo que muestra que ay en naturaleza animales irracionales invisibles y quáles sean*, Madrid, Imprenta Real, 1676.

Galán, Juan Eslava, *La Leyenda del Lagarto de la Malena y Los Mitos del Dragón*, Universidad de Granada and Ayuntamiento Jaén, 1992.

Galindo, Juan de Abréu, *Historia de la Conquista de las Siete Islas*, 1632.

Ganguli, Kisari Mohan, trans., *The Mahabharata*, published between 1883 and 1896.

Gardner, C., "Folk-Lore in Mongolia", *The Folk-Lore Journal*, Vol. 3, 1885.

Gardner, C., "Folk-Lore in Mongolia", *The Folk-Lore Journal*, Vol. 4, 1886.

Gaster, M., *Rumanian Bird and Beast Stories*, The Folklore Society, Sedgwick and Jackson, London, 1915.

Gerald of Wales (Giraldus Cambrensis), *Topography of Ireland*, 1187.

Gill, Walter, *A Second Manx Scrapbook*, 1932

Girgado, Luis Alonso, *Cuentos populares* [de Galicia], Tambre Narrativa, A Coruña, 1993.

Golden Legend: see Caxton.

Graves, Alfred Perceval, *The Irish Fairy Book*, T. Fisher Unwin, London, 1909.

Gregor, Reverend Walter, "Kelpie Stories", *The Folk-Lore Journal*, Vol. 7, 1888.

Gregor, Walter, "Kelpie Stories from the North of Scotland", *The Folk-Lore Journal*, Volume 1, 1883.

Gregor, Reverend Walter, "Some Folk-Lore of the Sea", *The Folk-Lore Journal*, Vol. 4, 1886.

Gregory, Pope, (Saint Gregory the Great), *Dialogues*, Book 3, Chapter 2; 6th century.

Gwynn, Edward J., *The Metrical Dindshenchas*, Royal Irish Academy, Dublin, 1903-1935. Reprinted 1991 by the School of Celtic Studies, Dublin Institute for Advanced Studies.

Hale, Leslie, *John Philpot Curran: His Life and Times*, Cape, London, 1958.

Hartland, Edwin Sydney, *English Fairy and Other Folk Tales*, 1890.

Haywood, John, *The Historical Atlas of the Celtic World*, Thames & Hudson, 2001.

Henderson, William, *Notes on the folk-lore of the northern counties of England and the borders,* The Folk-Lore Society, London, 1879.

Herity, Michael, ed., *Ordnance survey letters Wicklow and Carlow: letters relating to the antiquities of the counties of Wicklow and Carlow containing information collected during the progress of the ordnance survey 1838-1840* [by John O'Donovan], Four Masters Press, Dublin, 2013.

Huerta/Pliny: Huerta, Gerónimo Gómez de, *Historia Natural de Cayo Plinio Segundo*, 1599; Spanish translation with notes by Huerta of Pliny the Elder's *Naturalis Historia*, which he began in AD 77 and was unfinished at his death in the eruptions of Vesuvius in AD 79.

Hunt, David, *Legends of the Caucasus*, Saqi Publishers, London, 2012.

Hunt, William, "Columban", *Dictionary of National Biography*, Vol. 11, Smith, Elder & Co., 1887.

Hyde, Douglas, *Beside the Fire*, David Nutt, London, 1910.

Í Luínse, Amhlaoibh: see Ó Cróinín.

Ivanova, Mariya (2007). "The Chronology of the 'Maikop Culture' in the North Caucasus: Changing Perspectives", *Armenian Journal of Near Eastern Studies. II: 7–39.*

Jacobs, Joseph, *More English Fairy Tales*, 1894.

Jaimoukha, Amjad, The Nart Tales of the Circassians (online).

Jataka: see Cowell.

Jenkins, Chris, "Lady Godda – Goddess of Mercia", *White Dragon*, 1996.

Jonas the Monk, *Acta Sanctorum Ordinis S. Benedicti*, Vol. I, Venice, 1733.

Jones, Gwyn, and Thomas Jones, *The Maginogion*, Dent, 1949.

Joyce, P. W., *Old Celtic Romances*, Longmans, London, 1894.

Keating, Geoffrey, *The History of Ireland*, 1634.

Keightley, Thomas, *The Fairy Mythology*, 1870.

Keightley, Thomas, *Tales and Popular Fictions, Their Resemblance and Transmission from Country to Country*, 1834.

Kennedy, Patrick, *Legendary Fictions of the Irish Celts*, 1891.

Knox: "Folk-Tales from County Limerick collected by Miss D. Knox," *Folk-Lore: A Quarterly Review of Myth, Tradition, Institution, & Custom*, Volume 28, 1917, London.

Kürti, László, "The Way of the Táltos: A Critical Reassessment of a Religious-Magical Specialist", *Studia Mythologica Slavica III*, 2000, 89-114. Online as a pdf.

Larrañaga, Juan Garmendia, *Mitos y Leyendas de los Vascos: Apariciones, Brujas y Gentiles*, Haranburu Editor, Donostia-San Sebastián, 1995.

Lebor na hUidre, The Book of the Dun Cow, 12th century.

Leo the Deacon: see Talbot.
Lysaght, Moira, "Norbury, The Hanging Judge", *Dublin Historical Record*, Vol 30 No 2 Mar 1977.
MacKillop, James, *Dictionary of Celtic Mythology*, Oxford, 1998.
McLaughlin, Marie L., *Myths and Legends of the Sioux*, 1916. McLaughlin was "born and reared in an Indian community". She learned most of these tales from her mother, whose mother was a full-blooded Sioux.
McLaughlin, Roisin, *Early Irish Satire*, School of Celtic Studies, Dublin Institute for Advanced Studies, 2008.
MacManus, Dermot, *The Middle Kingdom: The Faerie World of Ireland*, Colin Smythe, Gerrards Cross, Bucks., U.K., 1959.
MacNeill, Máire, *Máire Rua: Lady of Leamaneh*, Whitegate, 1990.
Malaxecheverría, Ignacio, *Fauna Fantástica de la Península Ibérica*, Kriselu, San Sebastián, Spain, 1991.
Mallory, J. P., *In Search of the Indo-Europeans: Language, Archaeology, and Myth*, London, Thames & Hudson, 1999.
Marín de Cubas, Tomás Arias, *Historia de las Siete Islas de Canaria*, two versions: 1687 and 1694.
Mariño Ferro, Xosé Ramón, *Aparicións e Santa Compaña*, Edicións do Cumio, Vigo, 1998.
Marsh, Richard, *A World of Tricksters*, Legendary Books, Dublin, 2020.
Marsh, Richard, *Irish King and Hero Tales*, Legendary Books, Dublin, 2011.
Marsh, Richard, *Spanish and Basque Legends*, Legendary Books, Dublin, 2010.
Marsh, Richard, *Tales of the Wicklow Hills*, Legendary Books, Dublin, 2007.
Meyer, Kuno, ed/trans., *Betha Colmáin maic Lúacháin: The Life of Colman Son of Luachan; edited from a manuscript in the Library of Rennes*. Todd Lecture Series No. 17, Hodges, Figgis/Williams & Norgate, Dublin/London, 1911.

Meyer, Kuno, *Death-tales of the Ulster Heroes, The*, School of Celtic Studies, Dublin Institute for Advanced Studies, Dublin, 1906, reprinted 1993.

Miranda, Xosé, and Antonio Reigosa, *Contos fantásticos II*, Edicións Xerais de Galicia, 2001.

Moore, A. W., *Folk-Lore of the Isle of Man, The*, Brown & Son, Douglas, and Nutt, London, 1891.

Morganwg, Iolo, *Iolo Manuscripts*, translated from the Welsh by Taliesin Williams, Welsh Manuscript Society, 1848.

Morganwg, Iolo, *The Triads of Britain*, introduction and notes by Malcolm Smith, Wildwood House, London, 1977.

Morris, Lewis, *Celtic Remains*, published 1884, transcribed from a manuscript in 1778.

Moschus, John, *The Spiritual Meadow* in *Vitae Patrum: Lives of the Fathers of the Church*, 1628. *The Spiritual Meadow* is the last of ten volumes in the encyclopaedia *Vitae Patrum.*

Mosquera Paans, Miguel, *Lendas de Ourense*, Edicións do Cumio, Pontevedra, Spain, 2011.

Moule, H. J., "Batcombe Cross", *The Folk-Lore Journal*, Vol. 7, 1889.

Muruais, Andrés, *Reinado y Muerte del Urco: Colección de los Documentos en Prosa y Verso Publicados Durante el Carnaval de 1876 en Pontevedra*, 1876.

Muskheli, Veronika, "The Fate of Magically Strong Heroines in Central Asian Folktales", The Ellison Center for Russian, East European and Central Asian Studies: https://jsis.washington.edu/ellisoncenter/wp-content/uploads/sites/13/2016/05/Muskheli_REECASNW.pdf

Nennius ("The Irish Nennius"): *The Irish Version of the Historia Britonum of Nennius* [11th century], James Henthorn Todd, ed., Irish Archaeological Society, Dublin, 1848. This edition is based on manuscripts from the 11th to the 15th centuries.

New Ireland Review, April 1908. (Gormanston Foxes)

New Larousse Encyclopedia of Mythology, Hamlyn, 1959, 1968.

NFC: The National Folklore Collection, University College Dublin.

NFCS: The National Folklore Collection: Schools, University College Dublin. These are accounts of folklore and tales handwritten mostly by pupils, occasionally by their teachers, that the children collected from family and neighbours in the 1930s.

Noia Campos, Camiño, *Contos Galegos de Tradition Oral*, Edicións NigraTrea, Vigo, Spain, 2002.

Noia Campos, Camiño, *Cuentos Gallegos de Tradición Oral*, Edicións NigraTrea, Vigo, Spain, 2003. Selections from the 2002 edition.

North, Sir Thomas, *The Fables of Bidpai*, 1570; reprinted 1888. This is a version of *The Panchatantra*.

O'Curry, Eugene, from the *Book of Leinster*, folio 109, MS. H. 2. 18, Library of Trinity College.

Ó Cróinín, Seán, *Seanachas Amhlaoibh Í Luínse*, Comhairle Bhéaloideas Éireann, Baile Átha Cliath, 1980. (Folklore collected from Amhlaoibh Í Luínse.)

Ó Dónaill, Niall, *Foclóir Gaeilge-Béarla* [Irish-English Dictionary], Oifig an tSoláthair, Dublin, 1977.

O'Donovan, John, *Ancient Laws of Ireland*, A. Thom & Co., Dublin; Longmans/Turner, London, 1879.

O'Donovan, John, *Ordnance survey letters Wicklow and Carlow*: see Herity.

O'Farrell, Padraic, *Irish Ghost Stories*, Gill & Macmillan, Dublin, 2004.

O'Flaherty, Roderic, *Chorographical Description of West or h-Iar Connaught, A*, 1684; reprinted by The Irish Archaeological Society, Dublin, 1846.

O'Grady, Standish Hayes, *Silva Gadelica*, Williams and Norgate, London, 1892.

O'Hanlon, Rev. John, *Lives of the Irish Saints*, Vol. VI. Begun in 1875, nine of twelve projected volumes, one for each month, were completed before his death in 1905.

O'Kearney, Nicholas, "Feis Tighe Chonain", Introduction, *Transactions of the Ossianic Society for the Year 1854*, Vol. II, published 1855.

O'Keeffe, C. M., "Horses and Hounds of Ancient Ireland", *Ulster Journal of Archaeology*, Volume 7, 1859.

O'Kelly, William, *Historica Descriptio Hiberniae*, Vienna, 1703; new edition by Patrick O'Kelly, Dublin, 1828, 1844.

Ó hÓgáin, Dáithí, *The Lore of Ireland*, Collins Press, Cork, 2006.

Ó Súilleabháin, Seán, *A Handbook of Irish Folklore*, Singing Tree Press, Detroit, 1970. (Originally published 1942.)

O'Sullivan, Patrick V., *Irish Superstitions and Legends of Animals and Birds*, Mercier, 1991.

Ó Tuathail, Pádraig, ed., "Wicklow Traditions of 1798", *Béaloideas*, Vol 5, No. 2, Nollaig 1935.

Ovid, *Metamorphoses*, Sir Samuel Garth, ed., 1717. Translated by Garth, John Dryden, Alexander Pope, Joseph Addison, Nahum Tate, John Gay, William Congreve, and Nicholas Rowe.

Oxford English Dictionary, Clarendon Press, Oxford, 1989.

Panchatantra, The: see North and Thomas Scott.

Payne, John (trans.), *Book of the Thousand Nights and One Night, The*, 1882, 1901.

Percy, Thomas, *Reliques of Ancient English Poetry*, 1764.

Petrovitch, Woislav M., *Hero Tales and Legends of the Serbians*, 1914; Cosimo Classics, New York, 2007.

Pilpay: see North and Thomas Scott.

Piñeiro de San Miguel, Esperanza, and Andrés Gómez Blanco, *De lenda en lenda*, Galicia government publication, Ferrol, 1999.

Pliny: *Pliny's Natural History*, trans. Philemon Holland, 1601; edited by The Wernerian Club (Jonathan Couch), London, 1847.

Pliny, *Naturalis Historiae*, Carolus Mayhoff, ed., B. G. Teubneri, Leipzig, 1875.

Pliny: see also Huerta/Pliny.

Plummer, Charles, *Lives of Irish Saints*, Oxford University Press, 1922.

Plutarch, "Life of Alexander", *Parallel Lives*, AD 75.

Potanin, G. N., in "Folk-Lore in Mongolia", *The Folk-Lore Journal*, Volume 3, 1885.

Potanin, G. N., in "Folk-Lore in Mongolia", *The Folk-Lore Journal*, Volume 4, 1886.

Preston, Eileen Butler, *A Little Kept*, 1953. (Gormanston Foxes)

Price, Liam, *Place-names of Co. Wicklow, The, Vol. VII: The Baronies of Newcastle and Arklow*, Dublin Institute for Advanced Studies, Dublin, 1967 (reprinted 1983). This material was first published in *Proceedings of the Royal Irish Academy* in 1938 and 1941.

Prieto, Laureano, "La zoantropía en Galicia", *Zephyrus,* IV, 1953.

Raftery, Barry, and Jane McIntosh, eds., *Philip's Atlas of the Celts*, George Philip, London, 2001.

Reigosa, Antonio, Xoán R. Cuba, and Xosé Miranda, *Diccionario dos Seres Míticos Galegos*, Edicións Xerais de Galicia, 1999.

Risco, Vicente, "O lobo da xente", *Lar*, 1925.

Ritter, Tex, *Tex Ritter: Children's Songs and Stories*, phonograph record, Capitol, 1945. "The Phantom White Stallion of Skull Valley".

Rúa Aller, Francisco M., and Manuel E. Rubio Gago, *La Piedra Celeste: Creencias Populares Leonesas*, Diputación Provincial de León, Breviarios de la Calle del Pez, 1986.

Rudkin, Ethel, "The Black Dog", *Folklore* Vol. 49, 1938.

Sahagún, Fray Bernardino de, *Historia general de las cosas de Nueva España*, 1576, 1585.

Sainero, Ramón, *La Huella Celta en España e Irlanda,* Ediciones Akal, 1998.

Sainero, Ramón, *Orígenes Celtas del Reino de Brigantia: La Génesis de España, Los*, Abada Editores, Madrid, Spain, 2009.

Sanas Cormaic, 10th-century glossary by king-bishop Cormac mac Cuilennáin. See Stokes, *Three Irish Glossaries*.

Sánchez Vicente, Xuan Xosé, *Cultura Popular Asturiana: Unida y Pluralida, La*, Servicio de Publicaciones, Comunidad Autónoma del Principado de Asturias, Oviedo, Spain, 1985.

Sarl, Arthur J., *Horses, Jockeys & Crooks: Reminiscences of Thirty Years' Racing*, Hutchinson, London, 1935. Sarl was Racing Correspondent of *The People*.

Scott, Thomas D., *Fables of Pilpay, The*, Lumley, London, 1852. This is a version of *The Panchatantra*.

Scott, Sir Walter, *The Lady of the Lake*, 1810.

Scott, Sir Walter, *Peveril of the Peak*, 1823.

Scott, Sir Walter, *Letters on Demonology and Witchcraft*, 1884.

Scottish National Dictionary: http://www.dsl.ac.uk/

Shahnameh: see Ferdowsi.

Sordo Sotres, Ramón, *Mitología de Asturias y Cantabria: Entre los ríos Sella y Nansa*, Colección el Jogueru, Llanes, 1991.

Sordo Sotres, Ramón, *Mitos Asturianos*, Llanes, 1999.

Stokes, Whitley, "The Rennes Dindshenchas", *Revue Celtique* 15, 1894.

Stokes, Whitley, *Three Irish Glossaries*, Williams and Norgate, London, 1862.

Stokes, Whitley, "The Wooing of Luaine and the Death of Athirne", *Revue Celtique* 24 1903.

Súarez López, Jesús, *Folklore de Somiedo: Leyendas, Cuentos, Tradiciones*, Museo del Pueblo de Asturias: Archivo de la Tradición Oral, Ayuntamiento de Gijón, 2003.

Súarez López, Jesús, *Fórmulas Mágicas de la Tradición Oral Asturiana: Invocaciones, ensalmos, conjuros*, Gobierno del Principado de Asturias, Gijón, 2016.

Talbot, Alice-Mary, and Denis F. Sullivan, *The History of Leo the Deacon: Byzantine military expansion in the tenth century*. Intro., transl., and annotations, Dumbarton Oaks Research Library and Collection, Washington D. C., 2005.

Thackeray, William, *The Irish Sketch-book*, 1843.

Theodoret of Cyrus, *Historia ecclesiastica*, Book II, Chapter 26, AD 450.

Timoneda, Juan, ed/pub., *Rosa Española*, 1573 fol. 81r; in *Romancero Castellano*, G. B. Depping, Brockhaus, Leipzig, 1846.

Todd, James Henthorn (J. H.): see Nennius.

Todd, J. H., and Eugene Curry, "On Rhyming Rats to Death". *Proceedings of the Royal Irish Academy*, Vol. 5 (1850-1853).

Trevelyan, G. M., *A Shortened History of England*, Penguin Books, Harmondsworth, 1980.

Voragine, Jacobus de: see Caxton.

Voz de Galicia newspaper, A Coruña, Galicia.

Waldron, George, *A Description of the Isle of Man*, 1726, 1731, 1744.

Walshe, Patrick T., "The Antiquities of the Dunlavin-Donard District", *Journal of the Royal Society of Antiquaries of Ireland* 61, 1931.

Westropp, T. J., *Collectanea: Co. Clare Folk Tales & Myths*, (*Folklore* XXIV, 1913).

Wilde, Lady Francesca Speranza, *Ancient Legends, Mystic Charms, and Superstitions of Ireland*, 1887.

Witcutt, W. P., "The Black Dog", *Folklore* Vol. 53:3, 1942.

Yeats, W. B., ed., *Fairy and Folk Tales of the Irish Peasantry*, 1888.

Yellow Book of Lecan, The (YBL), 14th century.

Zalka, Csenge, *Tales of Superhuman Powers: 55 Traditional Stories from Around the World*, McFarland, North Carolina and London, 2013.

Online Sources

Álvarez, David, blog Naturaleza Cantábrica.

As Manx as the Hills website by Bernadette Weyde.

Bullfinch's Mythology on Gutenburg.org

Keightley, Thomas, *The Fairy Mythology*, 1870 on sacred-texts.com

Keightley, Thomas, *Tales and Popular Fictions, Their Resemblance and Transmission from Country to Country*, 1834.

Yeats, W. B., ed., *Fairy and Folk Tales of the Irish Peasantry*, 1888.

Many other sources are online.

About the Author

Richard is a storyteller in Ireland and world-wide. His Legendary Tours take people to the places in Ireland where the stories happened, and he tells them on location. He has worked on race tracks as hotwalker, groom, shedrow foreman and pony boy.

www.ingramcontent.com/pod-product-compliance
Lightning Source LLC
LaVergne TN
LVHW020533100826
845148LV00010B/1443
9780915330188